The Fall and Redemption of Dr. Samuel A. Mudd

The True Story of the Doctor Who Went to Prison for Helping Abraham Lincoln's Assassin, John Wilkes Booth

by

Robert Kenneth Summers

3rd Edition
March 2008

ISBN: 978-0-6151-9504-9

For

Beth and Nick

Table of Contents

Introduction..1

Part 1 - The Early Years..3
   A Man of His Times..3
   Religion...7
   Early Education...7
   Medical School..8
   Farm Life..10
   Civil War...11
   The Military Draft...13
   The End of Slavery..16

Part 2 - Assassination, Arrest, and Trial.....................................17
   Dr. Mudd's First Encounter with Booth..................................17
   Dr. Mudd's Second Encounter with Booth.............................18
   Dr. Mudd's Third Encounter with Booth.................................19
   Dr. Mudd's Fourth Encounter with Booth..............................19
   The Hunt for John Wilkes Booth..22
   The Alleged Conspirators...29
   Edman Spangler..29
   Samuel Arnold and Michael O'Laughlen................................30
   Prison and Penitentiary 31
   The Lincoln Conspiracy Trial..36
   Conviction...41

Part 3 - Fort Jefferson...44
   The Trip to Prison...44
   The Dry Tortugas...47
   The Prisoners' Arrival..49
   Promises, Promises...51
   Attempted Escape..52
   The Dungeon..54
   Colonel George St. Leger Grenfell...55
   Prison Life..57
   The Great 1867 Yellow Fever Epidemic...............................64

Part 4 - Home Again...72
   Dr. Mudd is Pardoned...72
   Spangler and Arnold are Pardoned..73
   Edman Spangler at the Mudd Farm.......................................75
   The Final Years...77
   The Death of Dr. Mudd...82
   Comment...84

Source Documents..85
   10-17-1852: Sam Mudd's Expulsion from Georgetown College.........................86
   03-05-1856: Dr. Samuel Mudd's 1856 Graduation Thesis..............................88
   01-13-1862: Dr. Mudd's Letter to Orestes A. Brownson..............................96
   04-22-1865: Dr. Mudd's Statement to Colonel Henry H. Wells.........................99
   05-16-1865: Testimony of Lieutenant Lovett and Detectives........................103
   06-16-1865: Mrs. Mudd's First Affidavit..109
   07-06-1865: Mrs. Mudd's Second Affidavit.......................................110
   07-10-1865: General Ewing's Request to President Johnson.........................113
   07-27-1865: Navy Paymaster William Keeler's Two Letters.........................118
   08-03-1865: Washington Evening Star Article on Trip to Fort Jefferson...........123
   08-22-1865: The Dutton Report & Dr. Mudd's Rebuttal.............................125
   09-01-1865: Captain Prentice to General Townsend...............................130
   09-04-1865: Mrs. Mudd's Letter to Judge Advocate General Joseph Holt.......132
   09-16-1865: Lieutenant Carpenter to General Townsend...........................135
   09-30-1865: Dr. Mudd's Description of His Escape Attempt........................137
   10-05-1865: Dr. Mudd's Letter to Jere Dyer.....................................140
   12-22-1865: Mrs. Mudd's Christmas Letter to President Johnson...................142
   01-01-1866: Dr. Mudd's New Year's Day Letter to Mrs. Mudd.......................144
   03-05-1867: Dr. Mudd's Letter to Mrs. Mudd.....................................146
   04-16-1867: Dr. Mudd's Letter to Tom Dyer......................................149
   09-04-1867: Letter from Fort Jefferson Surgeon Major J. Sim Smith...............151
   09-13-1867: Dr. Mudd's Letter to Mrs. Mudd.....................................153
   12-03-1867: The Butler Commission...154
   12-14-1867: Official Army Report of the 1867 Yellow Fever Epidemic.............155
   12-25-1867: Dr. Mudd's Letter to Dr. Whitehurst Regarding Epidemic.............160
   12-31-1867: Dr. Whitehurst's Letter to Dr. Crane...............................161
   02-29-1868: Major George P. Andrews Letter to Dr. Samuel A. Mudd.............163
   04-13-1868: Lizzie Smith's Letter to President Johnson.........................164
   02-08-1869: Dr. Samuel A. Mudd's Pardon..165
   04-19-1869: Letter from Dr. Mudd to Dr. Whitehurst after Pardon................167
   06-24-1869: Edman Spangler's Account of Life at Fort Jefferson.................168
   06-25-1873: Newspaper Article by Dr. Mudd on Epidemics & Infection...........173
   02-25-1878: Bill for the Relief of Dr. Samuel A. Mudd..........................176
   03-10-1883: Dr. Samuel Mudd's Guide to Health.................................177
   04-18-1892: Cincinnati Enquirer Article Concerning Dr. Mudd....................185
   08-07-1893: Conversation Between Dr. Mudd and Samuel Cox, Jr.................188
   12-18-1902: Samuel Arnold's Account of the Yellow Fever Epidemic.............189
   02-11-1909: Mrs. Samuel Mudd's Last Interview.................................192
   Profile: General August V. Kautz - Reminiscences of the Civil War.............196
   Profile: The Ships of Dr. Samuel A. Mudd......................................200
   Profile: Mary Eleanor "Nettie" Mudd...204
   Profile: The Author...205

Photographs...206

Research Notes..220

Index...225

Introduction

During the American Civil War, in the summer of 1864, the young actor John Wilkes Booth conceived a plan to kidnap President Abraham Lincoln and carry him to Richmond, Virginia where the Confederate government would presumably free the President in exchange for the Union's release of captured Confederate soldiers. When this impractical plan was abandoned a few months later, Booth determined to assassinate the President, and did so at Washington's Ford's Theater on Good Friday evening, April 14, 1865.

Booth broke his leg while fleeing from the theater, and after riding all night through Southern Maryland, stopped just before dawn at the farm of Dr. Samuel A. Mudd who set his broken leg. He left the Mudd farm later that day, but a week and a half later was cornered and killed in Virginia.

Many people were arrested during the Government's investigation of the assassination, but ultimately only eight of these, including Dr. Mudd, were put on trial for being part of Booth's conspiracy. All eight were found guilty. Four were hung. The other four, including Dr. Mudd, were sent to Fort Jefferson, a military prison located on a small Gulf of Mexico island about 70 miles west of Key West, Florida. In 1869, President Andrew Johnson pardoned Dr. Mudd who returned home to his family and farm and lived for another fourteen years until his death in 1883.

All historians agree that Dr. Mudd had nothing to do with planning or carrying out the assassination of President Lincoln. However, most also agree that he was guilty of helping Booth escape by not alerting the authorities to Booth's presence at his farm. General August V. Kautz, one of the nine members of the Military Commission that tried the eight alleged conspirators, said:

> Dr. Mudd attracted much interest and his guilt as an active conspirator was not clearly made out. His main guilt was the fact that he failed to deliver them, that is, Booth and Herold, to their pursuers.

Dr. Mudd was pardoned in large part because of his work during a 1867 yellow fever epidemic at his military prison, Fort Jefferson. Many soldiers survived the epidemic only because of Dr. Mudd's tireless work. Towards the end of the epidemic, Dr. Mudd himself contracted yellow fever and almost died. When the epidemic had finally run its course, 300 soldiers at Fort Jefferson signed a petition testifying to his bravery and asking President Johnson to pardon him. The petition said in part:

> He inspired the hopeless with courage, and by his constant presence in the midst of danger and infection, regardless of his own life, tranquilized the fearful and desponding.

After his release from prison, Dr. Mudd returned home to his wife and children. He lived fourteen more years, dying from pneumonia in 1883 at the age of 49.

Dr. Mudd has been the subject of many books and articles over the years. Some have been historically accurate. Others have not. This book includes the complete text of several key historical documents concerning Dr. Mudd to help you judge for yourself the accuracy of what you read about him. I hope you enjoy the book.

- Robert K. Summers

Part 1 - The Early Years

Sam Mudd first got into trouble when he was expelled from Georgetown College:

> The students whose names were stricken from the roll of matriculation in this instance were expelled by electricity, the telegraph being employed in requesting the parents of the offenders to remove them. From time to time a carriage rolled up, a student entered with his effects, and passed out of the College gate.[1]

One of the telegrams sent out from Georgetown College that day, Saturday, October 23, 1852, went to Henry L. Mudd, a large tobacco plantation owner who lived near Bryantown, Maryland. The message told him to come pick up his eighteen year-old son Samuel who was being expelled along with five other boys for leading a rowdy student protest. Three days later, on Tuesday, October 26, 1852, Henry Mudd arrived in his carriage at Georgetown College, collected his son Sam, and returned with him to the family farm.

Back home, Sam's parents considered what to do with their disgraced teenage son. Someone suggested medicine, an honorable occupation, and in short order Sam was apprenticed to his older cousin George Mudd, a practicing physician who lived and worked in nearby Bryantown. At the time, it was common for a young man who thought he might be interested in becoming a doctor to apprentice with a practicing physician before enrolling in medical school. Sam studied medicine under his cousin for the next two years. In the fall of 1854, Sam enrolled in the University of Maryland's Medical Department in Baltimore. In 1856, Sam's proud parents saw their son graduate as a newly minted Doctor of Medicine.

Over the next few years, the young doctor would get married, have the first four of his nine children, and settle into the respectable life of a Southern Maryland gentleman farmer/physician. However, the Civil War soon brought hard times to Southern Maryland. The end of slavery in Maryland brought economic collapse to planters who grew labor-intensive crops such as tobacco. Dr. Mudd's farm income plummeted as he was unable to raise a crop in the summer of 1864. To make matters worse, he was drafted into the Union Army that summer, and had to pay a $300 commutation fee to avoid serving.

In the fall of 1864, a neighbor introduced the young Dr. Mudd to someone who said he might be interested in buying his farm. The man was a young actor named John Wilkes Booth. Sam Mudd's life would never be the same.

A Man of His Times

The Mudd family of Southern Maryland traces its lineage back two and a half centuries to colonial times, when the first Mudd in America, Thomas Mudd, arrived from England.[2] Thomas sailed to America from Bristol, England on August 14, 1665 as a poor 18 year-old indentured servant. The summer he left England was the time of England's Great Plague – the Black Death – in which tens of thousands of people died, particularly the poor. The following year, 1666, the Great Fire of London finished what the plague had started – the complete ruin of the world's greatest city. Young Thomas Mudd's decision to leave England may well have saved his life.

---

[1] Shea, John Gilmary, *Memorial of the First Centenary of Georgetown College, D.C. Comprising a History of Georgetown University by John Gilmary Shea, LL.D. and an Account of the Centennial Celebration by a Member of the Faculty.* Page 180. P.F. Collier. New York. 1891.

[2] Mudd, Richard D., *The Mudd Family of the United States.* Volume 1. Second Edition. 1971. Page 26.

By the time he died in 1697, Thomas Mudd had become fairly prosperous, amassing more than 1,500 acres of prime farmland, some of which eventually passed down to Henry Lowe Mudd, Sam Mudd's father.

The main Mudd crop was always tobacco, a labor-intensive product. As the supply of indentured servants from Europe dried up, slaves were purchased to replace them. The 1696 will of Thomas Mudd gave four slaves to his wife Ann, and one slave to his daughter Barbara. From the beginning, the Mudds were slave owners, as were all their neighbors, including one by the name of George Washington whose 300-slave plantation at Mount Vernon, Virginia was just ten miles away across the Potomac River.

In her book *The Life of Dr. Samuel A. Mudd*, Dr. Mudd's daughter Nettie Mudd says there were more than a hundred slaves on Henry Lowe Mudd's large tobacco plantation, known as Oak Hill. The 1860 U.S. Slave Census lists 61 slaves. Whatever the exact number, Oak Hill was one of the largest tobacco plantations in Charles County, Maryland. Oak Hill was about five miles outside the small village of Bryantown, Maryland, which in turn was about 30 miles south of Washington, D.C.

Samuel Alexander Mudd was born December 20, 1833, the fourth of Henry and Sarah Mudd's ten children. He was born into a culture and a country which for hundreds of years had considered slavery to be a normal and legal part of life. It would take a civil war to root it out. Bryantown was a local center for the slave trade. In 1937, Richard Macks, an elderly former Charles County slave, recalled:[3]

> I was born in Charles County in Southern Maryland in the year 1844 ... the county where James (sic) Wilkes Booth took refuge in after the assassination of President Lincoln in 1865.

> ...In Bryantown there were several stores, two or three taverns or inns, which were well known in their days for their hospitality to their guests and arrangements to house slaves. There were two inns both of which had long sheds, strongly built, with cells downstairs for men and a large room above for women. At night the slave traders would bring their charges to the inns, [and] pay for their meals, which were served on a long table in the shed. Then afterwards they were locked up for the night.

> ...When I was a boy, I saw slaves going through and to Bryantown. Some would be chained, some handcuffed, and others not. These slaves were brought up from time to time to be auctioned off or sold at Bryantown, to go to other farms in Maryland, or shipped south.

The local newspaper serving Bryantown and the surrounding rural community when Sam Mudd was growing up was the *Port Tobacco Times and Charles County Advertiser*. Next to ads for fruit trees, agricultural lime, liquor, cigars, and furniture, almost every issue carried ads such as the following:

NOTICE

I want to purchase for some gentlemen in the South, for their own use, some FOURTY or FIFTY NEGROES of both sexes, at ages varying from twelve to twenty-five years. Persons wishing to sell will please address JOHN L. JOHNSON, Washington, D.C. - March 24, 1859.

---

[3] Federal Writers Project 1936-1938. Maryland Slave Narratives. Richard Macks. Applewood Books. Bedford, Massachusetts. Library of Congress, Washington, D.C.

$300 REWARD

RANAWAY from the subscriber, living near Port Tobacco, on the 26th of May last year, Negro Man WILLIAM BUTLER. William is about 30 years of age, five feet ten inches tall, of a dark copper complexion; when standing, stoops very much in his shoulders, and his legs bend back at the knee joint; very diffident when spoken to, but prompt and shrewd in reply. I will give Two Hundred dollars if taken in Charles County, and Three Hundred dollars if taken in any other portion of the State or in Alexandria or the District of Columbia, and secured so that I get him again. BARNES COMPTON - Jan 24, 1856.

A SERVANT WANTED

I wish to purchase, for my own use, a BOY from 15 to 20 years old. Jas. A. KEECH - Feb. 7, 1856

PUBLIC SALE

By virtue of an order of the Orphan's Court for Charles County, I will expose to Public Sale on Monday, the 28th day of December 1857 at the late residence of Isaac Bowie, deceased, EIGHT LIKELY NEGROES. Terms of sale: a credit of six months will be given, the purchaser giving bond, with approved security, bearing interest from the day of sale. GEORGE N. ROWE, Administrator of Isaac Bowie, deceased.

PUBLIC SALE

I will sell AT PUBLIC AUCTION in the town of PORT TOBACCO on Tuesday, 22d JANUARY instant, Fifteen or Twenty Valuable SLAVES of various ages and sexes. Terms: Cash, or drafts at six months with interest at date, accepted by good Houses in Baltimore or Alexandria. WM. D. MERRICK - Jan. 3, 1856

Slavery permeated the society into which Sam Mudd was born and raised. His community, his state, his country, and his church had condoned slavery for more than two centuries. Slaves were servants in his home and in the homes of his friends and neighbors. Slaves worked the fields of the family farm and all the neighboring farms. Slavery was a normal part of everyday life in much of America, including nearby Washington, D.C., the capital of the nation. It was therefore not surprising that Sam Mudd became a slave owner like his father and his neighbors before him.

At the Lincoln assassination conspiracy trial, there was testimony that Dr. Mudd once shot his slave Elzee Eglent in the leg with a shotgun for being "obstreperous".[4]

---

[4] Benn Pitman, *The Assassination of President Lincoln and the Trial of the Conspirators.* New York, N.Y.. Moore, Wilstach, and Baldwin. 1865. Testimony of Jeremiah T. Mudd. Page 191.

Another former slave of Dr. Mudd's, Mary Simms, testified at the trial that she ran away from Dr. Mudd's farm after he whipped her.[5]

Explaining why he once tried to escape from his imprisonment at Fort Jefferson, Dr. Mudd wrote:

> ...it is bad enough to be a prisoner in the hands of white men, your equals under the Constitution, but to be lorded over by a set of ignorant, prejudiced and irresponsible beings of the unbleached humanity, was more than I could submit to...[6]

Ten years after Dr. Mudd was released from prison, and four years before he died, the Baltimore Sun of March 7, 1879 printed the following short article:

> The name of Dr. Samuel A. Mudd, of Charles County, Md., was, by mistaking him for Dr. G. D. Mudd, also of Charles County, accidentally included in the list of a committee of Republicans which met in Baltimore lately while Dr. Samuel A. Mudd was in the city. Dr. Samuel A. Mudd, who was sent to the Dry Tortugas, writes that he "would not be considered so lost to honest principle and self-respect as to be found politically associated with men who, in my county, have endeavored to lower the white race, and have sacrificed every genteel feeling for the emoluments of office."

In Dr. Mudd's favor, some of his former slaves testified at the conspiracy trial that he was a good master, and his medical practice included caring for slaves as well as whites. James V. Deane, a former slave on the Mason plantation not far from Dr. Mudd's farm, said:

> When the slaves took sick, Dr. Henry (sic) Mudd, the one who gave Booth first aid, was our doctor. [7]

Another former slave, William Marshall, testified at the conspiracy trial that Dr. Mudd treated his wife when she was sick.[8] Dr. Mudd's sister Mary also testified at the trial that:

> During this time [early March 1865], on one of the days, a negro woman on the place was taken very sick of typhoid pneumonia. My brother saw her every day until the 23d of March.[9]

It should be noted that Dr. Mudd's racial views were not unusual for the time and place in which he lived. His views were the same of those of most of his friends, neighbors, clergymen, and half the population of the country. He was a typical man of his times.

---

[5] *Investigation And Trial Papers Relating To The Assassination Of President Lincoln*, 1865. Testimony of Mary Simms (NARA microfilm publication M-599). National Archives, Washington, D.C.

[6] Mudd, Nettie, *The Life of Dr. Samuel A. Mudd*, Fourth Edition. 1906. Page 131.

[7] Federal Writers Project 1936-1938. Maryland Slave Narratives. James V. Deane. Applewood Books. Bedford, Massachusetts. Library of Congress, Washington, D.C.

[8] Pitman, Benn, *The Assassination of President Lincoln and the Trial of the Conspirators*. Testimony of William Marshall. Page 172.

[9] Pitman, Benn, *The Assassination of President Lincoln and the Trial of the Conspirators*. Testimony of Mary Mudd. Page 196.

Religion

But how could devout Catholic families like the Mudds own slaves when the Catholic Church we know today strongly condemns slavery as intrinsically evil? The answer is that in Dr. Mudd's time the Catholic Church (and most Protestant churches in the South except the Quakers) not only condoned slavery, but also allowed priests and nuns to own slaves. For example, the Catholic Jesuit scholar Thomas Murphy reports that the Jesuits owned 272 slaves on six Maryland plantations.[10] Father Leonard Edelen, pastor of St. Francis Xavier Church, Newtown, Maryland, and his assistant pastor, Father Aloysius Mudd, had eleven slaves.

Even Catholic nuns had slaves. In *Carmel in America*, Father Charles Warren Currier writes about the Carmelite nuns of Port Tobacco, Maryland, located about ten miles from where Dr. Mudd lived:

> The first convent of religious women in the United States of America was founded in 1790, at a distance of about four miles from Port Tobacco, on the property formerly belonging to Mr. Baker Brooke. The place was henceforward called Mount Carmel... A portion of the property of the nuns, while they were at Mount Carmel, consisted of slaves. Many of the novices, on entering the community, brought their slaves with them. These were comfortably lodged in quarters outside the convent-enclosure and did the work of the farm. They were treated with great love and charity by the sisters, and were considered as children of the family. Their souls being regarded as a precious charge, for which the community was responsible to God, they were carefully instructed in their religious duties, and all their wants, both spiritual and temporal, faithfully attended to. On their part these poor creatures were devotedly attached to the community. Their number was about thirty, and twice a year the sisters would spin, weave and make up suits of clothing for them, besides spinning and weaving their own clothing.[11]

Families like the Mudds undoubtedly reasoned that if the Church condoned slavery, and if it was all right for priests and nuns to own slaves, then it was certainly all right for devout Catholic farmers to do the same.

On the second floor of Henry Lowe Mudd's home, in addition to the family bedrooms, was a chapel where the Mudd family prayed together and where visiting priests celebrated Mass. It was no surprise then, that Henry Mudd's son, Sam Mudd, would become a deeply religious man.

Early Education

The Mudd family also valued education highly. One wing on the ground floor of Henry Lowe Mudd's home included a schoolroom where their governess, Miss Peterson, home-schooled the Mudd children.

In 1849, at the age of 15, Sam Mudd left home to attend St. John's College in Frederick City, Maryland. At the time, there was not yet a clear-cut separation of high school and college as distinct academic entities. College was generally a six or seven year high school-college course. The first two or three years were called the Preparatory Department or Junior Department, and the last four years the Senior Department.

---

[10] Murphy, Thomas, S.J., *Jesuit Slaveholding in Maryland, 1717 – 1838*. New York, N.Y. 2001. Page xiii.

[11] Currier, Charles Warren, *Carmel in America, A Centennial History of the Discalced Carmelites in the United States, 200th Anniversary Edition*. Carmelite Press, Darien, Ohio. 1989. Chapter VIII - Mount Carmel in Maryland, Pages 70 and 83.

St. John's College offered a six year program, while Georgetown College in Washington, D.C. (now Georgetown University) offered a seven year program.[12]

St. John's College was a friendly rival to Georgetown College. Both were run by the Jesuits, known for their intellectual rigor and strict discipline. However, in the springtime at the end of his second year at St. John's, almost all the upper level collegiate students at St. John's withdrew from the school in protest over the school's strict discipline. Many families, unhappy with the situation at St. John's, looked for another school for their child to attend. The Mudds settled on Georgetown College, which 17 year-old Sam entered on September 17, 1851.

There were 176 boys in Sam Mudd's 1851 Georgetown College class. Many were from Maryland, Virginia, and Washington, D.C., but the majority were from other states, including Georgia, Louisiana, Tennessee, Pennsylvania, New York, Mississippi, Alabama, North Carolina, Kentucky, South Carolina, and Texas, and also from other countries, including Canada, England, Germany, Ireland, Chili, Mexico, Venezuela, Cuba, and Poland.

Boarding students were not allowed to leave the college grounds for any reason, except to go home for summer vacation. All letters not from parents were opened and read by administrators. Pocket money was discouraged. Any money from parents had to be deposited with the college Treasurer who dispensed it as he saw fit. Students were not allowed to have any books other than class textbooks, unless specifically permitted by the Prefect of Schools.

Young Sam's career at Georgetown College was cut short. Shortly after his sophomore year began, on October 17, 1852, he was expelled. Sam and a number of fellow students were protesting what they considered the unfair discipline of a fellow classmate, but they carried the protest a bit too far. The Jesuits identified Sam and five other boys as protest leaders, and expelled them as a warning to the other students. (See Source Documents).

The boys may have been emboldened by Georgetown's "Ki Yi Yi" student rebellion just two years earlier. In that 1850 rebellion, students yelled "Ki Yi Yi" while protesting punishment for an unauthorized student meeting. Stones were hurled, firecrackers exploded, and there was general chaos for several days. About 130 of the College's 180 students were expelled, or left in sympathy. In the end though, in order to save the school, the College allowed all the students to return in exchange for a formal apology.[13]

When the 1852 protest erupted, College administrators did not want to repeat their mistakes of 1850. They acted quickly to nip the protest in the bud, and expelled only the six protest leaders, one of whom was Sam Mudd. This quickly ended the protest, and none of the six were allowed to return to school.

Medical School

If Sam Mudd had not been expelled from Georgetown, he would probably not have become a doctor. He would most likely have completed his liberal arts education and become a successful businessman or

---

[12] Georgetown University, *Catalogue of the Officers and Students of Georgetown College, District of Columbia, for the Academic Year 1852-53*. Lauinger Library, Special Collections Division. 1852.

[13] Robert Emmett Curran, S.J., *The Bicentennial History of Georgetown University From Academy to University 1789-1889*. Volume 1. Washington, D.C., Georgetown University Press. 1993. Page 184.

politician. Instead, back at home, he had to rethink his goals, and began to consider medicine, a profession several other Mudd's had followed.

One of those Mudd doctors, Dr. George Dyer Mudd of Bryantown, took Sam under his wing. He became Sam Mudd's preceptor - his medical mentor and tutor. In the mid-1800's it was common for someone interested in medicine to gain one or two years practical experience and training by apprenticing with a practicing physician before enrolling in medical school. At the conspiracy trial, Dr. George Mudd testified:

> I am a practitioner of medicine in the village of Bryantown, Charles County, Md. Dr. Samuel A. Mudd was a student of medicine under me for many years. His father and my father were first-cousins.[14]

After two years back home training with Dr. George Mudd, 21 year-old Sam entered the University of Maryland Medical Department in Baltimore on October 9, 1854. Dr. George Mudd was listed as his official Preceptor.[15]

The physician training program lasted two years, from October to March each year. As was common in all medical schools of the time, the second year repeated the same lectures as the first year so that the students would be sure to master the subject matter. The University of Maryland Medical Department's Catalogue[16] said:

> The course of instruction in the University embraces the Principles and Practice of Surgery, Chemistry and Pharmacy, the Principles and Practice of Medicine, Anatomy and Physiology, Obstetrics, Materia Medica, Therapeutics, and Pathology, Experimental Physiology and Microscopy.

> Clinical Instruction in Medicine and Surgery is given at the Baltimore Infirmary, which contains a hundred and fifty beds, is in the immediate neighborhood, belongs to the University and is under the control and management of the Faculty.

The Baltimore Infirmary provided students hands-on experience with patients, training that most medical schools in the 1850's did not yet offer. The training that Sam Mudd received at the University of Maryland was among the best available in the United States at the time.

Only ten students were permitted to reside in the Baltimore Infirmary as clinical assistants. Sam Mudd was one of those students. In a letter to his wife during the 1867 yellow fever epidemic at Fort Jefferson, Dr. Mudd mentions working with yellow fever cases as a medical student:

> We had several cases in the Baltimore Infirmary during the epidemic that prevailed at Norfolk in 1855. I became acquainted with the pathology of the disease, but have acted here entirely upon

---

[14] Pitman, Benn, *The Assassination of President Lincoln and the Trial of the Conspirators*. Testimony of Dr. George Mudd. Page 206.

[15] University of Maryland, *Faculty of Physic Matriculation Book 1851-1892*, Health Sciences and Human Services Library, Baltimore, Maryland.

[16] *Catalogues Univ. of Maryland 1837-38 - 1879-80, Forty-Eighth Annual Circular of the Medical Department of the University of Maryland, Session 1855-56 and Catalogue of Matriculates, Session 1854-55*. Baltimore. Sherwood & Co., MDCCVLD.

my own theory, and with unprecedented success. I can say with truth that none have died that have been seen in time and had proper attention and nursing.[17]

The yellow fever experience he gained at the Baltimore Infirmary undoubtedly helped him save lives during the Fort Jefferson epidemic.

The Baltimore Infirmary is today the University of Maryland Medical Center, with 656 hospital beds, a shock trauma center, a cancer center, a heart center, a diabetes center, and a kidney, liver, and pancreas transplant center. It remains the primary teaching hospital for the University of Maryland School of Medicine.

Farm Life

Sam completed the two-year course of instruction, wrote his 40-page graduation thesis on dysentery (see Source Documents), and graduated on March 5, 1856. The young 23 year-old doctor then returned to his Charles County home to practice medicine.

The following year he married his childhood sweetheart Sarah Frances Dyer, who was known by family and friends as "Frankie" or "Frank", nicknames for Frances. Everything was going Sam Mudd's way. He was smart, well educated, and now had a beautiful new wife.

But there was even more to come. As a wedding present, Henry Mudd gave his son 218 acres of his best farmland, known as St. Catherine's, and built a new house for his son on the property. While the house was being built, Dr. and Mrs. Mudd lived with Jeremiah Dyer, Mrs. Mudd's bachelor brother. The Dyer farm was located just behind Dr. Mudd's farm, separated by the Zekiah Swamp. In 1859, Dr. and Mrs. Mudd moved into their new home.[18]

Sam Mudd enjoyed the robust good health that came with farm life. He was a good horseman who hunted foxes with his hound dogs. He was usually described as tall and thin, with reddish hair, and weighed about 150 pounds. In an 1867 letter he wrote from Fort Jefferson, he said to his wife: "I weighed a few days ago one hundred and forty-five, which is only a few pounds short of my usual weight." Red hair ran in the Mudd family. Of his nine children, we know that at least two, Samuel Jr. and Stella Marie, had red hair. Stella Marie, later to become Sister Mary Rosamunda, was described as having "flaming red hair" when she was born.[19]

To supplement the income of a newly minted doctor, Sam Mudd became a tobacco grower and slave owner like his father. According to the 1860 Federal Slave Census, Dr. Mudd had five slaves.[20] He acquired more after that, but the exact number is not known. Jeremiah Mudd testified at the conspiracy trial that Dr. Mudd "...was a large slave-owner." The 1860 Federal census listed the value of his real estate as $6,000 and the value of his personal estate as $6,500.

---

[17] Mudd, Nettie, *The Life of Dr. Samuel A. Mudd*, Fourth Edition. Page 265.

[18] Mudd, Nettie, *The Life of Dr. Samuel A. Mudd*, Fourth Edition. Page 27.

[19] Personal correspondence, privately held by Sisters of Holy Cross, Congregational Archives & Records, Bertrand Hall - Saint Mary's, Notre Dame, Indiana.

[20] 1860 Federal Slave Census, Bryantown, Charles County, Maryland, Page 55, Slave Owner - Samuel Mudd, Digital image. Ancestry.com.

Civil War

When the Civil War began in 1861, just two years after Dr. Mudd began farming, the Southern Maryland slave system and the economy it supported both began to disintegrate. In her 1906 book, *The Life of Dr. Samuel A. Mudd*, Nettie Mudd wrote:

> The Negroes, very soon after the war commenced, became imbued with the idea of freedom, and as this idea gained stronger hold in their minds their efficiency as servants diminished. When President Lincoln issued the Emancipation Proclamation on January 1, 1863, declaring the freedom of the slaves in the States that had seceded, the moral effect on the Negroes in Maryland was such that they were of little value to their owners. Their demoralization as laborers was almost complete. Subsequently, when slavery was abolished in the State by constitutional provision, they almost uniformly refused to work for their former owners, even for highly remunerative wages. Of course, in my father's home, there were experienced these conditions. He had to pay twice the value of their services to the emancipated colored people in order to make even a partial crop, or to retain them as servants about his dwelling.[21]

On April 16, 1862, a year after the Civil War began, and almost a year before his famous Emancipation Proclamation, President Lincoln signed a bill abolishing slavery in Washington, D.C. Many Southern Maryland slaves then fled to freedom in Washington. Others joined regiments of the Union Army's newly formed U.S. Colored Troops, eventually distinguishing themselves in several battles of the Civil War.

In August 1863, the Union Government established Camp Stanton in Benedict, Maryland, just ten miles from the Mudd farm. Camp Stanton recruited and trained free blacks and runaway slaves for the Union Army. This provided an unparalleled opportunity for more Southern Maryland slaves to escape their masters. Six regiments of the U. S. Colored Troops totaling over 8,700 African-American soldiers were trained at Camp Stanton.[22]

In 1864, the Union began drafting slaves into the Army, further depleting the supply of slave labor. Dr. Mudd and other Southern Maryland farmers were unable to raise a crop in the summer of 1864 due to the lack of slave labor. As a result of the loss of slave labor, farm income and land values in Southern Maryland fell sharply. Several people testified at the conspiracy trial that Dr. Mudd wanted to sell his farm.

Dr. William T. Bowman testified:

> I heard him say last summer when he could get no hands, that he could not till his land and he would like to sell it and would do so. I asked him what he expected to do in case he sold his land. He said he thought of going into the mercantile business in Benedict... Benedict is in an easterly direction from Bryantown, and is our usual port for Charles County... on the Patuxent River.[23]

---

[21] Mudd, Nettie, *The Life of Dr. Samuel A. Mudd*, Fourth Edition. Page 28.

[22] College of Southern Maryland, Southern Maryland Studies Center, *Hidden Identities: Southern Maryland Slaves & the United States Colored Troops at Camp Stanton, Maryland.* http://www.csmd.edu/library/smsc/NPS.html. 2006.

[23] Pitman, Benn, *The Assassination of President Lincoln and the Trial of the Conspirators.* Testimony of William T. Bowman. Page 178.

Farmers brought their produce to Benedict for sale. Steamboats transported produce and passengers between Benedict, Baltimore, and ports on the Rappahannock and Potomac rivers. Benedict also prospered from the new Union Army encampment at nearby Camp Stanton.

Dr. Mudd probably got the idea of a mercantile business from his brother-in-law, Jeremiah Dyer. Jere, as he was called, had gotten out of farming the previous year, 1863, and moved to Baltimore where he was in the mercantile business selling grain, tobacco, and other farm products.

Others testified similarly. Dr. J.H. Blanford testified:

> During the last eighteen months, I have several times heard Dr. Mudd speak, in general terms, of being dissatisfied with his place, and that he would sell if an advantageous offer were made to him.[24]

And Marcellus Gardiner testified:

> I have heard Dr. Samuel Mudd, on several occasions during the past two years, state that he wanted to sell out.

At the trial it was pointed out that Dr. Mudd did not have title to his farm. His father retained title. The question was, if he didn't have title to his farm, how could he talk to Booth about selling it? His brother, Henry L. Mudd, Jr., who handled his father's financial affairs, answered that question. He testified that:

> My father gave that farm to my brother. He has no deed for it, but he can get one any time he wants it.[25]

Dr. Mudd would eventually obtain title to his farm in 1878 when his father's will was probated.

In 1862, to help pay for the enormous cost of the war, Congress passed the Internal Revenue Tax Act of July 1, 1862. This new tax was the first on the incomes of individual U.S. citizens, and was assessed on annual incomes over $600. Businessmen, including physicians, were also required to pay an annual $10 business license. 1864 tax assessment records show that Dr. Mudd paid his $10 physician's license fee, but do not show that he was assessed any income tax. It therefore appears that Dr. Mudd's 1864 income was below $600 (about $12,000 in 2007 dollars).[26] The Civil War and the end of slavery had brought hard times to the people of Southern Maryland.

Dr. Mudd's financial situation was not helped by the addition of another mouth to feed. His fourth child, Samuel A. Mudd II, was born January 30, 1864. He now had to provide for a wife and four children from a small rural medical practice and a farm which produced little income.

---

[24] Pitman, Benn, *The Assassination of President Lincoln and the Trial of the Conspirators*. Testimony of Dr. J.H. Blanford. Page 200.

[25] Pitman, Benn, *The Assassination of President Lincoln and the Trial of the Conspirators*. Testimony of Henry L. Mudd, Jr. Page 198.

[26] Internal Revenue Assessment Lists, Maryland 1862-1866 (NARA microfilm publication M-771, 21 rolls) Alphabetical List of Persons in Division 14 of Collection District No. 5 of the State of Maryland, September 1864. National Archives, Washington, D.C.

But things were about to get worse. In July 1864, Sam Mudd was drafted into the Union Army.

The Military Draft

In March 1864, President Lincoln placed General Ulysses S. Grant in charge of all Union armed forces. In short order, Grant's aggressive tactics in the battles of the Wilderness, Spotsylvania, Cold Harbor, Petersburg, and the siege of Richmond led to a very large number of casualties which had to be replaced. The draft, and threat of the draft, was designed to produce these replacements.

Early Civil War drafts were conducted by the states, which set their own rules for who was subject to the draft and who was not. In Maryland, physicians were exempt. However, as it became clear that the war was not going to be over quickly, and that large numbers of men were needed to replace the large numbers of casualties, the draft process was federalized. Those who had been exempt under state law, including physicians such as Dr. Mudd, now found themselves subject to the Federal draft.

Following Congressional enactment of the Enrolment Act of 1863, President Lincoln issued a succession of draft calls totaling over one million men. Four major Civil War drafts were held during the summer of 1863, the spring of 1864, the fall of 1864, and the spring of 1865.

The law allowed drafted men to avoid serving by hiring a substitute, or by paying a $300 commutation fee, the main purpose of which was to place a cap on the cost of a substitute. Since $300 (about $6,000 in 2007 dollars) was a year's wages for a working man, the commutation fee was broadly criticized as something only the well-to-do could afford.

Despite the relatively small number of men they produced, the drafts were considered an overall success since their main purpose was to spur voluntary enlistments. The threat of the draft, together with the payment of enlistment bonuses, produced a Union Army consisting mainly of volunteer units. However, there were few volunteers from the Fifth Congressional District of Maryland where Dr. Mudd lived. The Provost Marshal for the Fifth Congressional District reported:

> There have been but few Volunteer Recruits obtained in this District, the political feelings of the people being generally against furnishing men for the Union Army. There have been only one hundred and twenty-three (123) obtained during the whole operations of the office. There were however, I suppose, several thousand Colored Volunteers obtained by the recruiting officers under General Birney and Colonel Bowman in the lower counties of this District.[27]

As the war continued, field commanders issued a steady stream of requests for replacements. The first draft in the summer of 1863 spurred a large number of enlistments, but few of those drafted actually entered the army due to the large number of exemptions for physical reasons and payment of the $300 commutation fee.

The need for more men continued. During the fall of 1863, the winter of 1863/64, and the spring of 1864, President Lincoln called for 700,000 more volunteers. However, the number of volunteers fell short of the number needed, so Congressional Districts not meeting their quotas were required to hold a draft to make up the deficit. The second of the Civil War's four drafts began in April 1864 and was completed in July.

---

[27] Historical Reports of State Acting Assistant Provost Marshals General and District Provost Marshals, 1865 - Historical Reports: Iowa (Statewide) - Massachusetts (10th District) (NARA microfilm publication M-1163), Page 6. Record Group 110, National Archives, Washington, D.C.

Maryland's Fifth Congressional District, where Dr. Mudd lived, having failed to meet its quota, began its draft on July 6th, but was interrupted by a rebel army raid. The draft was resumed on July 18th, and the following day, July 19, 1864, Dr. Samuel A. Mudd was drafted into the Union army.[28]

Here is an extract from the Provost Marshal's report describing the difficulties encountered during that draft:

> The July draft for the deficiency was progressing daily from the 6th of that month, when it was brought to a sudden and abrupt close by the Rebel raid through this section immediately after the Battle of Monocacy. Our demoralized troops retreated through this village (Ellicott's Mills) after that battle, until a stand was made here by Brig. Gen. Ricketts, who held the place until the 11th of July, when he fell back to Baltimore, leaving this place at the mercy of a large Rebel force then within three miles of the village. Upon the retreat of General Rickett's division I stopped drafting immediately and commenced packing up the papers and valuable documents of the office. These I hurried into a wagon which I pressed into service, and forwarded them to Baltimore for safety. Just as the papers were shipped, a telegram was received from Col. N.L. Jeffries, A.A. Pro. Mar. Gen., directing me to send all my public stores and property and come to Baltimore. There was at that time a large amount of clothing on hand, stored in the third story of the building occupied by the Board. I commenced immediately removing it. The clothing was got into the street just as Rickett's division was embarking on the cars for Baltimore, and his men broke open many of the boxes and helped themselves to such as they chose to take. I was utterly unable to restrain them, and, as it was reported and believed at the time that the Rebels were about to enter the place, and all the stores would fall into their hands, and Gen. Ricketts failed to protect the property, and the Rail Road Company would furnish no transportation for it, much was lost.
>
> I reported in Baltimore that night to Col. N.L. Jeffries. The next morning I obtained an armed guard through Col. Jeffries, and transportation from the Baltimore and Ohio Rail Road Company, and returned to Ellicott's Mills, and brought away the balance of the property.
>
> The business of the office was not again resumed until July 18, 1864, when I, being confined to my bed by sickness, was temporarily relieved from duty and Captain J.O.P. Burnside appointed acting Prov. Marshal for the District. The draft which had been interrupted by the Rebel raid was then resumed and finished, and the examination of drafted men recommenced; but before this examination was concluded, an order for another draft was received on the 19th day of September, 1864 to fill the quota under the call of July 18, 1864.[29]

The draft call of July 18, 1864 referred to above was a new appeal by President Lincoln for 500,000 more men. The second draft of the war was thus barely concluded before the third draft of the war was being scheduled.

---

[28] Descriptive List of Drafted Men Called into the Service of the United States from the 5th District of Maryland, May - Nov 1864. Page 214. Record Group 110. Entry 3759, National Archives, Washington, D.C. See also Entry 3760, List of Drafted Men, May 1864 - April 1865, and Entry 3765, Register of Medical Examination of Men Drafted Under the Call of May 19, 1864.

[29] Historical Reports of State Acting Assistant Provost Marshals General and District Provost Marshals, 1865. M-1163, Page 3A. RG 110, National Archives, Washington, D.C.

Congressional District Provost Marshals were required to have the results of drafts printed in a local newspaper. On July 20, 1864, the Baltimore Sun carried a front page story containing the names of all the persons selected in the previous day's Fifth Congressional District's draft. For the Fourth Election District of the Fifth Congressional District, the Sun reported that those selected were:

> Thomas Hancock; John R. Murray, constable; Toney Bruce, slave of A.S. Chapman; Henry Middleton, slave of J.T. Gardner; Thomas J. Boarman, colored; James Gross, colored; Alfred Proctor, colored; John A, Bean; Wm. M. Burch; Patrick Wade, slave of Mrs S.E. Mudd; Thos. Segar; J. Alexander Turner; Chilton Dent; T.H. Nighting; George Butler, colored; Frank Jones, slave of S.P.A. Chapman; Eavey Reeder, slave of John O. Norton; Geo. F. Burroughs; Alex. Hawkins, slave of Thos. Dent; John Hawkins, colored; Chas. Brooks, colored; Henry Gardner, slave of Thomas Carrico; Richard Bearman; Wesley Bond. slave of S.W.B. Hawkins; Harry Chapman, slave of Clinton Dent; T.S. Freeman; Wm. Jenkins, colored; Henry Stewart, slave of E.D. Boon; George Douglas, slave of John W. Hawkins; William Wood; B.R. Smith; **Samuel Mudd, physician**; Thomas Robey; Jos. Butler, colored; George W. Carrico; Rich'd Boon; James A. Morris; Charles Olden, slave of Catharine A. Hawkins; Constantine Mudd; Patrick Buckett, slave of Letty S. Hawkins; Rufus Robey.

As can be seen, many slaves and free blacks were also being drafted in the summer of 1864, thereby hastening the collapse of Southern Maryland's slave-based economy, and showing why Dr. Mudd was interested in selling his farm.

Like most other draftees, Dr. Mudd did not serve. The Maryland Fifth District Provost Marshal's draft records in the National Archives, perhaps incomplete due to the chaos of war, are silent on what happened to Dr. Mudd after he was drafted. There is no record that he was exempted from serving because he hired a substitute, or because he paid the $300 commutation fee, or because of any other reason. All that is known is that he did not serve, and that his name was not on any list of deserters or men failing to report for duty after being drafted. During the conspiracy trial, John C. Holland, Provost Marshal for the draft in the Fifth Congressional District of Maryland said of Dr. Mudd: "I am not acquainted with him."

Sam Mudd's father had paid for substitutes for Sam's brothers Henry and James, but substitutes were getting expensive.[30] At the time Sam Mudd was drafted, substitutes cost between $500 and $600 according to ads in the Baltimore Sun. They were getting expensive because the commutation fee option which had kept a lid on the cost of substitutes was cancelled on July 4, 1864, two weeks before Dr. Mudd was drafted. But Secretary of War Stanton ruled that persons drafted after July 4th in response to a call for troops made before July 4th could still pay the commutation fee. Since this exception applied to Dr. Mudd, it seems probable that he paid the $300 commutation fee instead of paying for a more expensive substitute.

It is unfortunate that Dr. Mudd did not serve in the Army. If he had, he probably would not have met John Wilkes Booth. He would also have also provided much-needed medical help to an Army in great need of such help. For example, just three days before he was drafted, the following front page ad appeared in the July 16, 1864 issue of the Baltimore American & Commercial newspaper:

---

[30] Tom Mudd, Mudd and Related Families, FHL Microfilm 1426475. Family History Library, Salt Lake City, UT.

State of Maryland
Surgeon's Office

A number of vacancies in the Medical staff of the Maryland Regiments still remain unsupplied. Candidates for these positions will apply by letter to the undersigned.

Chris C. Cox, M.D.
Surgeon General of the State of Maryland
No. 12 North Calvert Street

Before the Civil War began, the Union Army consisted of only 16,000 men. They were served by 114 doctors, or surgeons as the Army called its doctors. When the war began in April of that year, 24 of these surgeons resigned and 3 were dismissed for disloyalty, leaving only 84 surgeons to support the entire Army.[31]

But the need for doctors during the Civi War was enormous. By the time the war ended, more than 12,000 doctors saw service in the Union Army. About 5,500 of these were civilian contract doctors who worked mainly in Army general hospitals, many of which were in and around Washington, D.C. Civilian contract doctors held no military commission, but received the pay of first lieutenants. Many of the contract doctors also practiced civilian medicine on the side.

The End of Slavery

Three months after Dr. Mudd's draft scare, on November 1, 1864, the final nail in the coffin of the slave-based Southern Maryland economy was driven in when a new Maryland state constitution abolishing slavery took effect. In Baltimore that morning, church bells rang and Fort McHenry's sixty-five guns boomed in celebration. (Lincoln's January 1, 1863 Emancipation Proclamation freed the slaves in the rebellious states, but not in loyal border states such as Maryland which had stayed in the Union.)

Article 24 of the new Maryland constitution said:

> Hereafter, in this state, there shall be neither slavery nor involuntary servitude, except in punishment of crime, whereof the party shall have been duly convicted; and all persons held to service or labor as slaves are hereby declared free.

In Charles County where Dr. Mudd lived, only thirteen people voted for the new constitution. Nine hundred ninety-one, probably including Dr. Mudd, voted against it.[32]

Later that month, as Dr. Mudd pondered whether to continue working his farm by himself, or sell it and move, he was introduced to someone who said he might be interested in buying his property, a 26 year-old actor by the name of John Wilkes Booth.

---

[31] Gillett, Mary C. *The Army Medical Department 1818 - 1865.* Washington, D.C.. Center of Military History - United States Army. 1987.

[32] Charles Lewis Wagandt, The Mighty Revolution: Negro Emancipation in Maryland, 1862 - 1864. Baltimore. The Johns Hopkins Press. 1964.

Part 2 - Assassination, Arrest, and Trial

In April 1864, Union General Ulysses S. Grant ended the practice of exchanging Confederate and Union prisoners of war. Grant's purpose was to deny the Confederate army sorely-needed manpower, and to burden the Confederacy with feeding and caring for captured Union soldiers.

John Wilkes Booth had the wholly impractical idea that if he could somehow kidnap President Lincoln, the Union Government would exchange a large number of Confederate prisoners for Lincoln.

Booth's kidnap idea involved transporting a captured Lincoln from Washington, D.C. to the Confederate Government in Richmond. He planned to bypass the Union Army presence in Northern Virginia by leaving Washington over the Eastern Branch (now the Anacostia River) bridge, riding down the eastern side of the Potomac River through Confederacy-friendly Southern Maryland for thirty miles or so, ferry across the Potomac River into Virginia, and then ride to Richmond. Even though Grant's army blockaded Richmond, there were still ways for people to get in and out of the city.

Booth went to Southern Maryland in 1864 to familiarize himself with the road network and river-crossing points. He told people he met that he was looking for farm land to buy. It was on one of these trips, in November 1864, that he was introduced to Dr. Mudd at St. Mary's Catholic Church in Bryantown. Booth visited Bryantown again in December 1864, but did not meet Dr. Mudd during that visit.

Dr. Mudd's First Encounter with Booth

November 1864

The Catholic church closest to Dr. Mudd's farm was small St. Peter's Church, which sat by itself 2 ½ miles from the Mudd farm beside a country dirt road. Local Catholic families used St. Peter's for baptisms, weddings, funerals, and convenience. However, the preferred Catholic church was the larger St. Mary's Church in Bryantown, five miles from the Mudd farm. Church attendance then, as today, was as much a social event as a religious event. Attending church in Bryantown gave isolated farm families a chance to catch up on local gossip, do a little shopping, and for the men, a chance to enjoy an after-church drink with other men at the nearby Bryantown tavern.

John C. Thompson, the man who introduced Booth to Mudd, described his introduction of Booth to Dr. Mudd during his testimony at the conspiracy trial: [33]

> I reside in Charles County, Maryland. I had a slight acquaintance with a man named Booth; I was introduced to him by Dr. Queen, my father-in-law, about the latter part of October last, or perhaps in November. He was brought to Dr. Queen's house by his son Joseph. None of the family, I believe, had ever seen or heard of him before; I know that I had not. He brought a letter of introduction to Dr. Queen from some one in Montreal, of the name of Martin, I think, who stated that this man Booth wanted to see the county. Booth's object in visiting the county was to purchase lands; he told me so himself, and made various inquiries of me respecting the price of land there, and about the roads in Charles County. I told him that land varied in price from $5 to $50 per acre; poor land being worth only about $5; while land with improvements, or on a river, would be worth $50; but I could not give him much information in regard to these matters, and

_____

[33] Pitman, Benn, *The Assassination of President Lincoln and the Trial of the Conspirators*. Testimony of John C. Thompson. Page 178.

referred him to Henry Mudd, Dr. Mudd's father, a large landowner. He also inquired of me if there were any horses for sale in that neighborhood. I told him that I did not know of any, for the Government had been purchasing, and many of the neighbors had been taking their horses to Washington to sell. Booth told me, on the evening of his arrival at Dr. Queen's, that he had made some speculations or was a share-holder in some oil lands in Pennsylvania; and as well as I remember, he told me that he had made a good deal of money out of it, and I did not know but that he came down there for the purpose of investing.

On the next morning, Sunday, I accompanied him and Dr. Queen to Church at Bryantown. I happened to see Dr. Samuel A. Mudd in front of the Church before entering, and spoke to him, and introduced Mr. Booth to him. Mr. Booth staid at Dr. Queen's that night and the next day. About the middle of the December following, if my memory serves me, Mr. Booth came down a second time to Dr. Queen's; he staid one night and left early next morning. I never saw him but on these two occasions, and do not know whither he went when he left Dr. Queen's.

After Mass, Booth and Dr. Mudd joined the usual after-church gathering at Bryantown Tavern for a drink and conversation with neighbors. One of the men at the tavern was Thomas Harbin, a former Bryantown postmaster whom Booth knew by reputation to be a Confederate spy and mail courier. A man who knew the best routes between Southern Maryland and Richmond would be very valuable to Booth's kidnap plot. Booth asked his new acquaintance Dr. Mudd to introduce him to Harbin, then took Harbin to a private upstairs room where he told Harbin of his kidnap plot and asked him to join. (See Source Documents).

Harbin thought Booth was "crazy", but agreed to join his plot anyway. Nothing came of the kidnap plot, of course, but shortly before Booth was cornered and shot in Virginia, he unexpectedly ran into Harbin, who gave him food and directions.

Dr. Mudd's Second Encounter with Booth

The Next Day

Booth saw Dr. Mudd a second time the day after their introduction at Church. In a statement to detectives, Dr. Mudd described his initial introduction to Booth, and Booth's visit to his home the next evening: [34]

I have seen J. Wilkes Booth. I was introduced to him by Mr. J.C. Thompson, a son-in-law of Dr. William Queen, in November or December last. Mr. Thompson resides with his father-in-law, and his place is about five miles southwesterly from Bryantown, near the lower edge of what is known as Zechiah Swamp. Mr. Thompson told me at the time that Booth was looking out for lands in this neighborhood or in this county, he said he was not very particular where, if he could get such a lot as he wanted, whether it was in Charles, Prince Georges, or Saint Mary's county; and Booth inquired if I knew any parties in this neighborhood who had any fine horses for sale. I told him there was a neighbor of mine who had some very fine traveling horses, and he said he thought if he could purchase one reasonable he would do so, and would ride up to Washington on him instead of riding in the stage. The next evening he rode to my house and staid with me that night, and the next morning he purchased a rather old horse, but a very fine mover, of Mr. George Gardiner, Sr., who resides but a short distance from my house. I would know the horse if I should

---

[34] *Investigation And Trial Papers Relating To The Assassination Of President Lincoln*, 1865. Signed Statement of Dr. Samuel A. Mudd, April 21/22, 1865, witnessed by Col. Henry H. Wells. (NARA microfilm publication M-599). National Archives, Washington, D.C.

see him again. He is a darkish bay horse, not bright bay, with tolerably large head, and had a defect in one eye. Booth gave eighty dollars for the horse. I have never seen Booth since that time to my knowledge until last Saturday morning.

Dr. Mudd admitted, after the conspiracy trial was over, that the final sentence in his statement above was not true. He did see Booth again before the assassination. He met Booth in Washington on December 23, 1864, a month after Booth had stayed overnight at his house, and four months before Booth assassinated the President. Louis Weichmann was also at that meeting, and his testimony about it at the assassination trial was probably the tipping point that led to Dr. Mudd's conviction. Dr. Mudd confessed to this meeting only after the trial was over, but by then it was too late for the truth to do him any good.

Dr. Mudd's Third Encounter with Booth

Friday, December 23, 1864

The details of Dr. Mudd's third encounter with Booth in Washington are described in Louis Weichmann's trial testimony which follows in the Conspiracy Trial segment below.

Dr. Mudd's Fourth Encounter with Booth

Saturday, April 15, 1865

The fourth and last time Dr. Mudd saw Booth was when Booth sought medical assistance at the Mudd farm after the assassination.

On Good Friday evening, April 14, 1865, at a little after 10 o'clock, Dr. Mudd put aside his pipe and violin. Then he and his wife Sarah Frances checked to see that their four young children, Andrew, Lillian, Thomas, and baby Samuel were asleep, and went to bed themselves in their first floor bedroom at the back of the house. At about the same time, John Wilkes Booth crept up behind President Abraham Lincoln in his box at Ford's Theater in Washington, D.C., and shot him in the head.

Shouting "Sic Semper Tyrannis" (Death to Tyrants) Booth leaped from Lincoln's box onto the stage, breaking a bone in his left leg. Hobbling across the stage and through a back door, Booth got onto his horse in the alley and rode hard out of the city, across the Eastern Branch (Anacostia River) bridge, and then south through the dark Maryland countryside. This was the same escape route Booth had mapped out earlier in his plot to kidnap Lincoln. Meeting up with his accomplice David Herold, the pain in Booth's leg became so intense from the hard riding that he decided he had to abandon the escape route he had so carefully planned and try to find a doctor. He remembered that Dr. Mudd lived near Bryantown, and headed off on a detour to try to find his farm house.

During Booth's escape attempt, he and Herold crossed the Potomac River to the Virginia shore from Pope's Creek, Maryland. At the conspiracy trial, Jeremiah Dyer testified that a person traveling from Washington to Pope's Creek would have to detour out of his way at least seven or eight miles to get to Dr. Mudd's farm. [35]

---

[35] Pitman, Benn, *The Assassination of President Lincoln and the Trial of the Conspirators.* Testimony of Jeremiah Dyer. Page 180.

At about 4 AM, the exhausted Booth and Herold finally found Dr. Mudd's farm house. Herold knocked loudly on the door, awakening Dr. Mudd and his wife. Mudd went out, helped the injured Booth off his horse, and led him and Herold into the house. Dr. Mudd, a young 31 year-old physician, husband, father of four children, former slave owner and tobacco farmer didn't know it, but his life had just changed forever.

Dr. Mudd helped Booth up the stairs to the guest bedroom on the second floor. Working by lantern light, and quietly in order not to awaken his four young children sleeping in the adjoining bedroom, Dr. Mudd cut the boot off Booth's swollen left leg and examined it. He found a broken bone about two inches above Booth's left ankle, fashioned a splint for the leg, and told Booth to rest.

President Lincoln died in Washington at 7:22 AM. He had lived through the night without regaining consciousness. About 9 AM, Dr. Mudd had breakfast with his wife and David Herold. At mid-day, after checking his patient's condition, he had lunch. Then he and Herold rode to his father's adjoining farm to see if there was a buggy Herold could use to carry his injured companion. There wasn't, so he and Herold started to ride to Bryantown to see if one could be obtained there. Herold soon changed his mind and decided to return to Dr. Mudd's farm. Dr. Mudd continued to Bryantown alone to shop for his wife. When he arrived he saw that the town was full of soldiers and learned from the townspeople that President Lincoln had been assassinated by a man named Booth. He returned to his farm to find his two visitors leaving.

In a statement Mrs. Mudd later made about Booth's visit, she said that neither she nor her husband recognized the man with the broken leg was Booth, but that upon returning from Bryantown, Dr. Mudd told her he was suspicious of the two men. She wrote that he then decided to return to Bryantown:

> He then sent for his horse to go to Bryantown and tell the military authorities about those two men. I begged him not to go himself, but to wait till church next day and tell Doctor George Mudd or some one else living in Bryantown all the circumstances and have him tell the officers at Bryantown about it. He was very unwilling to delay and warned me of the danger from a failure to tell of these men at once. I told him if he went himself, Boyle who was reported to be one of the assassins and who had killed Captain Watkins last fall in that county might have him assassinated for it, and that it would be just as well for the authorities to hear it next day, because the crippled man could not escape. (See Source Documents: Mrs. Mudd's Second Affidavit).

After leaving Dr. Mudd's farm at sundown Saturday, Booth and Herold headed through the darkness towards the Potomac River, keeping to the woods to avoid capture by the Union soldiers now swarming through the area. After traveling about fifteen miles, they arrived around midnight at Rich Hill, the farm of Samuel Cox, a prosperous farmer and Southern sympathizer. Cox, suspecting they were the assassins everyone was looking for, would not let them into his house, but told them they could hide for the night in the woods on his farm.

Easter Sunday, April 16, 1865

Dr. Mudd's wife said her husband told her Saturday evening that there was danger in not reporting the two strangers' visit to the authorities. But she also said she convinced him to stay with her and their children that night and report the two men's visit in the morning. The next morning was Easter Sunday, the holiest day of the year for Christians. Families usually dress in their finest and go to church together on Easter Sunday morning. Dr. Mudd's family had the choice of two churches: St. Peter's, a small country church about two miles north of their farm, and St. Mary's, a larger church about five miles south of their farm, in Bryantown.

Surprisingly, instead of going to church in Bryantown where he could have reported the two strangers to the authorities, Dr. Mudd instead went in the opposite direction, to St. Peters. The President's assassination was a topic of great discussion at St. Peters that morning. After church, Dr. Mudd caught up with his cousin Dr. George Mudd who was riding back to his home in Bryantown. At the trial, Dr. George Mudd testified:[36]

> I had very little conversation with Dr. Mudd at church. He remarked that he regarded the assassination of the President, to use his own expression, was a most damnable act. He overtook me on the road after church, and stated to me that two suspicious persons had been at his house; that they came there on Saturday morning a little while before daybreak; that one of them had a broken leg, or a broken bone in the leg, which he bandaged; that they got while there something to eat; that they seemed laboring under some degree, or probably quite a degree, of excitement - more excitement than probably should necessarily result from the injury received; that they said they came from Bryantown, and were inquiring the way to Parson Wilmer's; that while there one of them called for a razor, and shaved himself; I do not remember whether he said shaved his whiskers or moustache, but altered somewhat, or probably materially altered, his features; he did not say which it was that had shaved himself, that he himself, in company with the younger one, or the smaller one of the two, went down the road toward Bryantown, in search of a vehicle to take them away from his house; that he arranged or had fixed for them a crutch or crutches (I do not remember which) for the broken-legged man; and that they went away from his house, on horseback, in the direction of Parson Wilmer's. I do not think he stated what time they went.
>
> When I was about leaving him, he turning into his house, I told him that I would state it to the military authorities, and see if any thing could be made of it. He told me that he would be glad if I would, or that he particularly wished me to do it; but he would much prefer if I could make the arrangement for him to be sent for, and he would give every information in his power relative to the matter; that, if suspicions were warrantable, he feared for his life on account of guerrillas that were, or might be, in the neighborhood. This was about half-past 11 o'clock in the forenoon, and when I parted with him, I was within fifty yards of his house.
>
> As I left Dr. Samuel Mudd, I went toward Bryantown. I dined at his father's house that day, and on my way toward Bryantown I stopped to see a patient, and it was nightfall before I got to the village of Bryantown. What Dr. Samuel Mudd had told me I communicated to the military authorities at Bryantown the next morning.

Dr. Mudd clearly did not give his cousin the impression that alerting the authorities to the visit of the two strangers was a matter of any great importance. Instead of going immediately to Bryantown with the news, George Mudd had a leisurely lunch at Dr. Mudd's father's home, visited some patients on his way back to Bryantown, and then went home for the night. The next morning, when he finally got around to telling the military authorities about Dr. Mudd's visitors, he obviously didn't lend any sense of urgency to the story. The military didn't begin to look into the story until the next day, Tuesday.

---

[36] Pitman, Benn, *The Assassination of President Lincoln and the Trial of the Conspirators.* Testimony of Dr. George D. Mudd. Page 211.

About the same time that Dr. Mudd was attending church that Easter Sunday morning, Samuel Cox sent his son to see his foster-brother and neighbor, Thomas A. Jones. Jones had been employed by the Confederate government during the war to transport Confederate agents and mail across the Potomac between Maryland and Virginia.

Jones later wrote:[37]

> The next morning, which was Easter Sunday, soon after breakfast, Samuel Cox, Jr, adopted son of my foster-brother, Samuel Cox, came to my house, Huckleberry, and told me his father wanted to see me about getting some seed-corn from me. He added, in an undertone, "Some strangers were at our house last night."
>
> Even had I not heard the evening before of the assassination of Mr. Lincoln, knowing Cox as I did, I would have been sure he had sent for me to come to him for something of more importance than to talk about the purchase of seed-corn. But putting together the intelligence I had the evening before received from the two soldiers, the fact that strangers had been at Cox's the previous night and that Cox had now sent for me, I was convinced that he wanted to see me in reference to something connected, in some way, to the assassination.

When Jones arrived, Cox told him that Lincoln's assassins had come to his farm during the night, and that his farm overseer, Franklin Robey, had hidden them in a pine thicket about a mile away. He asked Jones to help them get across the Potomac into Virginia, and Jones agreed. For the rest of that week, until Friday, April 21st, Jones would bring food and supplies to Booth and Herold in the pine thicket, asking them to be patient until it was safe to cross the Potomac.

The Hunt for John Wilkes Booth

Monday, April 17, 1865

On Monday morning, George Mudd finally told Lieutenant Dana about the two strangers. The story apparently was not presented to Dana as an urgent matter, since Dana didn't bother to assign detectives to investigate until the next day.

Also on Monday, five of the alleged conspirators were arrested. Samuel Arnold was arrested at Fortress Monroe, Michael O'Laughlen was arrested in Baltimore, Mary Surratt and Lewis Powell were arrested at the Surratt boarding house in Washington, and Edman Spangler was arrested at his boarding house a few blocks away.

Late Monday evening, Major James R. O'Beirne, Washington's Provost Marshal, ordered Lieutenant Alexander Lovett to proceed to Southern Maryland and arrest anyone suspected of being implicated in

---

[37] Jones, Thomas A., *J. Wilkes Booth: An Account of His Sojourn in Southern Maryland after the Assassination of Abraham Lincoln, His Passage Across the Potomac, and His Death in Virginia.* Chicago. Laird & Lee, Publishers. 1898. Page 66. Reprinted in *Thomas A. Jones, Chief Agent of the Confederate Secret Service in Maryland*, by John M. and Roberta J. Wearmouth, Port Tobacco, Maryland. Stones Throw Publishing. 1995.

the assassination of President Lincoln. Nine cavalrymen and two Special Officers (military detectives) of Major O'Beirne's force, Simon Gavecan and William Williams, were assigned to assist Lovett.[38]

Tuesday, April 18, 1865

Enroute to Bryantown, another of Major O'Beirne's Special Officers, Joshua Lloyd, joined Lieutenant Lovett's group. Around noon on Tuesday, Lieutenant Lovett and his men arrived in Bryantown, where Lieutenant Dana told him of Dr. George Mudd's report of two strangers at Dr. Samuel Mudd's farm.

Lieutenant Lovett immediately interviewed George Mudd, who repeated his story of the two strangers who had visited Samuel Mudd's farm. Lovett then took George Mudd and his men to the farm.

When they arrived, Dr. Mudd was out working in the fields. While waiting for him to return, Lieutenant Lovett interviewed Mrs. Mudd. She told about the two strangers coming to their house early Saturday morning, and how Dr. Mudd set the broken leg. She also mentioned that the man with the broken leg had shaved off his moustache, and that as he was coming down the stairs to leave the house in the afternoon, his chin whiskers became detached. She said she thought his beard was false. When asked about this later, Dr. Mudd said he didn't know if the beard was real or false.

When Dr. Mudd came in from the fields, his cousin George Mudd told him why Lieutenant Lovett and his men had come to see him. Lovett then proceeded to interview Dr. Mudd about his visitors.

At the trial, Lieutenant Lovett testified that Dr. Mudd told him that he did not recognize either of the two men, that they had stayed but a short time, leaving that same morning, and that he first learned of President Lincoln's assassination on Easter Sunday morning at church. None of these claims proved to be true.

After interviewing Dr. Mudd for about an hour, Lieutenant Lovett and his men left. He wrote in his report:

> Dr. Mudd seemed to be very much reserved and did not care to give much information. I was then satisfied that it was Booth and Herold, and made up my mind to arrest Doctor Mudd when the proper time came.

At the trial, Lieutenant Lovett was asked about Dr. Mudd's demeanor when he was being questioned:[39]

Q: You say that the Doctor seemed to be very much excited and alarmed?

A: He seemed to turn very pale and blue about the lips like a man that is frightened at something.

Q: Like what?

---

[38] *Investigation And Trial Papers Relating To The Assassination Of President Lincoln*, 1865. Report of 1st Lieutenant Alex. Lovett to Col. H.L. Burnett, J.A., May 2, 1865 (NARA microfilm publication M-599), National Archives, Washington, D.C.

[39] *Investigation And Trial Papers Relating To The Assassination Of President Lincoln*, 1865. Testimony of Lieutenant Alex. Lovett, May 16, 1865. (NARA microfilm publication M-599). National Archives, Washington, D.C.

A: Like a man that might be frightened at something he had done. I do not mean that he was afraid of us.

Q: You state that Dr. Mudd appeared very much frightened. Had you, or not, addressed any threat to him of any kind?

A: No sir. I was in citizen's clothes at the time. I addressed no threat to him.

Wednesday, April 19, 1865

While Dr. Mudd worked quietly on his farm, the Government still had no definite idea where Booth was. Some thought Booth was hiding in Washington. Others thought he had escaped north to Canada, or west to Chicago, or east to the Chesapeake Bay, or even to London. Several men resembling Booth's description had been arrested in error. The two strangers who had been at Dr. Mudd's farm may or may not have had something to do with the assassination. Dr. Mudd had said he didn't recognize them.

Near Washington, George Atzerodt was found at the home of a relative, and arrested as a suspected conspirator in the assassination of President Lincoln. Six of the eight persons who would stand trial for conspiring to assassinate President Lincoln had now been arrested. Only David Herold and Dr. Mudd remained free.

Thursday, April 20, 1865

On Thursday, the Federal Government posted a $100,000 reward ($2,000,000 in 2007 dollars) for information leading to the arrest of Booth ($50,000), John Surratt ($25,000), and David Herold ($25,000). Surratt had served as Booth's right-hand man during Booth's planning to kidnap Lincoln. When that plan fell apart, Surratt left Washington, and was in Elmira, New York when Booth assassinated the President.

The reward poster included the following statement:

All persons harboring or secreting the said persons, or either of them, or aiding or assisting their concealment or escape, will be treated as accomplices in the murder of the President and the attempted assassination of the Secretary of State, and shall be subject to trial before a Military Commission and the punishment of DEATH.

Dr. Mudd worked on his farm Thursday, hoping he had seen the last of detectives hunting for Booth. But he hadn't. He would be arrested the next day. Thursday night would be the last night he would sleep at home for the next four years.

Friday, April 21, 1865

On Friday morning, Lieutenant Lovett procured a fresh squad of mounted men of the 16th New York Cavalry and returned to Dr. Mudd's farm for the purpose of arresting him. Lovett was again accompanied by Special Officers Simon Gavecan, William Williams, and Joshua Lloyd.

At the trial, Lieutenant Lovett testified:

When he found that we were going to search the house he said something to his wife, and she brought down a boot and handed me the boot.

He said that he had to cut it off the man's leg in order to set the leg. I turned down the top of the boot and saw some writing on the inside, saw the name "J. Wilkes" written in it. I called his attention to it, and he said he had not taken notice of that before.

With the discovery of the boot, Booth's pursuers now knew with certainty the route he had taken after escaping from Washington.

With Dr. Mudd under arrest, and Booth's boot in hand as evidence, Lovett and his men left the farm. During the ride back to Bryantown, Dr. Mudd surprised Lieutenant Lovett by disclosing for the first time that he knew John Wilkes Booth. Lovett testified:

After I left, we got our horses, and going on the main road I told one of the men to show him Booth's photograph. The man held it up to him and he said it did not look like Booth.

He said it looked a little like him across the eyes. Shortly after that he said he had an introduction to Booth last fall, in November or December. He said a man named Johnson had given him the introduction... at church, I think he said.

This was a major revelation. Dr. Mudd had repeatedly insisted that he did not recognize the stranger, but he now admitted that he had personally met Booth and therefore knew what he looked like.

Colonel Henry H. Wells

Arriving in Bryantown around noon, Lieutenant Lovett took Dr. Mudd to the Bryantown jail where he turned him over to Colonel Henry H. Wells, Provost Marshal of defenses south of Washington. At the trial, Wells testified that he questioned Dr. Mudd three times that Friday over the course of five to six hours, and more than twelve times in all over the course of the next three days.[40]

In the end, Dr. Mudd's story of the visit of the two strangers was written down, signed by Dr. Mudd, and notarized by Colonel Wells. See the Source Documents section for the full text of Dr. Mudd's statement.

At the trial, Colonel Wells testified that Dr. Mudd told him that he knew the man with the broken leg was Booth while Booth was still at his house, but that he did not learn of Lincoln's assassination until late Saturday night or Sunday morning, after Booth had left his farm.

At the trial, Colonel Wells was asked:

Q: Can you state at what time Dr. Mudd professed to have recognized Booth as the man to whom he had been introduced. Was it during their stay at his house, or after they left?

A: It was during their stay at the house.

Q: You understood him to admit that he recognized him as Booth before he left?

A: Yes.

---

[40] *Investigation And Trial Papers Relating To The Assassination Of President Lincoln*, 1865. Testimony of Col, Henry H. Wells, May 16, 1865. (NARA microfilm publication M-599). National Archives, Washington, D.C.

General Ewing then questioned Colonel Wells further about when Dr. Mudd admitted he recognized Booth while Booth was at his home.

Q: Please state as near as you can, Dr. Mudd's exact words when he spoke of the reflection and recollecting that it was Booth who had been at his house.

A: Do you wish me to state all that he said?

A: All relating to that point.

A: On showing him the photograph he said that he should not have recollected the man from the photograph; and he said that he did not know him or remember him when he first saw him, but that on reflection he remembered that he was the man who was introduced to him in November last, or in the fall.

Q: Those were the words?

A: I will not quite say that they were the exact words; but as nearly as I can give them.

Q: There was nothing but that in his conversation on that point, was there?

A: That was the substance of it. Of course, it was said many times over and varied somewhat, but that was the general tenor of what he said on that subject.

Q: He did not say whether this reflection on which he would recognize the man with the broken leg as the one to whom he had been formerly introduced, was reflection after the man left, or not?

A: It was, as I understood.

Q: But he did not say?

A: I think he did say. He left the impression very clearly on my mind that it was before the man left.

Q: But are you unable to say that he said that?

A: Certainly, I am not able to say that he mentioned the precise time when the reflection occurred to him, in so many words, but I know what impression the general scope and tenor of his language left on that subject. He gave as a reason for not remembering him at the first, that the man was very much worn and debilitated, and he said that he seemed to make an effort to keep the lower part of his face disguised, and that when he came to think, reflect, he remembered that it was the man to whom he was introduced. He did not, however, I think, say to me that that reflection or that memory came to him at any particular moment.

This was a damaging admission. Dr. Mudd had slipped in telling Colonel Wells that he recognized Booth while Booth was still at his farm. But, if it was true that he had not heard of Lincoln's assassination until after Booth had left, he could not be faulted for failing to tell the authorities that Booth was at his farm.

Wells testified:

> I asked him then if he at this time had heard of the murder of the President. He said he had not. I think, however, he remarked to me in one of these interviews that he heard of that for the first time either on Sunday morning or late in the evening of Saturday. I think - so my impression is - that in any event it was after the person had left his house.

Subsequent testimony showed that Dr. Mudd's claim was not true - that in fact he learned of the assassination before Booth left his house. Neighbors Francis R. Farrell and John F. Hardy testified that Dr. Mudd told them of Booth's assassination of Lincoln, and Dr. Mudd said in his written statement that he visited with Farrell and Hardy before Booth left his farm. By his own statement, Dr. Mudd unwittingly confirmed that he knew of the assassination while Booth was still at his house.

Colonel Wells was asked about Dr. Mudd's demeanor when being questioned:

> Q: Did Dr. Mudd seem unwilling to give you this information?

> A: Dr. Mudd's manner was so very extraordinary that I scarcely know how to describe it. I will undertake, if you desire me, to do it as well as I can.

> Q: I wish you would.

> A: He did not seem unwilling to answer a direct question that I asked, but I discovered almost immediately that unless I did not ask the direct question, important facts were omitted.

> Q: Was he alarmed?

> A: He did seem very much embarrassed.

> Q: You said that at the last interview he was very much alarmed from some statements that you made to him. What were the statements you made to him?

> A: I said to him that it seemed to me he was concealing the facts, and that I did not know whether he understood that that was the strongest evidence of his guilt that could be produced at that time, and might endanger his safety.

In Dr. Mudd's written statement prepared that Friday afternoon, he said he had not seen Booth again between Booth's November visit to his farm and the assassination. Colonel Wells was asked about this at the trial:

> Q: I understand you to say that Dr. Mudd stated distinctly that he had not seen Booth since that introduction in November last?

> A: Yes sir, until the Saturday morning when he arrived at his house.

Unfortunately for Dr. Mudd, just three days earlier the judges had heard Louis Weichmann testify in detail about a meeting Dr. Mudd had with Booth in Washington between the November visit and the assassination. Dr. Mudd had been caught in a major fabrication.

Meanwhile, Thomas Jones decided it was time to try to get Booth and Herold across the Potomac. That night, he led the two men from their hiding place to the Potomac shore, and helped them into a small boat. Booth and Herold then set off into the dark Potomac but the current prevented them crossing to the Virginia shore. They wound up on the Maryland shore again, some distance from where they started, and found a place to hide until they could try to cross again the next night.

Saturday, April 22, 1865

In Washington, Colonel Henry L. Burnett, the military prosecutor assigned by Secretary of War Stanton to build criminal cases against the alleged conspirators, had been following reports concerning Dr. Mudd. Following Dr. Mudd's arrest and statement to Colonel Wells, Burnett ordered that Dr. Mudd be transferred from the Bryantown jail to the Old Capitol Prison in Washington. His order said:[41]

> Send forthwith a sufficient cavalry force to bring Dr. Mudd and his family to this city at once and report to me on their arrival. Take the necessary precautions to bring safely and hold securely after their arrival.

By specifying "and his family" Colonel Burnett clearly intended that Mrs. Mudd was also to be arrested. She and Dr. Mudd had told the same story to investigators, so she had also placed herself under suspicion. In the end though, probably due to the fact that she had four small children at home, she was not arrested.

Late Saturday night, Booth and Herold set out again in their small boat. This time they successfully crossed the Potomac, landing at Gambo Creek on the Virginia shore.

Sunday, April 23, 1865

On Sunday, Dr. Mudd remained in the Bryantown jail, awaiting transfer to Washington.

In Virginia, a Confederate sympathizer, Mrs. Quesenberry, fed Booth and Herold and sent them to a Dr. Stewart who she thought would treat Booth's painful broken leg. However, Dr. Stewart refused to admit the two men to his house, only allowing them to spend Sunday night in his slave quarters.

Monday, April 24, 1865

On Monday, Dr. Mudd arrived at the Old Capitol Prison in Washington, D.C.

In Virginia, Booth and Herold continued their flight, finally arriving at the Richard Garrett farm where Booth, using a false name, was allowed to spend the night indoors for the first time since leaving Dr. Mudd's farm. Herold continued down the road to Bowling Green, Virginia, where he spent the night.

Tuesday, April 25, 1865

Herold rejoined Booth at the Garrett farm where they rested for the day. That night, becoming suspicious of the two men, the Garretts did not let them sleep in their home, making them sleep in the barn.

---

[41] *Investigation And Trial Papers Relating To The Assassination Of President Lincoln*, 1865. Order to Col. J.A. Foster from Col. Henry L. Burnett, Judge Advocate, April 22, 1865. (NARA microfilm publication M-599). National Archives, Washington, D.C.

Wednesday, April 26, 1865

Union soldiers hunting for Booth had learned he was at the Garrett farm. About 2 A.M., they arrived at the farm, cornering Booth and Herold in the barn. Herold surrendered, but Booth refused to surrender and was fatally shot. He lingered in pain until about 7 AM when he finally died.

The twelve day hunt for Booth was finally over.

The Alleged Conspirators

The eight persons arrested for conspiracy in the assassination of President Abraham Lincoln were David Herold, George Atzerodt, Samuel Arnold, Michael O'Laughlen (also known as Michael O'Laughlin), Edman Spangler (also known as Edmund, Edward, or Ned Spangler), Lewis Powell (also known as Lewis Payne), Mary Surratt, and Dr. Mudd.[42]

There was little question as to the guilt of David Herold, Mary Surratt, Lewis Powell, and George Atzerodt.

David Herold had accompanied Booth during the entire twelve-day escape attempt, from the night of the assassination until he was captured at the Garrett farm.

Mary Surratt, the mother of John Surratt, was the owner of the Washington boarding house where Booth and his fellow conspirators plotted against Lincoln. She denied knowing of Booth's conspiracy against Lincoln, but the evidence against her was compelling.

Lewis Powell admitted that he was part of the plot against Lincoln, and that he tried to kill Secretary of State William H. Seward.

George Atzerodt admitted that he had agreed to murder Vice President Andrew Johnson, but lost his nerve and failed to do so.

The Court did not believe the remaining four defendants had anything to do with planning or carrying out the assassination of President Lincoln, but thought their association with Booth nevertheless warranted conviction for conspiracy. Edman Spangler, Samuel Arnold, and Dr. Mudd would spend the next four years of their lives in prison together. Michael O'Laughlin would die in prison and never return home. In prison, the four men would develop bonds of friendship that none of these very different men could have ever imagined. In fact, Edman Spangler lived with Dr. Mudd and his family during the final months of his life.

Edman Spangler

Edman Spangler was born August 10, 1825 in York, Pennsylvania. He worked his whole life as a carpenter. He first met John Wilkes Booth as a young man while working on a carpentry job for Booth's father, the famous actor Junius Brutus Booth. In 1861, Spangler moved to Washington to work as a carpenter at the new Ford's Theater. There, he became reacquainted with John Wilkes Booth who was now a famous actor like his father.

---

[42] Pitman, Benn, *The Assassination of President Lincoln and the Trial of the Conspirators*. Charge and Specification. Page 18.

Spangler's boss, John T. Ford, considered Spangler a valued employee, and a man innocent of any involvement in Lincoln's assassination. To his everlasting credit, John Ford continued to assert Spangler's innocence and fight for his release during the entire four years Spangler was in prison.[43]

Spangler lived frugally. He slept at Ford's theater, taking his meals at a nearby boarding house. He was a friendly, good-hearted, hard working, and dependable man. His only vice was drinking with his friends, but it never interfered with his work. His spare-time passion was crabbing in the nearby Chesapeake Bay.

In a classic case of being in the wrong place at the wrong time, Spangler was in the alley behind Ford's Theater when Booth rode up there to assassinate the President. Booth dismounted, asked Spangler to hold the reins of his horse, and went inside the theater. Spangler, who had scene-shifting duties to perform, asked another person to hold the reins and went inside to perform his duties during the play Our American Cousin.

In the confusion and pandemonium that reigned after Booth shot the President, jumped to the stage, and ran from the theater, observers mistakenly thought Spangler had assisted Booth, and reported this to the authorities. The unfortunate carpenter was arrested and ultimately convicted of helping Booth escape, although the military judges signaled their uncertainty of his guilt by giving him the relatively light sentence of six years.

In prison, Spangler and Mudd would become friends. Spangler taught Mudd carpentry, and Mudd credited Spangler with saving his life during the 1867 yellow fever epidemic. Spangler spent the last few months of his life at the Mudd farm, where he died in 1875.

Samuel Arnold and Michael O'Laughlen

Samuel Arnold and Michael O'Laughlen were both born in 1834 and both grew up in Baltimore.[44]

Arnold's father owned one of Baltimore's largest bakeries. In 1848 he attended St. Timothy's Hall boarding school near Baltimore where he became friends with another student by the name of John Wilkes Booth. When the Civil War broke out, Arnold and two brothers joined the Confederate Army, fighting with the First Maryland Infantry. Discharged for medical reasons, Arnold worked for a while with his brother in Georgia, but returned to Baltimore in 1864.

In 1845, the Booth family bought a house across the street from the O'Laughlen's. John and Mike soon became good friends. As they grew older their paths took them in separate directions, with Booth pursuing his acting careen and O'Laughlen working in the family hay and feed business. When the Civil War started, O'Laughlen joined the Confederate First Maryland Infantry. He was discharged in June 1862, and then divided his time between Baltimore and his brothers' family business in Washington, D.C.

Although Arnold and O'Laughlen both grew up in Baltimore and both had served in the same Confederate Army unit, they had never met. That changed in August 1864 when John Wilkes Booth invited both men to a meeting at his Baltimore hotel room.

---

[43] Mudd, Nettie, The Life of Dr. Samuel A. Mudd, Fourth Edition. Page 181.

[44] Kauffman, Michael W., American Brutus: John Wilkes Booth and the Lincoln Conspiracies. New York. Random House. 2004. Page 133.

Booth proposed to the two men a plan to capture President Lincoln and exchange him for Confederate prisoners needed to replenish the Confederate Army's ranks. Union General Grant had stopped prisoner exchanges as a way to starve the South of fighting men. To their ultimate regret, the two men agreed to join Booth's plan.

Several months passed without Booth taking any action to carry out his plan. Then, in a Washington D.C. restaurant on March 15, 1865, Booth brought Arnold and O'Laughlen together for the first time with his other kidnap conspirators, Lewis Powell, David Herold, George Atzerodt, and John Surratt. Booth proposed that the group handcuff Lincoln in his box at Ford's Theater, lower him by rope from the box to the theater stage, carry him out of the theater to a waiting carriage, and then flee from the city with the captured Lincoln.

Arnold, who had agreed to help capture Lincoln in a country setting, was stunned by the complete impracticality of Booth's plan, and said so. Besides, he argued, since General Grant had resumed prisoner exchanges, what was the point of continuing the kidnap plot? The meeting broke up with nothing planned.

Two days later Booth learned the President was scheduled to attend a play at Campbell Hospital on the outskirts of the city. This was more of the country setting Arnold had in mind. Booth quickly assembled the conspirators, but Lincoln had a change of schedule and never went to Campbell Hospital. At this point, Arnold and O'Laughlen concluded that the idea of kidnapping Lincoln was going nowhere, told Booth they were finished with the plot, and returned to Baltimore.

Booth assassinated President Lincoln a month later on Good Friday evening, April 14, 1865. Tracking Arnold through a letter he had written to Booth, detectives arrested Arnold at his new job at Fortress Monroe the following Monday morning. Arnold implicated O'Laughlen, who was arrested at his sister's house in Baltimore.

Arnold and O'Laughlen were as surprised as everyone else at Booth's assassination of Lincoln. They admitted they were part of Booth's original plot to kidnap Lincoln, but denied having anything to do with Lincoln's assassination. The court believed them. It spared them from hanging, but sentenced them to life imprisonment. O'Laughlen would not survive prison as the others did. He died in the prison's great 1867 yellow fever epidemic. After Mike O'Laughlen's death, Dr. Mudd said of him:[45]

> I never met with one more kind and forbearing, possessing a warm friendly disposition and a fine comprehensive intellect. I enjoyed greater ease in conversational intercourse with him than any of my prison associates.

Prison and Penitentiary

The six men arrested as conspirators in the assassination - David Herold, Lewis Powell, George Atzerodt, Samuel Arnold, Michael O'Laughlen, and Edman Spangler - were held under close military guard on the Navy ironclads Montauk and Saugus anchored in the Eastern Branch (now Anacostia River) of the Potomac River, near the Navy Yard. A short distance downstream from the Navy Yard, where the Eastern Branch joined the main Potomac River, was the Washington Arsenal, the present-day site of Fort Lesley J. McNair.

---

[45] Mudd, Nettie, *The Life of Dr. Samuel A. Mudd*, Fourth Edition. Page 295.

Others arrested in connection with the Lincoln assassination were held at the Old Capitol Prison, located opposite the U.S. Capitol on the present-day site of the U. S. Supreme Court. One of those was Mrs. Surratt, owner of the boarding house where John Wilkes Booth and his co-conspirators often met. She had been arrested on April 17th, three days after the assassination.

On April 29th, Secretary of War Edwin Stanton ordered that Mrs. Surratt and the six men being held on the Navy vessels be transferred to the penitentiary on the grounds of the Washington Arsenal.[46] The men were transferred later that night and Mrs. Surratt the next day. Seven of the eight persons who would be tried for conspiracy were now incarcerated at the Arsenal, which would also be the site of their trial.

Dr. Mudd arrived at the Old Capitol Prison from Bryantown on April 24th. While seriously annoyed with Dr. Mudd and other Southern-Marylanders who had not fully cooperated in the hunt for Booth, the Government wanted to put on trial only those persons who had actually conspired with Booth. Dr. Mudd was being held as a witness, not as a conspirator. But that was about to abruptly change with the arrest and interrogation of Louis Weichmann.

Louis Weichmann was arrested and brought to the Old Capitol Prison on April 30th, the same day Mrs. Surratt was moved from there to the Arsenal. Weichmann had been a boarder at Mrs. Surratt's boarding house, and was a long-time friend of her son John. Because of his closeness to the Surratt's, Weichmann was terrified that the Government would try him as a conspirator. John T. Ford, the owner of Ford's Theater where President Lincoln was shot, was also under arrest at the Old Capitol Prison. A few years later, Ford recalled conversations he had with Weichmann at the prison:[47]

> It was about the 20th or 21st of April (Note: Ford's recollection was off by about 10 days) that I was accosted by a young man who said his name was Weichmann and that he had been a school mate at Charlotte Hall, Maryland with Mrs. Surratt's son, that he was holding a Government position in Col. Hoffman's Commissary of Prisoners Office and that he boarded at Mrs. Surratt's house. He was greatly agitated and begged my advice as to how he should act and said that he had been away with the officers in pursuit of John H. Surratt for the purpose of Identification but the trip had no result and further that he was to go before Secretary Stanton to be interrogated.

> ... When he urged me to advise him, he said he had no others accessible to go to who could realize his situation. I answered, simply tell the truth, be right in all you say - don't be frightened or influenced any other way.

> ... It was two days afterwards when we had another conversation and in the meanwhile it was known in the prison that Weichmann and others had been taken to the War Department and had an interview with Secretary Stanton. He told me of it and seemed unnerved and beyond the power to control his terror. He said Mr. Stanton had told him that the blood of the murdered president was as much on his hands as on Booth's, that his association with the other conspirators and various other incidents were sufficient to justify at least the suspicion, and he had not told the Government all, which he must do for his own safety. He was during this recital shaking with freight and I could say nothing to him except a few assuring words that Mr. Stanton

---

[46] Letter from Edwin M. Stanton, Secretary of War, to General Winfield Hancock, May 1, 1865. Edwin M. Stanton Papers. Manuscripts Division, Library of Congress, Washington, D.C.

[47] John T. Ford's Statement, John T. Ford Papers, Maryland Historical Society, Baltimore, Maryland.

was a harsh lawyer and evidently had in his mind to frighten him thoroughly for a purpose. His nervous condition was so pitiful that the wags among the prisoners took advantage of it.

... It was probably two days later I met him again. He exhibited considerable self control and said he had been again to the War Department and had made up his mind to stand by the Government - which he repeated several times within the few minutes we were together.

Weichmann had calmed down because he realized the Government needed him as a witness against the alleged conspirators, and he knew that a person appearing as a witness could not also be tried as a defendant. If he fully cooperated with the Government and told them all he knew, he had nothing to fear.

When Dr. Mudd saw Weichmann at the Old Capitol Prison, he must have become very worried. Weichmann had been at the December 1864 meeting in Washington that Dr. Mudd had with John Wilkes Booth, John Surratt, and Weichmann. Dr. Mudd had signed a sworn statement that this meeting did not happen. Booth was dead and John Surratt was in hiding. Weichmann was the only person who could tie Dr. Mudd to this meeting, and Weichmann was now under arrest and being grilled by the Government.

Because of his intimate knowledge of what took place at the Surratt boarding house, Weichmann was interrogated personally by Secretary of War Edwin Stanton. In a book Weichmann wrote after the trial, he recounted Stanton's reaction when he told Stanton of Dr. Mudd's meeting with Booth:[48]

He [Stanton] now requested me to state who had introduced me to John Wilkes Booth. "Dr. Samuel A. Mudd," answered I. "Did you say Dr. Mudd?" queried Mr. Stanton. "Yes, sir." And then I related the story of the meeting of Booth, Mudd, Surratt, and myself...

Then Stanton, half rising from his desk, and bringing down his clenched hand on the table with much force, exclaimed with great earnestness to General Burnett, "By God, put that down, Burnett; it is damned important."

This changed everything. Dr. Mudd had been caught in a lie of major proportions. The Government now considered Dr. Mudd to be a conspirator, not a witness. On May 4th, he was transferred to the Arsenal Penitentiary and placed in cell 176. Like the others before him, he surrendered his personal effects, was handcuffed, and had chains put on his feet. An armed guard was posted outside his cell, and the iron door shut. This cell would be his home for the next two and a half months. [49]

Dr. Mudd and the other alleged conspirators were the first prisoners the forty year-old Penitentiary had seen for three years. In 1862, the prison had been converted to a war-time storage depot for ordnance supplies. The prison contained 224 cells. 160 of these were in a four-tier central cellblock. The other 64 were in a three-tier adjoining cellblock. The three-tiered cellblock also contained office space and quarters

---

[48] Weichmann, Louis J., A True History of the Assassination of Abraham Lincoln and of the Conspiracy of 1865. Edited by Floyd E. Risvold. Vintage Books, New York, 1975. Page 226.

[49] Letter from General John F. Hartranft to General Winfield Hancock, May 5, 1865. Records of Brevet General John Frederick Hartranft as Special Provost Marshal for the Trial and Execution of the Assassins of President Lincoln. Record Group 393 - U.S. Army Continental Commands, National Archives, Washington, D.C. Microfilm. Original documents held at Bureau of Archives and History, Pennsylvania Historical and Museum Commission, Harrisburg, Pennsylvania.

for the warden. Dr. Mudd and the others were held in this cellblock. The trial courtroom was conveniently located on the third floor of the warden's section.[50]

Brevet Major-General John F. Hartranft was appointed Military Governor, or warden, of the Arsenal Penitentiary for the duration of the trial. To avoid fraternization between guards and prisoners, a different set of soldiers was assigned to the prison each day. The soldiers were chosen from among the best in Washington, and were not told their assignment until they arrived at the prison. Guards were rotated to a different post every two hours, and were never assigned to the same post during their 24 hours of service. Prisoners were forbidden to talk to the guards, and were not allowed to have knives, spoons or other articles they might use to escape, or take their own life.

> Each prisoner was manacled and confined in a separate cell, attended by a guard; and the heads of the male prisoners were enveloped in mufflers, as one of them, while on board of the monitor, had endeavored to commit suicide by dashing out his brains.[51]

During their first month at the Arsenal prison, whenever they were in their cells, the prisoners were required to wear a padded hood that covered their entire head. There was an opening at the mouth to allow for eating, but no openings to see out of. The hood was tied around the neck and induced a terrible feeling of claustrophobia. After Edman Spangler was pardoned in 1869, he wrote about the use of the hood in an article for the New York World Newspaper, dated June 24, 1869:

> "Spangler, I've something that must be told, but you must not be frightened. We have orders from the Secretary of War, who must be obeyed, to put a bag on your head." Then two men came up and tied up my head so securely that I could not see daylight. I had plenty of food, but could not eat with my face so muffled up. True, there was a small hole in the bag near my mouth, but I could not reach that, as my hands were wedged down by the iron. At last, two kind-hearted soldiers took compassion on me, and while one watched the other fed me.

> ... The next morning someone came with bread and coffee. I remained there several days, suffering torture from the bag or padded hood over my face. It was on Sunday when it was removed and I was shaven. It was then replaced.

> ... On every adjournment of the court, I was returned to my cell, and the closely-fitting hood placed over my head. This continued until June 10, 1865, when I was relieved from the torture of the bag, but my hands and limbs remained heavily manacled.

In his *Reminiscences of the Civil War*, General August V. Kautz, a member of the Military Commission that tried the eight prisoners, recalled his shocked reaction when the prisoners were brought into court the first time on May 9th wearing hoods, chains, and black cloaks:

---

[50] Kauffman, Michael M., *Fort Lesley McNair and the Lincoln Conspirators.* Lincoln Herald. Winter 1978. Page 176.

[51] Poore, Ben: Perley, *The Conspiracy Trial for the Murder of the President and the Attempt to Overthrow the Government by the Assassination of its Principal Officers.* J.E. Tilton & Company. Boston. 1865. Page 9.

The prisoners in the number of eight were brought in behind a railing. They were masked and chained, and clad in black dominos so that we could not identify the prisoners. The Commission decided that they must be brought in so that we could recognize the different prisoners and be able to identify them. The mystery and apparent severity with which they were brought into the court room partook so much of what my imagination pictured the Inquisition to have been, that I was quite impressed with its impropriety in this age. The prisoners were never again brought into court in this costume.

At some point that day, either in the courtroom or afterwards, Dr. Mudd was not hooded like the other prisoners. General Hartranft's superior, General Winfield Hancock, asked why he wasn't hooded. General Hartranft replied:[52]

Dr. Mudd has been treated since he has been in this prison precisely the same as each of the other prisoners, except that he has not been hooded, which was in accordance with your instructions. I disclaim all intention of granting to Dr. Mudd any privileges.

No further mention is made in the prison records of Dr. Mudd not being hooded like the other prisoners.

Although the prisoners no longer wore the hated hoods in the court room, the hoods were replaced as soon as they left the court room and returned to their cells. On June 6th, General Hartranft wrote to his superior:

The prisoners are suffering very much from the padded hoods, and I would respectfully request that they be removed from all the prisoners except 195. This prisoner does not suffer as much as the others, and there may be some necessity for his wearing it, but I do not think there is for the others.

Four days later, on the evening of June 10th, the hoods were removed from all the prisoners except Lewis Powell in cell 195, and never used again.

---

[52] Letter from General John F. Hartranft to General Winfield Hancock, May 10, 1865. Records of Brevet General John Frederick Hartranft as Special Provost Marshal for the Trial and Execution of the Assassins of President Lincoln. Record Group 393 - U.S. Army Continental Commands, National Archives, Washington, D.C. Microfilm.

The Lincoln Conspiracy Trial

The public was clamoring for the Government to act, and it did - with breath-taking speed. President Lincoln was shot on April 14, 1865. Two weeks later, on May 1st, President Johnson ordered creation of a Military Commission. The members of the Commission were:

Major-General David Hunter
Major-General Lewis Wallace
Brevet Major-General August V. Kautz
Brigadier-General Albion P. Howe
Brigadier-General Robert S. Foster
Brigadier-General T.M. Harris
Lieutenant-Colonel David R. Clendenin
Brevet Brigadier-General James Ekin
Brevet Colonel C.H. Tompkins.

Brigadier-General Joseph Holt, Judge Advocate General, was appointed the Judge Advocate and Recorder of the Commission. Congressman John A. Bingham of Ohio and Brevet Colonel Henry L. Burnett were designated as Assistant Judge Advocates.

When the Commission opened the trial on May 9th, the prisoners were still frantically trying to secure defense attorneys. Dr. Mudd tried to secure the services of attorney Robert James Brent, a former Maryland Attorney General, but this was unsuccessful. At his wits end, he asked several non-lawyers to represent him. These included his cousin Henry Alex Clarke who owned a Washington coal company, his cousin Dr. George Mudd, and another physician, Dr. James Morgan. All of these non-attorneys wisely declined to act as Dr. Mudd's legal counsel. Finally, Dr. Mudd's wife was able to find legal counsel, and it was very, very good legal counsel. On May 11th, two powerhouse attorneys, Frederick Stone and Thomas Ewing, Jr. appeared as defense counsels for Dr. Mudd and were accepted by the court.[53]

Frederick Stone was a highly respected lawyer from Port Tobacco, Maryland. Born in 1820, he grew up in Charles County, Maryland and graduated from St. John's College in Annapolis. He was admitted to the bar in 1841. Frederick Stone was the grandson of Michael J. Stone, the younger brother of Thomas Stone, a signer of the Declaration of Independence. He was a member of the Maryland House of Delegates in 1864 and 1865, and a Member of Congress from 1867 to 1871, representing Maryland's Fifth Congressional District where Dr. Mudd lived. From 1881 to 1890 he was an Associate Judge of the Maryland Court of Appeals.

Thomas Ewing, now a civilian attorney, had served with great distinction as a Union Major-General during the Civil War. He was born to a prominent Ohio family in 1829. His father was a U.S. Senator, and his brothers Hugh and Charles were also Union generals. His brother-in-law was Union General William Tecumseh Sherman. At the age of 19, young Thomas Ewing Jr. worked as private secretary to President Zachary Taylor. He studied law at Cincinnati Law School and was admitted to the bar in 1855. He subsequently married and practiced law in Leavenworth, Kansas. In 1861 he was elected the first Chief Justice of the Supreme Court in the new state of Kansas. When the Civil War broke out, he resigned as Chief Justice to serve as a Colonel in the Eleventh Kansas Volunteers. He was soon promoted to Brigadier-General, and then to Major-General. He would take the lead role in Dr. Mudd's defense.

---

[53] *Investigation And Trial Papers Relating To The Assassination Of President Lincoln*, 1865. (NARA microfilm publication M-599). National Archives, Washington, D.C.

Counsels for Mary Surratt also appeared and were accepted by the court on May 11th. Defense counsels for the other defendants were arranged shortly thereafter.

With the trial underway, an observer[54] described the scene in the courtroom:

A large room in the north-east corner of the third story of the old Penitentiary, near the cells in which the prisoners were confined, was fitted up for the trial. It is about thirty by forty-five feet square, with a ceiling about eleven feet high, supported by three wooden pillars. Four windows, with heavy iron gratings, afforded tolerable ventilation; and there are two ante-rooms for the accommodation of the court and of the witnesses. The room was whitewashed and painted for the occasion, a prisoner's dock was constructed along the western side. The floor was covered with cocoa-nut matting, and the tables and chairs were new. Gas was introduced, in case the court should protract its sittings until after dark.

The members of the Court, who were all in full uniform, took their seats around a large table parallel with the north side of the room... At the foot of the table at which the Court sat was another, occupied by Judge Advocate General Holt, with his Assistants, Hon. Mr. Bingham and Colonel Burnett. On this table, as the trial progressed, were deposited the weapons deposited by witnesses, the machine used by the Rebel War Department as a key to communications written in cipher, the articles found on the dead assassin's person, with a mass of law-books, notes of testimony, &c.

In the center of the room was a stand for witnesses... Behind the witness-stand, and parallel with the southern side of the room, was a long table, which was occupied by reporters and correspondents during the public sessions of the court. At the foot of this table sat the counsel for the prisoners after they had been introduced.

The prisoner's "dock" was a platform raised about one foot from the floor, and about four feet broad, with a strong railing in front of it. Along this "dock" sat the prisoners. Mrs. Surratt had the left-hand corner to herself; a passage-way to the door leading to the cells intervening between her and the seven male prisoners, who sat sandwiched with six soldiers who wore the light-blue uniform of the Veteran Reserve Corps. Dr. Mudd wore handcuffs connected with chains; but the "bracelets" of the other male prisoners were joined by wide bars of iron ten inches long, which kept their hands apart. All of the prisoners, including Mrs. Surratt, wore anklets connected by short chains, which hamper their walk; and heavy iron balls were also attached by chains to the limbs of Payne and Atzerodt, attendants carrying them as they go to and from their cells. As the prisoners entered and left the room, their fetters clanking at every step, they formed an impressive procession. As seen by the court and the gentlemen of the press, they sat in the following order:

Samuel Arnold, a young Baltimorean, had a rather intelligent face, with curly brown hair and restless dark eyes. He was a schoolmate of the President's assassin; and, at the breaking-out of the Rebellion, he joined the rebel army. An original conspirator, his courage failed him; and he went some weeks before the assassination to Fortress Monroe, where he was clerk to a sutler when arrested.

---

[54] Poore, Ben: Perley, *The Conspiracy Trial for the Murder of the President and the Attempt to Overthrow the Government by the Assassination of its Principal Officers*. J.E. Tilton & Company. Boston. 1865. Page 9 ff.

Samuel A. Mudd, M.D., was the most inoffensive and decent in appearance of all the prisoners. He was about forty years of age, rather tall, and quite thin, with sharp features, a high forehead, astute blue eyes, compressed pale lips, and sandy hair, whiskers, and mustache. He took a deep interest in the testimony, often prompting his counsel during the cross-examinations.

Edward Spangler was a middle-aged man, with a large, unintelligent-looking face, evidently swollen by an intemperate use of ardent spirits, a low forehead, anxious-looking gray eyes, and brown hair. He was born in the interior of Pennsylvania, where he has respectable connections; and, after having been employed in Ford's Theater in Baltimore as a stage-carpenter, came to Washington with Mr. Ford when he built the house in which Mr. Lincoln was assassinated. Doleful as Spangler looked when in court, the guards declared that he was the most loquacious and jovial of the prisoners when he was in his cell.

Michael O'Laughlin, like Arnold, was a Baltimore friend of the principal assassin, and at one time a soldier in the rebel army. He was a rather small, delicate-looking man, with rather pleasing features, uneasy black eyes, bushy black hair, a heavy black mustache and imperial, and a most anxious expression of countenance, shaded by a sad, remorseful look.

George B. Atzerodt was a type of those Teutonic Dugald Dalgettys who have taken an active part in the war for the suppression of the Rebellion, - sometimes on one side, and sometimes on the other, as bounties, or chances to pillage, were presented. He was born in Germany, but was raised and lived among the "poor white trash" in Charles County, Md.; working as a blacksmith until the war broke out, when he became a blockade-runner. He was a short, thick-set, round-shouldered, brawny-armed man, with a stupid expression, high cheek-bones, a sallow complexion, small grayish-blue eyes, tangled light-brown hair, and straggling sandy whiskers and mustache. He apparently manifested a stoical indifference to what was going on in the Court, although an occasional cat-like glance would reveal his anxiety concerning himself. Evidently crafty, cowardly, and mercenary, his own safety was evidently the all-absorbing subject of his thoughts.

Lewis Payne was the observed of all observers, as he sat motionless and imperturbed, defiantly returning each gaze at his remarkable face and person. He was very tall, with an athletic, gladiatorial frame; the tight knit shirt, which was his only upper garment disclosing the massive robustness of animal manhood in its most stalwart type. Neither intellect nor intelligence was discernible in his unflinching dark gray eyes, low forehead, massive jaws, compressed full lips, small nose with large nostrils and stolid, remorseless expression. His dark hair hung over his forehead, his face was beardless, and his hands were not those of a man who had been accustomed to labor. Report said that he was a Kentuckian by birth, and one of a family of notorious desperadoes; one of his brothers having been such a depraved criminal, that the rebels hung him. But, for weeks after the trial commenced, all that was certainly known of him was, that he was the ruffian who made the ferocious series of assaults on Secretary Seward and his family.

David E. Herold was a doltish, insignificant-looking young man, not much over one and twenty years of age, with a slender frame, and irresolute, cowardly appearance. He had a narrow forehead, a somewhat Israelitish nose, small dark hazel eyes, thick black hair, and an incipient mustache which occupied much of his attention. Few would imagine that any villain would select such a contemptible-looking fellow as an accomplice.

Mrs. Mary E. Surratt, who was a belle in her youth, had borne her five and forty years or more bravely; and, when she raised her veil in court that some witness might identify her, she exposed rather pleasing features, with dark gray eyes and brown hair... Whether she was guilty or innocent, it was easy to perceive that she desired to make a favorable impression upon the court, and to inspire feelings of pity.

The trial would take a month and a half. Testimony concerning Dr. Mudd was presented intermittently during the course of the trial. The prosecution called sixteen witnesses to testify against Dr. Mudd. The defense, led by General Ewing, called more than sixty witnesses to testify in his defense.

One line of attack against Dr. Mudd was an attempt to show that he was disloyal and sympathetic to the Confederate cause. However, General Ewing was effective in blunting this by calling many character witnesses who testified to his good character and loyalty. As a slave owner, Dr. Mudd had objected to the Union Government's abolition of slavery, but he had never expressed a desire to see the country split in two.

The prosecution's main line of attack, however, went to show that Dr. Mudd knew of the assassination while Booth was in his house, that he recognized Booth despite any disguise he may have had, and that he failed to notify the authorities of the assassin's presence. The Lovett and Wells testimony detailed above went to the heart of these issues.

The Military Commission may well have been inclined to forgive Dr. Mudd's alleged transgressions. After all, many others, including John Lloyd, Samuel Cox, and Thomas Jones had had a hand in helping Booth elude his pursuers, and the Government had not charged any of them with conspiracy. Samuel Chester, Booth's actor friend, had known all about Booth's plot to kidnap Lincoln, and said nothing to the authorities, but he was not put on trial either.

The testimony which probably tipped the Military Commission against Dr. Mudd was, ironically, testimony which was favorable to him. This was the testimony of Louis J. Weichmann.

Louis J. Weichmann

Louis J. Weichmann testified about a meeting that he, John Surratt, John Wilkes Booth, and Dr. Mudd had in Washington on December 23, 1864, between the time Booth first met Dr. Mudd in Bryantown, and when Booth showed up at Dr. Mudd's house after the assassination. Weichmann was slightly off on his recollection of the date. He testified the meeting was in January rather than December.

The problem for Dr. Mudd was that he had told investigators, and sworn in writing, that he did not see Booth between those two events. By trying to hide this meeting from investigators, Dr. Mudd appeared to have something serious to hide.

Louis Weichmann was a long-time friend of John Surratt, who remained in hiding in Canada during the conspiracy trial. He had gone to school with Surratt, lived at the Surratt boarding house where Booth and his fellow conspirators often met, and was considered by his fellow workers at the War Department to be a Southern sympathizer. John Surratt later said the only reason Weichmann never became an active member of Booth's gang was because Weichmann couldn't ride and shoot. Nevertheless, Weichmann came across as a believable witness at the trial.

Dr. Mudd had gone to Washington on December 23, 1864 to do some last minute Christmas shopping with his cousin Jeremiah Mudd.[55] After checking in at the Pennsylvania House hotel, they had something to eat and then wandered over to the National Hotel, where the two men became separated in the crowd.

Dr. Mudd stepped outside to Pennsylvania Avenue, and was spotted by Booth, who was staying at the National. Booth said he was just on his way to meet a man named John Surratt to inquire about Southern Maryland real estate. Dr. Mudd was acquainted with the Surratt family since they had run the Surrattsville post office and tavern not far from Mudd's farm. Booth told Dr. Mudd that the Surratts now lived in a boarding house about five blocks away. He asked Dr. Mudd to accompany him and introduce him to Surratt. Dr. Mudd agreed.

Weichmann's testimony described what happened next:[56]

> About the 15th of January [note: actually December 23, 1864] last I was passing down Seventh Street, in company with John H. Surratt, and when opposite Odd Fellows' Hall, some one called "Surratt, Surratt;" and turning round, he recognized an old acquaintance of his, Dr. Samuel A. Mudd of Charles County, Md.; the gentleman there [pointing to the accused, Samuel A. Mudd] He and John Wilkes Booth were walking together. Surratt introduced Dr. Mudd to me, and Dr. Mudd introduced Booth to both of us. They were coming down Seventh Street, and we were going up. Booth invited us to his room at the National Hotel. When we arrived there, he told us to be seated, and ordered cigars and wines for four. Dr. Mudd then went out into a passage and called Booth out, and had a private conversation with him. When they returned, Booth called Surratt, and all three went out together and had a private conversation, leaving me alone. I did not hear the conversation; I was seated on a lounge near the window. On returning to the room the last time, Dr. Mudd apologized to me for his private conversation, and stated that Booth and he had some private business; that Booth wished to purchase his farm, but that he did not care about selling it, as Booth was not willing to give him enough. Booth also apologized and stated to me that he wished to purchase Dr. Mudd's farm. Afterward they were seated round the center-table, when Booth took out an envelope, and on the back of it made marks with a pencil. I should not consider it writing, but from the motion of the pencil it was more like roads or lines.

> ... After their return to the room, we remained probably twenty minutes; then left the National Hotel and went to the Pennsylvania House, where Dr. Mudd had rooms. We all went into the sitting-room, and Dr. Mudd came and sat down by me; and we talked about the war. He expressed the opinion that the war would soon come to an end, and spoke like a Union man. Booth was speaking to Surratt. At about half-past 10, Booth bade us good night, and went out. Surratt and I then bade Dr. Mudd good night. He said he was going to leave next morning.

> ... There was nothing in the conversation between Dr. Mudd, Booth, and Surratt, at the National Hotel, that led me to believe there was anything like a conspiracy going on between them.

As can be seen, Weichmann's testimony about Dr. Mudd's meeting with Booth was actually quite favorable. Weichmann said that Dr. Mudd "spoke like a Union man" and "there was nothing in the

---

[55] Pitman, Benn, *The Assassination of President Lincoln and the Trial of the Conspirators.* Testimony of Jeremiah Mudd. Page 190.

[56] Pitman, Benn, *The Assassination of President Lincoln and the Trial of the Conspirators.* Testimony of Louis J. Weichmann. Page 114.

conversation between Dr. Mudd, Booth, and Surratt, at the National Hotel, that led me to think there was anything like a conspiracy going on between them."

Booth was a famous actor, and a public figure. He enjoyed and sought out the company of people who would confirm his popularity. It would not be too much of a stretch to say that he was the Brad Pitt of his generation. Normally, Dr. Mudd would have enjoyed talking about his relationship with Booth. But after the assassination, any relationship with Booth was toxic. One has only to recall the terrified Peter denying Jesus three times to understand the fearful Dr. Mudd's denial of recognizing Booth at his farm, denial of knowing of the assassination while Booth was there, and denial of his Washington meeting with Booth.

Although Weichmann's testimony about Dr. Mudd's meeting with Booth did not implicate Dr. Mudd in any way with Booth's plot against Lincoln, Dr. Mudd was unfortunately stuck with his story that the meeting never took place. After hearing Weichmann's testimony, the Military Commission understandably concluded that Dr. Mudd was trying to hide his meeting with Booth for some incriminating reason. This, together with their belief that Dr. Mudd had helped Booth escape by not reporting him to the authorities, probably sealed Dr. Mudd's fate.

Conviction

When the trial was over on June 30th, all eight defendants were convicted. Writing after the trial, General August V. Kautz, a member of the Military Commission, wrote:[57]

The defense lasted through until about the 19th of June when we began to hear the arguments in behalf of the prisoners. An attempt was made at the close to prove insanity on the part of Payne (Note: Payne was one of Lewis Powell's aliases), who finally defeated the attempt of his counsel by maintaining his sanity, that he knew what he was doing when he tried to kill Mr. Seward. The interest of the case centered mostly about Mrs. Surratt and Payne. Dr. Mudd attracted much interest and his guilt as an active conspirator was not clearly made out. His main guilt was the fact that he failed to deliver them, that is, Booth and Herold, to their pursuers.

Mrs. Surratt was shown to have been active in the conspiracy to kidnap, prior to the capture of Richmond. That she was a willing participant in his death was not clearly made out. My own impression was that she was involved in the final result against her will by her previous connection with the conspiracy. Booth was a fanatic in the matter and craved a notoriety that would appear heroic if he survived the act, and prove martyrdom if he perished. He, no doubt, held most of his confederates in the conspiracy under the impression that it was organized for the purpose of kidnapping, who would have been deterred if they had known that they might be required to kill.

During the many weeks that the court was in session, I never saw the face of Mrs. Surratt. She sat behind the railing farthest away, and her face was constantly screened by a large palm leaf fan. I could not even recognize her picture for she was entirely unknown to me. I presume this is the case with every member of the court. All the other members of the court are indelibly impressed on my mind. Herold was a simpering foolish young man, so short of stature that he appeared like a boy and never seemed impressed with the gravity of his position. He must have been simply a plastic tool in Booth's hands.

---

[57] Reminiscences of the Civil War, August V. Kautz Papers. Manuscripts Division, Library of Congress, Washington, D.C.

Payne was a sullen character whose expression rarely changed. He seemed to be fully aware that he had taken a desperate chance and lost, and had the nerve to abide the result manfully. He was manly and strong in every respect, but how much moral character there was in his makeup was not apparent on the surface.

Atzerodt looked the hired assassin and the testimony went to show that he failed to perform his part in the compact, which was to kill Genl. Grant, either from want of courage or want of sufficient intelligence. He excited no sympathy from anyone.

Dr. Mudd was the most intelligent looking and attracted most attention of all the prisoners. There was more work done in his defense. His subsequent career showed him to be a man of more character and intelligence than anyone of the prisoners.

Spangler does not seem to have been a conspirator knowingly. He was simply a tool of Booth's and held his horse for him, and cut the stick with which Booth held the door to the box, in which Mr. Lincoln was in at the theater. His greatest crime was his ignorance, and that he did not see the ends to which he was being used.

Arnold was shown to have been associated with the conspirators, but what part he performed and to what extent he was implicated was not shown to the Commission. He was a good-looking, amiable young man, who seemed to have gotten into bad company. The same degree and character of guilt applied to O'Laughlen.

All of the prisoners had counsel but the greatest effort was made in behalf of Mrs. Surratt and Dr. Mudd. The Hon. Thom. Ewing made an elaborate defense of Mudd and Mr. Johnson, by proxy, defended Mrs. Surratt, through Mr. Aiken.

On July 5th, President Johnson approved the sentences of the Military Commission and issued the following Executive Order:

Executive Mansion, July 5, 1865.

The foregoing sentences in the cases of David E. Herold, G. A. Atzerodt, Lewis Payne, Michael O'Laughlin, Edward Spangler, Samuel Arnold, Mary E. Surratt, and Samuel A. Mudd, are hereby approved, and it is ordered that the sentences of said David E. Herold, G. A. Atzerodt, Lewis Payne, and Mary E. Surratt be carried into execution by the proper military authority, under the direction of the Secretary of War, on the 7th day of July, 1865, between the hours of 10 o'clock, A.M., and 2 o'clock, P.M., of that day. It was further ordered, that the prisoners, Samuel Arnold, Samuel A. Mudd, Edward Spangler, and Michael O'Laughlin be confined at hard labor in the Penitentiary at Albany, New York, during the period designated in their respective sentences.

Andrew Johnson, President.

Lewis Powell, David Herold, George Atzerodt, and Mary Surratt were quickly hung as ordered on July 7th.

A week after the executions, President Johnson issued a second Executive Order, changing the location where Dr. Mudd, Spangler, O'Laughlen, and Arnold would be imprisoned from the penitentiary at Albany to the military prison in the Dry Tortugas islands of Florida. The four men were not told of the change of plans.

The second Executive Order read:

Executive Mansion July 15, 1865

The Executive Order, dated July 5, 1865, approving the sentences in the cases of Samuel Arnold, Samuel A. Mudd, Edward Spangler, and Michael O'Laughlin is hereby modified, so as to direct that the said Arnold, Mudd, Spangler, and O'Laughlin, be confined at hard labor in the military prison at Dry Tortugas, Florida, during the period designated in their respective sentences.

The Adjutant-General of the Army is directed to issue orders for the said prisoners to be transported to the Dry Tortugas, and to be confined there accordingly.

Andrew Johnson, President

Two days later, July 17, 1865, the New York Tribune carried a story about Dr. Mudd and his three companions following the end of the trial. About Dr. Mudd, it said "Mudd seems in very good spirits over his escape from the gallows. He says very little about the trial. He acknowledged that the testimony of the witness Weichmann in reference to himself is correct."

If Dr. Mudd was quoted correctly, his statement that Weichmann's testimony was correct is his first admission that he lied about not seeing Booth between November 1864 and the morning after the assassination. He would make the same admission to others during his trip to the Dry Tortugas.

Part 3 - Fort Jefferson

The Trip to Prison

At one o'clock in the morning on Monday, July 17, 1865, a soldier awakened Dr. Samuel Mudd in his cell at Washington's Arsenal prison and ordered him to get up.[58]

Most people's nightmares are over when they wake up, but Dr. Mudd's was just beginning. He and three other Arsenal prisoners, Edman Spangler, Samuel Arnold, and Michael O'Laughlen, were rousted from their cells and taken in irons to a nearby wharf on the Potomac River. At the wharf, they were put aboard the side-wheel Army steamer State of Maine. The four prisoners assumed they were being put aboard the State of Maine for transport to New York, and from there to the Federal penitentiary in Albany, where they had been told they would serve their sentences.

About two o'clock in the morning, the State of Maine splashed away from the wharf and picked up speed as it slipped through the night down the Potomac River. By sunup, the ship was in the Chesapeake Bay, and by late afternoon it arrived at Fortress Monroe, located at Hampton, Virginia where the Chesapeake Bay empties into the Atlantic Ocean.

One of the ships lying at anchor off Fortress Monroe that afternoon was the Navy side-wheel steamer U.S.S. Florida. At 6:30 P.M., the Florida's commander, Captain William Budd, noted in his log book[59] that he had taken aboard as passengers Brigadier General Dodd, Colonel Turner, Captain Dutton, and Doctor Porter, all of the U.S. Army. Also taken aboard were "4 Rebel Prisoners, with a guard of 28 men & their rations." He would soon learn that his "4 Rebel Prisoners" were the four men who had been convicted but not hung in the Lincoln conspiracy trial.

At 7 P.M., the Florida raised anchor and set out to sea. She quickly left the Chesapeake Bay, entered the Atlantic Ocean, and turned south. One week and a thousand miles ahead lay the Dry Tortugas.

Samuel Arnold described their trip on the U.S.S. Florida:[60]

> No sooner were we upon the gunboat than we were ordered into the lower hold of the vessel. It required, in our shackled condition, the greatest care to safely reach there, owing to the limited space, eight inches of chain being allowed between our ankles. After leaving the second deck we were forced to descend upon a ladder whose rounds were distant so far apart that the chains bruised and lacerated the flesh and even the bone of the ankles. We remained in the sweltering hole during the night in an atmosphere pregnant with disagreeable odors, arising from various articles of subsistence stored within, and about 8 o'clock next morning we passed through another ordeal in our ascent to the deck, which was attended with more pain than the descent, owing to the raw condition of our wounds.

---

[58] Arnold, Samuel B., *Memoirs of a Lincoln Conspirator*, Edited by Michael W. Kauffman, Heritage Books, Bowie, Maryland. 2003. Page 62.

[59] Log Book, U.S.S. Florida: July 26, 1865 to December 31, 1865, Volume 5 of 26, Entry 118. Record Group 24: Records of the Bureau of Naval Personnel, National Archives, Washington, D.C.

[60] Arnold, Samuel B., *Memoirs of a Lincoln Conspirator*, Edited by Michael W. Kauffman, Heritage Books, Bowie, Maryland. 2003. Page 63.

All intercourse with the crew was prohibited, guards being stationed around us, and we were not permitted to move without being accompanied by an armed marine. Subsistence of the grossest kind was issued, in the shape of fat salt pork and hard-tack. We remained on deck during the day, closely watching, as far as we were able, the steering of the vessel by the sun, and found we were steaming due South. The course was unchanged the next day and I began to suspect that fatal isle, the Dry Tortugas, was our destined home of the future.

From this time out we remained on deck, our beds being brought up at night and taken between decks in the morning. Arriving off Hilton Head, S.C., and whilst lying in port, we were informed by General Dodd that he was sailing under sealed orders, but as soon as we left the port he would announce our destination. We remained there during the night, having received some guests on board, and the officers amused themselves with dancing and carousing. About 12 o'clock in the day we were informed that the Dry Tortugas was our destination. Of it I had no idea beyond that gathered through the columns of the press, in which it had been depicted as a perfect hell, which fact was duly established by imprisonment on its limited space. After the second day on the ocean the irons were removed from our feet during the day, but replaced at night, and we were permitted from this day out the privilege of being on deck on account of the oppressive heat of the climate, where we could catch the cool sea breeze as it swept across the deck in the ship's onward track over the bounding ocean.

During the voyage to Fort Jefferson, Edman Spangler found paper and pencil and wrote a short letter to a friend. The letter was printed in the August 28, 1865 edition of the Washington Evening Star:

A gentleman in this city received a letter from Spangler, written previous to his arrival at the Dry Tortugas, written with a lead pencil, as follows:

On Board St'r Florida, bound to the Island of Dry Tortugas, Fla. – Friend: Still thinking of old times, and wishing I was seated in your saloon drinking a nice glass of whiskey, instead of in this hot and sunny clime. The last drink I had was in your house, and you may put it down as a settled fact it will be the last for six long years to come, and may be forever before I get another. You must not forget me now in my sunny home. When joy shall swell your heart, and the welkin is made to ring with the light and cheerful voices of yourself and my former companions, stop for a moment to cast a lingering but bright thought upon him who was life, all life, amidst you, wish him a companion of your festival, and I will feel happy in my exile – banished and in a burning clime – Dry Tortugas, thirteen hundred miles from you. Extend your hospitality to the gentleman who brings this to you. Good bye: sometimes think of me and my companions, though they are unknown to you personally.

– Edward Spangler

The transfer of the prisoners to Fort Jefferson took place in great secrecy. The Government wanted to quickly place the prisoners beyond the reach of the civil courts which might release them for a variety of reasons. The Government was also still concerned that the assassination may have been part of a larger Confederate conspiracy and that others in the plot, or sympathetic to the plot, might try to free the convicted prisoners. The transfer only became known after the Florida was at sea, when it was reported in the newspapers of Tuesday, July 19, 1865.

Following is a letter to Dr. Mudd's lawyer, General Thomas Ewing, Jr. from his law partner Orville Hickman Browning, complaining about the Government's secret transfer of the prisoners to Fort Jefferson.

Washington D.C.   July 19, 1865
Dear General:

The Intelligencer & Chronicle both announce this morning that Mudd, Spangler, Arnold, and O'Laughlin were taken on Monday from the Arsenal to Fortress Monroe, and there placed on board a vessel provisioned for thirty days, and that it is supposed they have been sent to the Dry Tortugas.

Irregular as this may be, it is, in all probability, true. The Chronicle is, no doubt, advised in the procedures and would hardly have made the announcement unless satisfied of the fact.

The authorities have probably determined that the question shall not be brought before the judicial tribunals, and have made this disposition of the prisoners to preclude a bearing upon habeas corpus. If their destination is as supposed, they are beyond the reach of law, and will have to await the course of events to bring them relief.

Dr. Blanford & wife were here on Saturday, desiring an interview with Dr. Mudd, but did not get it. Stanton was reported out of town, and Holt and others said they had no authority to grant passes. They called late in the afternoon. I told them to return on Wednesday, and I would go, in person, and make an effort to gain their admission, but on Monday the prisoners were removed!

I supposed, of course, they were going to Albany, and told Blanford I thought we had better not be precipitate in applying for a habeas corpus, but wait a few months and give time for passion to cool, and reason to resume its sway. He entirely agreed with me. We, and the public, are likely to have time enough for reflection....

Yours truly,

O.H. Browning

The Government also did not tell the prisoners' families of the transfer to Fort Jefferson. Mrs. Mudd last saw her husband when she visited him in the Arsenal prison on July 6th, the day before the four hangings. Two weeks later, she read in the papers that Dr. Mudd was on his way to the Dry Tortugas. Mrs. Mudd described her discovery:[61]

I came home and only a few days later read in the papers that Spangler, Arnold, O'Laughlin and my husband were on their way to the Dry Tortugas. Two days after this I received a letter from the Doctor, which was written on board the ship and mailed at Charleston, where a short stop was made. In this letter he asked me to not give up hope; to take care of the little ones and at some future day he would be at home with us. This seemed to give me courage, and I began to work with renewed efforts to try to secure his release.

---

[61] Mudd, Nettie, *The Life of Dr. Samuel A. Mudd*, Fourth Edition. Page 39.

The Dry Tortugas

In late December 1824 and early January 1825, about five years after Spain sold Florida to the United States for five million dollars, U.S. Navy Commodore David Porter inspected the Dry Tortugas islands. He was on the lookout for a site for a naval station that would help suppress piracy in the Caribbean. Unimpressed with what he saw, he notified the Secretary of the Navy that the Dry Tortugas were unfit for any kind of naval establishment. He reported that they consist of small sand islands a little above the surface of the ocean, have no fresh water, scarcely land enough to place a fortification, and in any case are probably not solid enough to bear one.

While Commodore Porter thought the Dry Tortugas were unfit for a naval station, others in the Government thought the islands were a good location for a lighthouse to guide ships around the area's reefs and small islands. A small island called Bush Key, later called Garden Key, was selected as the site for the new lighthouse. Construction began in 1825 and was completed in 1826. The 65-foot lighthouse was constructed of brick with a whitewashed exterior. A small white cottage for the lighthouse keeper was constructed beside the lighthouse.

In May 1829, Commodore John Rodgers stopped at the Dry Tortugas to evaluate the anchorage. Contrary to Commodore Porter's experience, Rogers was delighted with what he found. The Dry Tortugas, he reported, consisted of 11 small keys and surrounding reefs and banks, over which the sea broke. There was an outer and an inner harbor. The former afforded a safe anchorage at all seasons, and was large enough to let a large number of ships ride at anchor. Of more importance, the inner harbor combined a sufficient depth of water for ships-of-the-line, with a narrow entrance of not more than 120 yards. Rogers said that if a hostile power should occupy the Dry Tortugas, United States shipping in the Gulf would be in deadly peril, and "nothing but absolute naval superiority" could prevail. However, if occupied and fortified by the U.S., the Dry Tortugas would constitute the "advance post" for a defense of the Gulf Coast.

A series of engineering studies and bureaucratic delays consumed the next 17 years, but the construction of Fort Jefferson was finally begun on Garden Key in 1846.[62] The new fort would be built so that the existing Garden Key lighthouse and the lighthouse keeper's cottage would be contained within the walls of the fort. The parade ground side of the cell in which Dr. Mudd lived for most of his time at Fort Jefferson looked out directly onto the lighthouse tower and lighthouse keeper's cottage. The lighthouse would continue to serve a vital function in guiding ships through the waters of the Dry Tortugas Islands until the current metal light tower was installed atop an adjacent wall of the fort in 1876. The original brick lighthouse tower was taken down in 1877, eight years after Dr. Mudd left Fort Jefferson.

The design of the fort called for a three-tiered six-sided 420 heavy-gun fort, with two sides measuring 325 feet, and four sides measuring 477 feet. The walls met at corner bastions, which are large projections designed to allow defensive fire along the faces of the walls they joined. The heavy guns were mounted inside the walls in a string of open casemates, or gunrooms, facing outward toward the sea through large openings called embrasures. Fort Jefferson was designed to be a massive gun platform, impervious to assault, and able to destroy any enemy ships foolhardy to come within range of its powerful guns. If a fully constructed and manned Fort Jefferson had ever been put to the test, it would have surely been a one-sided fight.

---

[62] Manucy, Albert C., *The History of Fort Jefferson National Monument, Part One: The Fort at Garden Key 1846-1860*. Florida Works Progress Administration, Project 194, District Five, Key West, Fla. Page 14ff. Library of Congress Main Reading Room.

Fort Jefferson occupies about ten acres, roughly the same size as Yankee Stadium. The brick walls containing the gun rooms occupy approximately the same area as Yankee Stadium's stands. Inside the fort, the grassy central area, known as the Parade ground, is about the same size as the stadium's playing field. Living quarters for soldiers and officers, gunpowder magazines, carpenter shop, bakery, chapel, theater, kitchens, storehouses, and other buildings required to maintain the fort were located around the periphery of the Parade ground. The remaining central grassy area was used for drills, inspections, a small garden, and sports. including baseball, which was exploding in popularity as America's "national pastime." Most of the structures are gone now, victims of the tropical climate, hurricanes, and fires.

Fort Jefferson was essentially a very small and densely populated city. Almost 2,000 people lived there during the Civil War years just before Dr. Mudd arrived. The peak military population was 1,729, but there were also many civilians, a fluctuating number of military and civilian prisoners, and a few slaves, living there. They were all engaged in the construction and maintenance of the fort. Occupations included machinists, carpenters, plasterers, bakers, butchers, painters, blacksmiths, masons, and general laborers. There were also lighthouse keepers and their families, cooks, a civilian doctor and his family. A number of officers brought their families, including children, and a limited number of enlisted personnel brought wives who served as laundresses (typically four per company). The 22 slaves working at Fort Jefferson in 1863 were freed shortly after Lincoln's Emancipation Proclamation.

With the war over, the population began to decline and had dropped to 1,013 by the time Dr. Mudd arrived in July 1865. Of these, 486 were soldiers or civilians and 527 were prisoners. When Dr. Mudd was released in March 1869, the population had dropped to 282, of whom only 35 were prisoners.

The military prisoners at Fort Jefferson were a rough crowd. Their offenses included murder, manslaughter, robbery, grand larceny, and desertion. In June 1867, Post Commander George P. Andrews issued Special Order No. 78 which said:

> The attention of the officers of this Post is called to the fact that atrocious crimes have been committed by prisoners at this Post who seem to think they cannot be reached by law.

> In future every sentinel must use his bayonet and cartridge, and no sentinel who faithfully tries to do his duty shall ever see the inside of the guard house; if a prisoner refuses to obey orders the sentinel must shoot him, and then use his bayonet, at the same time calling for the guard. The responsibility for obedience to this order will be borne by the commanding officer.

Construction of Fort Jefferson was still under way when Dr. Mudd and his fellow prisoners arrived in 1865, continued all during the time they were imprisoned there, and for several years thereafter, but was never completely finished. By 1888, the military usefulness of Fort Jefferson had waned, and the cost of maintaining the fort due to the effects of frequent hurricanes and the corrosive tropical climate could no longer be justified.

In 1888 the Army turned the fort over to the Marine-Hospital Service to be operated as a quarantine station. In 1935 President Franklin Roosevelt set aside Fort Jefferson and the surrounding waters as a national monument. In 1992 the area was designated as Dry Tortugas National Park to protect the historical and natural features.

Fort Jefferson has been called Shark Island, Devil's Island, Death Island and other similar names, but to the people who lived there, Fort Jefferson was just Fort Jefferson, or as the prisoners sometimes referred to it, Hell.

The Prisoners' Arrival

After a seven day journey, the U.S.S. Florida arrived at Fort Jefferson at 11:30 A.M. on July 24, 1865. Rain squalls kept the temperature down to 85 degrees, not too bad for the Florida Keys at the end of July. A pilot came out from the fort to guide the Florida to an anchorage.[63] At 2 P.M., an officer from the fort came aboard to escort General Dodd and other officers ashore. An hour later, Dr. Mudd and his companions were taken ashore. O'Laughlen would never leave Fort Jefferson, dying two years later during the great 1867 yellow fever epidemic. Dr. Mudd, Arnold, and Spangler would not leave the island prison until March 1869, after receiving pardons from President Johnson.

Samuel Arnold describes the event:

> We arrived in sight of Fort Jefferson, Dry Tortugas, Fla., on July 24, 1865. When nearing the grim-looking walls, a signal gun was fired from the gunboat, which was responded to by the officer in command of the fort, and soon the officer of the day made his appearance on board, and was informed of the object of the visit of the boat, etc. Within a very short time we were placed within a small boat, were conveyed to the fort, and placed within one of the many casemates existing there.
>
> The officers who had had us in charge remained at the fort a sufficient length of time to have, as it is called, a lark. After three months of torture both of body and mind, we thought that we had at last found a haven of rest, although in a government Bastile, where, shut out from the world, we would dwell and pass the remaining days of our life. It was a sad thought, yet it had to be borne.
>
> We were now left under the charge of Col. Charles Hamilton, 110th New York Volunteers, who was at that period commandant of the post. He gave us instructions relative to the rules in force, stating the consequences which would attend any breach in discipline, finally impressing upon our minds that there was a dark and gloomy dungeon within the fort, to which offenders against the rules were consigned, over whose entrance was inscribed the classic words: "Whoso entereth here leaveth all hope behind."

Anyone entering or leaving Fort Jefferson did so through the Sally Port entrance. When Dr. Mudd and his companions arrived, the casemates, or gunrooms, on the second tier of the Sally Port wall were used to house prisoners, so this is likely where they were first assigned to live. Construction of the second tier casemates had been suspended because the weight of the fort was causing it to sink into the ground.

Each new prisoner was given a number. Arnold was prisoner 1523, Dr. Mudd was prisoner 1524, O'Laughlen was prisoner 1525, and Spangler was prisoner 1526. The military also referred to Dr. Mudd, Spangler, Arnold, and O'Laughlen as their 'state' prisoners to distinguish them from all the other Army and civilian prisoners at Fort Jefferson.

---

[63] Log Book, U.S.S. Florida: July 26, 1865 to December 31, 1865, Volume 5 of 26, Entry 118. Record Group 24: Records of the Bureau of Naval Personnel, National Archives, Washington, D.C.

Dr. Mudd and his fellow state prisoners were assigned to work according to their skills. [64] Dr. Mudd was assigned to work in the prison hospital. Samuel Arnold, who had attended Georgetown College, was assigned to clerical work in the office of the fort's commanding officer. Edman Spangler worked at his profession in the carpentry shop. [65] Arnold said "Spangler's trade was a godsend at this time and proved so on more than one occasion afterwards." O'Laughlen was assigned to work as a laborer helping with construction of the fort.

Following is the first letter Mrs. Mudd received from her husband after his arrival at Fort Jefferson. He had apparently written earlier letters, but because of erratic mail service, she had not yet received them. Recall that friends and family usually addressed Mrs. Mudd by her nicknames of "Frank" or "Frankie."

Fort Jefferson, Dry Tortugus, Florida,
August 24, 1865

Dearest Frank:

To-day one month ago we arrived here. Time passes very slowly and seems longer than that period - years gone by, apparently no longer. What do you think? I have received no letter or news whatever from home since being here. One or two of those who came down with me have received letters, containing no news, and do not advert to the possibility or the subject of release.

You know, my dear Frank, that that subject is the all absorbing one of my mind. Frank must be sick - the little children are sick - some may be dead, or some other misfortune has happened, are questions frequently revolving in my mind and heart, and the dear ones at home are unwilling to break the cruel intelligence to me.

My dear Frank, were it not for you and those at home, I could pass the balance of my days here perfectly content or satisfied. Without you and the children, what is life for me - a blank, a void. Then, my dear Frank, if you have any regard for me, which you know I have never doubted, let me hear from you and often. I have written to you by every mail that has left this place, and surely some have been received. I wrote to you aboard the boat before arriving here. Mail, sometimes, arrives here in five days from New York.

This place continues to be unusually healthy, and the only fear manifested is that disease may be propagated by the arrival of vessels and steamers from infected ports. At this time there is a vessel lying at quarantine with all hands aboard sick with fever of some description, - several have died, and there is not one well enough to nurse the sick - no volunteers from among the prisoners going to them, so the chances of life are small.

I am now in the hospital. I have little or no labor to perform, but my fare is not much improved. My principal diet is coffee, butter and bread three times a day. We have had a mess or two of Irish potatoes and onions, but as a general thing vegetables don't last many days in this climate before decomposition takes place. Pork and beef are poisonous to me; and molasses when I am able to

---

[64] Report of Lieutenant G.S. Carpenter, Sept. 16, 1865, Letters Sent Relating to Prisoners: Fort Jefferson, Florida Headquarters. Record Group 393, Entry 2. National Archives, Washington, D.C.

[65] Fort Jefferson, Florida, Provost Marshall, Records Relating to Prisoners, List of Prisoners and How Employed, October 9, 1868. Record Group 393, Entry 56. National Archives, Washington, D.C.

buy it, and occasionally (fresh) fish, when Providence favored, are the only articles of diet used. I am enjoying very good health, considering the circumstances.

Sweet, dearest Frank, write to me soon on the receipt of my letter. I am afraid letters have been intercepted from either you or myself. If I don't hear from you soon, I am afraid I will become alike indifferent and careless. I have written to Jere, Ewing, Stone, Ma and Papa some several letters - others, one or two, and not one syllable have I received.

I am afraid when the silence is broken, the news will be so great as to endanger the safety of the boat. My dear Frank, I have nothing to interest you - several hundred prisoners have been released and gone home recently to their families.

My anxiety increases upon the arrival of every boat and mail, and I envy the departing homeward bound. Give my love to all - kiss the children and believe me, truly and sincerely, your husband, S.A. MUDD

Promises, Promises

Throughout his entire imprisonment, Dr. Mudd experienced a dizzying roller coaster ride of rising hopes for imminent release followed by sinking drops to the depths of despair as such hopes were dashed. His hopes for release were fed by well-wishing family members, various friends, and paid lawyers. In letters home he would often speak hopefully of his imminent release based on their encouragement. When such hopes were routinely dashed, he finally asked that people stop telling him he was going to be released. But of course they didn't stop, and Dr. Mudd's wild emotional roller coaster ride continued for almost four years.

President Andrew Johnson was the source of much of the optimism for Dr. Mudd's release. From the very beginning of Dr. Mudd's imprisonment, President Johnson made regular private promises to Mrs. Mudd and others that he would release Dr. Mudd as soon as he could politically do so. One of Johnson's promises was recounted in a February 1866 letter that Jeremiah Dyer wrote to his sister, Mrs. Mudd. He describes a meeting he had with John T. Ford, the theater owner who was lobbying President Johnson and other public figures to release his former employee Edman Spangler.[66]

Dyer's letter said in part:[67]

I stopped in Washington to see Ford, but learned he was not in the city, so yesterday I went over and had a long interview with him. He told me he had a long interview with the President the day before, and had every assurance he would release Sam at the earliest moment he could consistently do so; the President also remarked to him, he (Sam) was a mere creature of accident, and ought not to have been put there, but in the present state of political excitement he did not think it prudent in him to take any action, as it would be another pretext for the radicals to build capital on.

… I have not the least doubt Sam will be released as soon as Johnson can do so with propriety, and I really think the day is not far distant.

---

[66] Mudd, Nettie, *The Life of Dr. Samuel A. Mudd*, Fourth Edition. Page 181.

[67] Mudd, Nettie, *The Life of Dr. Samuel A. Mudd*, Fourth Edition. Page 165.

According to John T. Ford, President Johnson thought that Dr. Mudd "was a mere creature of accident, and ought not to have been put there." Nevertheless, Johnson did keep him there because, as he told John Ford, he feared his political enemies would use Dr. Mudd's release against him.

The period following the end of the Civil War was a time of intense political struggle over reconstruction policies. One of the many complaints against Johnson was his extensive use of the pardon power to free former Confederate leaders. This worked against Dr. Mudd, whose pardon would surely have provided the basis for more political attacks against Johnson, and could conceivably have cost him the presidency.

Attempted Escape

In September 1865, two months after Dr. Mudd arrived, he tried to escape from Fort Jefferson. Control of Fort Jefferson was being transferred from the 161st New York Volunteers to the 82nd United States Colored Infantry. Prisoners had received good treatment under the 161st, as evidenced by the following letter written by Dr. Mudd to Captain William R. Prentice, the departing commander of the 161st:

Fort Jefferson, Tortugas, Florida, Sept. 19th. '65
Captain W.R. Prentice

My Dear Sir:

I did not observe until this morning the token of your friendship and kindness. I accept with pleasure the volume, ("Les Miserables") and often as my eyes shall scan its consoling pages - my mind shall revert with gratitude towards the Donor for the kind consideration received. You will please excuse my present poverty for a more suitable reciprocation of good feeling, and accept a small medal - usually worn by members of the Catholic Church, as a monitor and in honor of the Blessed Virgin, Mother of Christ.

With many regrets at your early withdrawal from the Chief Command of the Post and contemplated departure homeward - a pleasant trip - a happy future - I am very respectfully and truly

Your Obedient Ser'vt
Saml. A. Mudd M.D.

As a recent slave owner and a person convicted of conspiring to kill the president who had freed the slaves, Dr. Mudd was understandably fearful of his treatment by the incoming 82nd United States Colored Infantry. On September 25, 1865, he attempted to escape from Fort Jefferson by stowing away on the Army supply ship Thomas A. Scott, but was captured.

On its previous trip to Fort Jefferson, the Thomas A. Scott had left the fort bound for New York with eight escaping prisoners hidden aboard. Dr. Mudd thought he would he would try to escape the same way, but he was discovered hiding on the Thomas A. Scott, brought back to the Fort, and put in chains.

Writing to his brother-in-law Jeremiah Dyer, Dr. Mudd described his failed escape attempt:

... Providence was against me. I was too well known and was apprehended five or ten minutes after being aboard the steamer. They were so much rejoiced at finding me, they did not care to look much farther; the consequence was, the boat went off and carried away four other prisoners, who no doubt will make good their escape.

... For attempting to make my escape, I was put in the guard-house, with chains on hands and feet, and closely confined for two days. An order then came from the Major for me to be put to hard labor, wheeling sand. I was placed under a boss, who put me to cleaning old bricks. I worked hard all day, and came very near finishing one brick. The order also directs the Provost Marshal to have me closely confined on the arrival of every steamer and until she departs.

... I would have succeeded, only for meeting a party aboard, who knew me, before I could arrive at my hiding-place. I was informed on almost immediately, and was taken in custody by the guard.

Dr. Mudd's observation that he worked hard all day cleaning old bricks, nearly finishing one brick, illustrates the sardonic humor which appears from time to time in his letters.

Major George E. Wentworth, Fort Jefferson's new commanding officer, reported Dr. Mudd's escape attempt to the Army Adjutant General in Washington, D.C.:

Hdqrs Fort Jefferson Fla.
September 25, 1865.

Sir:

I have the honor to report that this morning upon searching the U. S. Transport Thos A Scott before her departure for New York, Dr Saml A Mudd was found secreted in the Lower Hold of the vessel under some planks. I immediately placed him in the dungeon in irons. From the position in which he was found I thought that he must have secured aid from some Party or Parties on board the steamer.

I went to the dungeon in which Dr. Mudd was confined, and threatened him with some punishment unless he disclosed the name of the parties who assisted him. He at last stated that a man by the name of Kelly, one of the crew of the steamer, assisted him. I immediately ordered his arrest and now have him confined in irons.

From the evidence of one James Healy, Coal Passer on the Steamer Scott whose deposition has been taken, I am of the opinion that Kelley was bribed by Dr. Mudd as I understand that Mudd has offered money to parties here to get them to do him favors. Henry Kelley is a young man. I should think about 18 years old. I would respectfully request that orders be given me in regard to the disposition of this man Kelly.

I am Very Respectfully
Your Obt. Serv't
George E. Wentworth, Major 82d. U.S.C. Infty, Commanding

Dr. Mudd apologized to Major Wentworth for having tried to escape, sending him the following note:

To the Major Commanding

Sir,

I acknowledge to having acted contrary to my own judgment & honor, in my attempted escape. I assure you it was more from the impulse of the moment & with the hope of speedily seeing my disconsolate wife & four little infants. Mr. Kelly did not secrete me aboard, but, promised to do so only. Before I was detected I had made up my mind to return if I could do so without being observed by the guards. I am truly ashamed of my conduct, & if I am restored again to the freedom of the Fort & former position, no cause shall arise to create your displeasure, & I shall always counsel subordination to the ruling authorities. By complying or relieving me from my present humble locality - you will merit the gratitude of your humble servant, a devoted wife & four dear little children. I do not complain of the punishment, but I feel that I have abused the kindness & confidence reposed, & would be glad exceedingly to comply with any other honorable acquirement, whereby, I may be able to wash away, the folly of my weakness.

Truly & Respectfully Yrs &c
Saml A. Mudd

The Dungeon

Following Dr. Mudd's attempted escape he was placed in a small cell in the guardhouse, located next to the Sally Port entrance. After a couple of days, he was allowed outside to work during the day, but was required to sleep in the guardhouse at night. On October 18th, he was transferred along with Arnold, O'Laughlen, Spangler, and George St. Leger Grenfell to a large empty ground-level gunroom in the bastion at the south end of the Sally Port wall. This was the "dark and gloomy dungeon" the post commandant had warned Dr. Mudd and his companions about when they arrived at Fort Jefferson.

Spangler, Arnold, and O'Laughlen were transferred to the dungeon along with Dr. Mudd because the authorities had heard, incorrectly it turned out, that there was a plan under way to free the four men.

The dungeon was the most secure place in the fort. It had a locked wooden door, a slate floor, slimy wet brick walls and ceiling, and two gun ports. Although one port was open, the other was closed with metal shutters. As a result, there was no cross ventilation and the light admitted by the single open port was insufficient to brighten the room. Immediately outside the small open port was an area where the fort's toilets emptied into the 70-foot wide moat. The architects had assumed the moat would be flushed clean by tidal action, but that often didn't happen. Inside the dungeon, the smell from the moat was inescapable. The moat surrounded the fort, so the wind carried the smell into the fort no matter which way the wind was blowing. In a January 22, 1866 letter which he wrote from the dungeon, Dr. Mudd said:

> The atmosphere we breathe is highly impregnated with sulphuric hydrogen gas, which you are aware is highly injurious to health as well as disagreeable. The gas is generated by the numerous sinks that empty into that portion of the sea enclosed by the breakwater, and which is immediately under a small port hole – the only admission for air and light we have from the external port.

The food in the dungeon was as bad as the air. Sam Arnold wrote:

> The rations issued at this time were putrid, unfit to eat, and during these three months of confinement I lived upon a cup of slop coffee and the dry, hard crust of bread. This is no

54

exaggeration, as many others can testify to its truthfulness. Coffee was brought over to our quarters in a dirty, greasy bucket, always with grease swimming upon its surface; bread, rotten fish and meat, all mixed together, and thus we were forced to live for months, until starvation nearly stared us in the face.

Six days a week, Dr. Mudd and the others were let out of the dungeon to work at hard labor. On Sundays and holidays they were confined all day inside the noxious cell. The men wore leg irons while working outside, but the irons were removed when inside the dungeon. Dr. Mudd suffered quite a bit both mentally and physically during his time in the dungeon. In a letter to his wife he said:

My legs and ankles are swollen and sore, pains in my shoulders and back are frequent. My hair began falling out some time ago, and to save which I shaved it all over clean, and have continued to do so once every week since. It is now beginning to have a little life. My eyesight is beginning to grow very bad, so much so that I can't read or write by candlelight.

John Ford, Spangler's boss at Ford's Theater, described Dr. Mudd's condition at this time in a letter he wrote to General Ewing. He said:

I am anxious to get a settlement with the Govt and then take measures with you looking to Spangler's pardon.

I heard from him the other day by a returned prisoner. He is doing well and is a general favorite but is compelled to wear irons. Dr. Mudd looks very badly. His hair is nearly all out and he is nearly half crazy. With Arnold he is compelled by a Negro guard to sweep the Sally Port continually. I believe that is the name. He is ironed, as well as Arnold.

On January 26, 1866, following a complaint by Mrs. Mudd to President Johnson a month earlier, Dr. Mudd and the other men were no longer required to wear leg irons. Shortly thereafter they were released from the dungeon and moved into the empty casemate gun room directly above the Sally Port entrance. The casemates on this second tier of the Sally Port wall were never fitted out with cannons, and instead were used to house the general prisoner population. The casemate above the Sally Port entrance would be the home for Dr. Mudd, Spangler, Arnold, and O'Laughlen during the remainder of their time at Fort Jefferson.

Colonel George St. Leger Grenfell

The other man in the dungeon with Dr. Mudd and his companions was Colonel George St. Leger Grenfell. Born in London on May 30, 1808, Grenfell was a British soldier of fortune who claimed to have fought in Algeria, in Morocco against the Barbary pirates, under Garibaldi in South America, in the Crimean War, and in the Sepoy Mutiny. He came to America in 1862 and became an officer in the Confederate Army, serving with calvaryman John H. Morgan, General Braxton Bragg, and General J.E.B. Stuart. He resigned from the Confederate Army in 1864 to join a plot to take over the governments of Ohio, Indiana, and Illinois and establish a Northwestern Confederacy.[68]

When the plan to take over Chicago was discovered, Grenfell and some 150 others were arrested. In what became known as the "Chicago Conspiracy", Grenfell was tried, convicted, and sentenced to hang. Through the efforts of the British Minister in Washington, his sentence was commuted to life imprisonment

---

[68] Starr, Stephen Z., *Colonel Grenfell's Wars: The Life of a Soldier of Fortune.* Louisiana State University Press. Baton Rouge. 1971.

at Fort Jefferson. Like Dr. Mudd and his companions, Colonel Grenfell was considered to be a 'state' prisoner.

Shortly after Grenfell arrived, Dr. Mudd wrote to his brother-in-law Jeremiah Dyer:

> We are all at this moment in chains. Neither Colonel Grenfel nor myself has been taken out to work the past two or three days, but suffered to remain passively in our quarters. He is quite an intelligent man, tall, straight, and about sixty-one or two years of age. He speaks fluently several languages, and often adds mirth by his witty sarcasm and jest. He has been badly wounded and is now suffering with dropsy, and is allowed no medical treatment whatever, but loaded down with chains, and fed upon the most loathsome food, which treatment in a short time must bring him to an untimely grave. You will confer an act of kindness and mercy by acquainting the English Minister at Washington, Sir F.A. Bruce, of these facts.

In an April 16, 1867 letter to Tom Dyer, his wife's brother in New Orleans, Dr. Mudd writes of Grenfell again:

> Colonel St. Ledger Grenfel is kept in close confinement under guard. A few days ago, being sick, he applied to the doctor of the Post for medical attention, which he was refused, and he was ordered to work. Feeling himself unable to move about, he refused. He was then ordered to carry a ball until further orders, which he likewise refused. He was then tied up for half a day, and still refusing, he was taken to one of the wharves, thrown overboard with a rope attached, and ducked; being able to keep himself above water, a fifty pound weight was attached to his feet. Grenfel is an old man, about sixty. He has never refused to do work which he was able to perform, but they demanded more than he felt able, and he wisely refused. They could not conquer him, and he is doing now that which he never objected doing.

In a 1926 Saturday Evening Post article, author George Allan England provided a description of Colonel Grenfell, as told to him by a former Fort Jefferson lighthouse keeper:

> All sorts and conditions were herded into the prison of Dry Tortugas. The greatest mystery man of them all was a fiery swashbuckler known as Col. St. Leger Grenfell.

> "He was a queer bird altogether," one William Felton told me at Key West. Felton was long a custodian at the fort, and can rock on his front porch and spin yarns about it by the hour. "Grenfell was sure one tough lookin' customer, six foot tall, black-haired, an' with black eyes under big, bushy eyebrows. He had a tremendous black beard, too, an' wore a red flannel shirt open at the neck, an' his pant legs tucked in high boots. Folks said he was a son of Sir Roger Grenfell, a earl, or somethin' swell like that."

Colonel Grenfell was afflicted with yellow fever during the height of the epidemic in September 1867. In letters to his wife, Dr. Mudd writes "Colonel Grenfel is quite sick with the disease; he was taken yesterday. I will do all that is possible to save him." And, "Colonel Grenfel is quite sick; his case is doubtful." But in the end, Dr. Mudd was able to save his life and Colonel Grenfell recovered.

Dr. Mudd's final mention of Colonel Grenfell is in an April 14, 1868 letter to his wife. In it he says:

> We have heard nothing from Grenfel since he escaped on the 6th of last month. All hands may have perished, it being quite stormy at the time.

Colonel Grenfell, a highly experienced sailor, and three others had escaped from Fort Jefferson in a small boat. The military report of the escape said:

> …Private William Noreil of Company I 5th US Arty who had been on duty posted as a sentinel over the boats within the boom, did between the hours of 11 o'clock P.M. and 1 A.M. desert his post, taking possession of a small boat and carrying with him the following named prisoners – G. St. Leger Grenfell, J.W. Adare, James Orr and Joseph Holroya.
>
> I am impressed with the belief that Grenfell had considerable money in his possession by and through which he bribed the sentinel.
>
> The surveying steamer Bibb which was lying in the harbor was dispatched in pursuit of them about 8 o'clock the same morning but after cruising the whole day failed either to overhaul or hear anything concerning them.

Most assumed that Grenfell and the others perished at sea, but there were persistent rumors he had survived. On June 5, 1868, the following announcement, originally published in the Mobile Alabama Advertiser, appeared in the New York Times.

> St. Leger Grenfell - The public was greatly gratified not long since to learn that this gallant English soldier had escaped his prison at the Dry Tortugas, and in his love of liberty at the risk of life, he had trusted himself to the mercies of a frail boat in an attempt to cross the Florida Straits to Cuba. We have the pleasure of stating that his voyage was made in safety, and that a letter has been received from him in Havana, sending his thanks and acknowledgments for kind treatment to some of the army officers at Tortugas, and stating that he was just about to sail for Old England. We do not doubt that every gentleman officer belonging to the garrison of his prison guard rejoices at his escape.

Most historians believe that notices such as this about Grenfell were fabrications. All that is known for sure is that Grenfell was never heard from again.

Prison Life

Daily life at Fort Jefferson was dictated by the rhythm of a busy army post. In the morning, bugle calls announced the time to rise and shine, to assemble for morning roll call, and for breakfast. The morning gun was fired as the flag was raised over the fort. Lunch, supper, and various events in between were announced by bugle calls. In the evening, bugle calls announced retreat, evening roll call, and bedtime taps. The evening gun was fired as the flag was lowered for the night. During the night, fort sentries loudly announced the regular changing of the guards.

Unfortunately for Dr. Mudd and his companions, they had front row seats to the sights and sounds of all this activity. For most of their time at Fort Jefferson, they lived in a casemate directly over the Sally Port near the area where most of this activity took place. Dr. Mudd wrote:

> We have three sentries within ten feet of our door that cry out the hours of the night at the pitch of their voices, which awakens us and destroys all sleep.[69]

---

[69] Mudd, Nettie, *The Life of Dr. Samuel A. Mudd*, Fourth Edition, Page 194.

Prisoners were primarily housed in casemates on the unfinished second tier of the Sally Port wing. When they were released from the dungeon, Dr. Mudd, Spangler, Arnold, and O'Laughlen were moved to a casemate in this wing, directly above the Sally Port entrance. They lived here for the next three years until their release from Fort Jefferson - except Mike O'Laughlen who died from yellow fever in 1867. Colonel Grenfell lived in a nearby casemate in the same wing.

Casemates were designed to be gunrooms for cannons, not living quarters for people. There was little privacy. They were designed to be open to the elements and to each other to allow gun smoke and noise to dissipate quickly. The east side of Dr. Mudd's casemate was open to the long line of adjoining casemates. The west side was a brick wall since this was the last in the row of casemates. The south side of the casemate cell was the interior of the brick Sally Port wall. There were three vertical slits in this wall, starting about seven feet above the floor. These openings admitted some air but were too high to serve as windows.

The entire north side of Dr. Mudd's casemate was open to the interior of the fort. On the parade ground immediately in front of the casemate sat two structures seemingly out of place inside the walls of a fort. The first structure was a small cottage surrounded by a white picket fence. The other structure, immediately behind the cottage, was a working 65-foot lighthouse, tended by the lighthouse keeper who lived in the cottage with his family. The lighthouse had been in operation before Fort Jefferson was thought of, and continued in operation while Fort Jefferson was built around it.

Dr. Mudd's casemate was directly above the Sally Port entrance. A stone cap on the Sally Port entranceway extended slightly above the outer edge of their casemate floor, causing rainwater to collect and pool on the floor. To drain the water, the men gouged a hole into the cement floor, with a line of small trenches running into the hole. The water that collected in the hole was scooped up and thrown outside. The high humidity and tropical rains caused constantly wet, damp living quarters. In a letter home, Dr. Mudd wrote:

> After every rain, our quarters leak terribly, and it's not unusual to dip up from the floor ten and twelve large buckets of water daily. We have a hole cut into the floor and little trenches cut, so as to concentrate the aqueous secretion, which facilitates the dipping process and freeing the room from noxious miasma.[70]

Sam Arnold wrote of the same problem:

> Often during our confinement in the place buckets were used to bail out the collected water, it having been found necessary to dig deep holes and gutters to catch the water, thereby preventing our quarters becoming flooded all over. For months --- yes, over a year --- were we quartered in this filthy place, having as companions in our misery every insect known to abound on the island, in the shape of mosquitoes, bedbugs, roaches and scorpions, by which, both night and day, we were tormented.[71]

The military eventually provided dry floor planking to relieve this condition. Spangler's carpentry skills undoubtedly came in handy in installing the planking. Arnold's reference to living in "this filthy place" for over a year apparently referred to the length of time they had to live there while it was wet and flooded,

---

[70] Mudd, Nettie, *The Life of Dr. Samuel A. Mudd*, Fourth Edition, Page 199.

[71] Mudd, Nettie, *The Life of Dr. Samuel A. Mudd*, Fourth Edition, Page 185.

before the dry planking was provided. They lived in the Sally Port casemate the entire three years from their release from the dungeon in February 1866 until their release from Fort Jefferson in March 1869.

Hurricanes were a constant threat. For example, on Sunday, October 22, 1865, while Dr. Mudd was imprisoned in the dungeon, a violent hurricane struck.[72] Trees were uprooted. The cattle pen in the middle of the parade ground collapsed and the cattle roamed free in frightened confusion. With the wind still howling in the darkness before dawn the next morning, the upper story of the south section of the officers quarters blew out, killing Lieutenant John W. Stirling in his bed and injuring Captain R.A. Stearns. The walls and roofs of many other fort buildings were severely damaged. It would take months to repair the damage.

Summertime temperatures at Fort Jefferson hovered in the 90's. Temperatures over 100 degrees were not uncommon. The high temperatures combined with the high humidity produced a broiling sensation that could not be escaped. The winter months provided some relief, but could still be uncomfortable. On January 22, 1866, in the middle of his first 'winter' at Fort Jefferson, Dr. Mudd wrote to his wife:

During the day, owing to the overpowering light and heat, my eyes are painful and irritated.... The weather here since the beginning of winter has been as warm as summer with you.... It sounds strange to read of heavy snows and persons freezing to death, in the papers.

Trying to ease his wife's concerns about the tropical climate, Dr. Mudd wrote to her:

You seem to manifest some uneasiness on my account, apprehending the injurious effects of the heat upon my feeble constitution. In this regard I must remark that the climate being more moist and equable, is not liable to the evil and depressing effects, as with you. Heat in the sun here is very great, yet rarely attended with "sun stroke"; no fatal case from this cause having occurred since I have been here. Whenever there is a breeze, which is generally the case, it is always pleasant. A strict eye is kept to the cleanliness of the place, and being remote from the main land we have no fears of any infectious or epidemic disease. Unsuitable diet, beef, pork, etc. are more frequent causes of disorders and disease than locality or climate. We stand in need of a vegetable and fruit diet, of which this place is woefully deficient.[73]

The damp tropical conditions also provided a prefect breeding ground for insects of all kinds. At one point, Dr. Mudd wrote:

I am nearly worn out, the weather is almost suffocating, and millions of mosquitoes, fleas, and bedbugs infest the whole island. We can't rest day or night in peace for the mosquitoes.

He had no way of knowing that the mosquitoes were not just pests, but killers, carrying the deadly yellow fever virus.

---

[72] Bearss, Edwin C., Historic Structure Report, Historical Data Section, Fort Jefferson: 1846-1898. Fort Jefferson National Monument, Monroe County, Florida. Page 288 ff. Library of Congress, Washington, D.C.

[73] Mudd, Nettie, The Life of Dr. Samuel A. Mudd, Fourth Edition, Page 197.

Before his attempted escape in September 1865 Dr. Mudd had been working in the prison hospital. After his attempted escape he was assigned to manual labor - sweeping down various parts of the fort. But in February 1867, he was assigned to the carpentry shop. In a February 20, 1867 letter, Dr. Mudd wrote:

I have had my occupation changed to that of the carpenter's shop, which affords me more exercise and a greater diversion to my thoughts. I occupy my time principally in making little boxes, ornamenting them with different colors and varieties of wood.

He worked in the carpentry shop until the yellow fever epidemic began in August 1867. Between the end of the yellow fever epidemic in November 1867 and his pardon in February 1869, Dr. Mudd was again detailed to the carpentry shop, but also sometimes worked as a clerk in the Provost Marshall's office.

The carpentry job was very important in Dr. Mudd's daily life. It provided useful and creative work to help keep his mind off his troubles. The carpentry shop, blacksmith, lime house, and bakery were located together inside the fort in the southwest corner of the parade ground. Edman Spangler worked in the carpentry shop his entire time at Fort Jefferson. Under his tutoring Dr. Mudd became quite a good journeyman carpenter.

As he gained experience, Dr. Mudd began to make rather intricate items such as walking canes, cribbage boards, jewelry boxes, and even items of furniture, some of which contained beautiful inlaid patterns. Several of these items have survived and are on display at the Dr. Samuel A. Mudd House Museum in Waldorf, Maryland.

There was no fresh water on the Tortugas islands. This is of course how the islands came to be called the Dry Tortugas. Cisterns built into the fort's foundation caught and stored rainwater, but this water was not of sufficient quality or quantity to meet the needs of the fort. The primary source of drinking water was from steam condensers, but at the time Dr. Mudd arrived, the single old condenser then in operation could not produce enough drinking water for the almost 2,000 people at the fort, and water rationing was imposed. Over the course of the next year, the water situation steadily improved as the old condenser was repaired, an additional condenser was installed, and the number of soldiers and prisoners declined significantly. By the end of 1866, there was an ample supply of potable water at Fort Jefferson.

Nothing fresh could be grown on the island in any quantity. Food and other supplies arrived on a military steamer twice a month from New Orleans. The quality of the food was a source of constant complaint. But it was bad for everyone, prisoners and soldiers alike, since everyone ate the same food.

Watermelons, bananas, and pineapples sometimes arrived on ships from Cuba, but at exorbitant prices. Fresh vegetables were rare. Canned tomatoes and beans were sometimes available. Bread, butter, molasses, and coffee were a staple. Sea turtles, some weighing as much as two or three hundred pounds, were sometimes caught by the soldiers and added variety to the diet.

Dr. Mudd was mostly a vegetarian at Fort Jefferson. Meat was of such bad quality he never ate it. He said:

All articles of meat, salt and fresh, are repulsive. I can't bear the sight of them.

In the final year of his imprisonment, Dr. Mudd was allowed to tend a small vegetable garden in the center of the Parade field. In April 1868, he writes lovingly of his little garden, saying:

> There are a great quantity of ripe tomatoes, peas, beans, and collards in the garden, now suitable for table use. The corn is in silk, and soon there will be roasting ears.

Here is what Sam Arnold thought of the food:

> Food issued was horrible in the extreme. Many were suffering dreadfully from scurvy and chronic troubles. The bread was disgusting to look upon, being a mixture of flour, bugs, sticks and dirt. Meat, whose taint could be traced by its smell from one part of the fort to the other; in fact, rotten, and to such an extent that dogs ran from coming in contact with it, was served. No vegetable diet was served of any description, and the coffee, which should have been good, as good quality was issued, was made into a slop by those who had charge of the cookhouse.

Arnold was apparently not exaggerating. A soldier serving at Fort Jefferson at about the same time wrote:

> I have just been to dinner we had boiled Pork Potatoes & a piece of Bread & a dish of Rain water with wiggles in it we drink lots of wiggles & the Bread is well filled with Black Bugs about 1/4 of an inch long we pick out some of them & eat the rest there is scarcly anything that turns my stomach now it has got to be proof against dirt & nastiness.

The bad food and living conditions affected everyone's health. Scurvy was a major medical problem at Fort Jefferson, resulting from the lack of fruits and vegetables containing vitamin C. Arnold and Dr. Mudd both suffered from rheumatism. Dr. Mudd lost weight – he normally weighed about 150 pounds. But when the prison diet later improved and dry floor planking was installed in their casemate cell, the prisoners' health improved somewhat.

Shortly before his release, Dr. Mudd wrote to his wife that his hair was much thinner than when he left home, and that he had shaved off his moustache and trimmed his goatee quite short. He said he scarcely recognized himself when he looked in a mirror.

Many military posts, including Fort Jefferson, had convenience stores run by civilian businessmen known as sutlers. Soldiers complained that the prices were high and the quality low, but they had nowhere else to go. There was no competition at isolated Fort Jefferson. Sutlers sold clothing, ink, pencils, writing paper, preserves, tobacco, canned food, pins, mirrors, pocketknives, toothbrushes, hairbrushes, and a wide variety of other everyday items. Emily Holder,[74] the wife of a Fort Jefferson assistant surgeon, wrote that she was able to buy a stove and other necessities for setting up housekeeping from the sutler's store. Whiskey was also available from the sutler's store, and drunkenness on the part of soldiers was a common disciplinary problem at the fort.

The sutler store at Fort Jefferson was located outside the walls of the fort. Prisoners could purchase items at the store with the three dollars per month credit they were given there. Some prisoners also received money from home, or earned money doing odd jobs at the fort. Dr. Mudd received some spending money from his family, and also earned some money by making small ornamental boxes which sold in Key West.

---

[74] Holder, Emily, *At the Dry Tortugas During the War.* Californian Illustrated Magazine. January 1892.

In an 1867 letter to his wife, he said:

> Do not give yourself any uneasiness about my fare, etc. We can supply our few wants by making little boxes, frames, etc., which are in great demand. Today we contributed to the Southern Relief Fair at Key West little articles, which were worth to us over seventy-five dollars. Our work-boxes sell readily at twenty-five and thirty cents apiece.

Spangler also made extra spending money. Dr. Mudd wrote that:

> Spangler made money by trafficking with the soldiers, and we are mainly indebted to him for something extra to the crude, unwholesome, and sometimes condemned Government ration that was issued to us.[75]

Prisoners also received food and other items in packages from home. Dr. Mudd and his fellow prisoners received clothing, canned fruit and vegetables, tobacco, and sometimes even whiskey, although the whiskey often mysteriously disappeared from the packages before being given to the prisoners.

Friends and family supported Dr. Mudd during his imprisonment by sending him letters and newspapers as well as spending money and food. Two mail boats a week normally arrived at Fort Jefferson, but sometimes the boats were delayed due to quarantine procedures designed to protect against yellow fever and other diseases. Dr. Mudd's mail usually encountered additional delays as it passed through the fort's military censor. While the mail from family and friends was usually upbeat about his chances for release, the newspapers allowed him to form a more realistic view of the political climate and his likelihood of release.

Fort Jefferson also had a small library that both prisoners and soldiers could use. In an October 18, 1867 letter to his wife, Dr. Mudd said: "I have access to a very choice library of over 500 volumes." Records show that the small library also subscribed to newspapers such as the New York Herald, the Washington Chronicle, and the London Illustrated News. Samuel Arnold, who usually worked as a clerk in the office of the fort's commanding officer, was sometimes placed in charge of the library when the regular Army librarian, Private Alfred Herbert O'Donoghue, was away.

A soldier wrote:

> We have a good library, pretty well stocked with books, and receive also some New York papers, besides other publications; so that in this respect we are very fortunate, isolated as we are from the outer world.

Alfred O'Donoghue, the Librarian, was a highly over-qualified Army Private. He graduated from Trinity College, Dublin, Ireland in 1857, and was a correspondent for the Dublin Daily Express and the London Times before immigrating to the United States in 1863 and joining the Union Army. After service at Fort Jefferson, he left the military and moved to Missouri where he married and became a successful editor and lawyer.

---

[75] Mudd, Nettie, *The Life of Dr. Samuel A. Mudd*, Fourth Edition. Page 294.

O'Donoghue also established and ran a Fort Jefferson school for soldiers who could not read or write. He held classes for about 35 illiterate soldiers Monday through Friday from 3 P.M. to 5 P.M.

There was obviously little opportunity for entertainment at a military prison located on a desert island. However, although neither Dr. Mudd nor Samuel Arnold mentioned it in their writings, the officers and civilians at the fort did organize plays for entertainment. Both soldiers and prisoners were able to attend. Alfred O'Donoghue wrote[76] that the fort had:

> ...a very good theatre, gotten up entirely, at very great cost and labor and well supported, by the present battalion. There are performances nearly every week. The plays are sent on from New York, and the dramatic company is kept pretty well informed in theatrical matters. The great difficulty that the managers labor under is the want of female characters, personated by real women. Soldiers do not, as a rule, make good lady characters, and especially here, the face of every man being so well known, their employment in the female department destroys the illusion of reality so necessary to good playing. A shout of derisive laughter often greets the false woman in expansive crinoline; the awkwardness of the figure and long stride betray the deception. Besides, despite of care, very ridiculous accidents in the dress arrangement will sometimes occur, pins will get out of place, and skirts will fall, betraying the masculine trowsers.

> For a brief period we had indeed a real live woman character; the very pretty and very talented wife of a non-commissioned officer, since promoted to another department, consented to act with the boys. Her acting and deportment were both excellent, and the enthusiasm on such occasions among the audience was unbounded. On the evening previous to her departure a benefit was given her, and a goodly pile of greenbacks raked in.

Although Dr. Mudd didn't mention the theatrical performances in his letters, his fellow prisoner, Colonel Grenfell, did. But Grenfell didn't agree with O'Donoghue that the fort had "a very good theater." A grumpy Grenfell wrote in a January 15, 1868 letter to his Confederate Army friend Colonel Henry Lane Stone that:

> A learned physician, Dr. Mudd, has descended to playing the fiddle for drunken soldiers to dance to or form part of a very miserable orchestra at a still more miserable theatrical performance.

Dr. Mudd actually played the violin, often referred to as a fiddle.

There were no ministers permanently stationed at Fort Jefferson, but Dr. Mudd practiced his religion as well as he could. He said his rosary regularly:[77]

> ... I have not omitted saying my beads a single day since living on this horrid island.

> ... after the discourse, I repaired to my quarters, took my usual supper, said my beads, and enjoyed for a time a promenade up and down my gloomy quarters, ...

---

[76] O'Donoghue, Alfred, *Thirty Months at the Dry Tortugas*. Galaxy Magazine. Feb 1869, Volume 7 issue 2.

[77] Mudd, Nettie, *The Life of Dr. Samuel A. Mudd*, Fourth Edition, Pages 152, 154, and 176.

... I shall say to-day a pair of beads for your intention.

From time to time a Catholic priest would visit Fort Jefferson, hear confessions, and say mass for the soldiers, workmen, and prisoners there. Dr. Mudd wrote:[78]

... I heard mass yesterday. There are many Catholics among the citizen laborers, and we have quite a large congregation, nearly all going to communion.

... I have had the happiness to go to confession and communion... Bishop Verot and Father O'Hara visited us on the 28th.

... I had the consolation of going to confession, and receiving holy communion on the 8th.

... I went to confession and communion... The name of the priest is Father Allard.

The Great 1867 Yellow Fever Epidemic

Yellow fever is a viral infection transmitted by mosquitoes. In the initial stages the victim suffers headache, muscle aches, fever, loss of appetite, vomiting, jaundice, kidney failure, and bleeding. Those who do not recover from this stage can then experience multi-organ dysfunction including liver and kidney failure, brain dysfunction, seizures, coma, shock, and death. Yellow fever gets its name from the jaundice that affects many patients, causing yellow eyes and yellow skin.

In the mid-1800's neither the cause nor the treatment of yellow fever was understood. It would not be until 1900 that Dr. Walter Reed and his assistants would prove that yellow fever was caused by the bite of an infected Aedes Aegypti mosquito, and not by person-to-person transmission. Dr. Reed found that eradicating mosquitoes eradicated yellow fever.

Today, in addition to mosquito eradication, a safe and effective vaccine is available to prevent contracting yellow fever. However, there is still no cure for yellow fever once it is contracted. All that can be done is to treat the symptoms.

The 1867 yellow fever epidemic at Fort Jefferson was part of a wider yellow fever epidemic that killed thousands of people along the gulf coast from Texas to Florida, and northward up the Mississippi valley to Memphis, Tennessee. At Fort Jefferson, the epidemic began on August 18, 1867 when a soldier in Company K was felled with the disease. On the 20th, a second Company K soldier was stricken, and on the 21st two more were stricken. (See Official Army Report of the 1867 Yellow Fever Epidemic in Source Documents).

On August 22nd, Private James Forsythe, 5th U.S. Artillery, was the first to die. Private Joseph Enits died next, on August 30th. The fever spread to Company L and to the officers' servants. Company I, housed in the barracks adjoining the hospital, was then attacked. Company M escaped the plague until September 7th when 30 men were stricken.

The prison doctor, Brevet Major Joseph Sim Smith, an 1858 graduate of Georgetown University Medical School, contracted the disease on September 5th. Dr. Mudd then volunteered to take over caring for the

---

[78] Mudd, Nettie, *The Life of Dr. Samuel A. Mudd*, Fourth Edition, Pages 155, 158, 199, 232.

sick until a replacement for Dr. Smith arrived, and the commanding officer, Major Valentine H. Stone, agreed.

Dr. Smith died on September 8th. The next day, Smith was replaced by 60 year-old Dr. Daniel W. Whitehurst from Key West. For the next two months, Drs. Mudd and Whitehurst worked day and night to treat those afflicted with yellow fever, which included nearly everyone at the fort, soldiers and prisoners alike. Samuel Arnold and Michael O'Laughlen both contracted the disease. Arnold survived, but O'Laughlen died on September 23rd. Dr. Mudd himself contracted the disease on October 4th, forty-seven days after the epidemic had begun.

Dr. Mudd recounts the story of the yellow fever epidemic in a long letter to his wife:

October 27, 1867

I will now, as near as I can, by a pen description, give you an idea of the embarrassment I labored under upon assuming the duties as surgeon of the post, that were unexpectedly thrust upon me, and the track followed by the germs or poison, as evidenced by the appearance of disease.

Thus on the 4th of September, seventeen days after the epidemic of yellow fever had broken out, the surgeon, Dr. J. Sim Smith, a gentleman much respected and beloved by the garrison, was himself attacked with the fever, and by his illness, the Post was left without a physician in the midst of a fearful pestilence. The thought had never before entered my mind that this contingency might arise, and consequently I found myself unprepared to decide between the contending emotions of fear and duty that now pressed to gain ascendancy. Memory was still alive, for it seemed as yesterday, the dread ordeal through which I had passed. Tried by a court not ordained by the laws of the land, confronted by suborned and most barefaced perjured testimony, deprived of liberty, banished from home, family and friends, bound in chains as the brute and forced at the point of the bayonet to do the most menial service, and withal denied for a time every luxury, and even healthy subsistence, for having exercised a simple act of common humanity in setting the leg of a man for whose insane act I had no sympathy, but which was in the line of my professional calling. It was but natural that resentment and fear should rankle in my heart, and that I should stop to discuss mentally the contending emotions that now rested upon a horrid recollection of the past. Can I be a passive beholder? Shall I withhold the little service I might be capable of rendering the unfortunate soldier who was but a tool in the hands of his exacting officer? Or shall I again subject myself to renewed imputations of assassination? Who can read the motives of men? My motive might be ever so pure and praiseworthy yet one victim of the disease might be sufficient to start up the cry of poison and murder.

Whilst these disagreeable thoughts were revolving a fellow-prisoner remarked, saying: "Doctor, the yellow fever is the fairest and squarest thing that I have seen the past four or five years. It makes no distinction in regard to rank, color, or previous condition - every man has his chance, and I would advise you as a friend not to interfere." Another said it was only a little Southern opposition to reconstruction, and thought the matter ought to be reported to Congress in order that a law might be passed lowering the temperature below zero, which would most effectually put an end to its disloyalty.

But I must be more serious; and you will perceive that the time had now arrived in which I could occupy no middle ground. I felt that I had to make a decision, and although the rule of conduct upon which I had determined was not in accord with my natural feelings, yet I had the sanction of my professional and religious teachings and the consciousness of conforming to that holy precept, "Do ye good for evil," which alone distinguishes the man from the brute.

It being our breakfast hour on the morning of the 5th, and thinking it required some condescension on the part of the commanding officer to call upon an humble prisoner to serve in the honorable position of surgeon of the post, I concluded to spare him this disagreeable duty, and instructed Mr. Arnold, a fellow prisoner and roommate, who was acting clerk at headquarters, to inform Major Stone, then commanding, that should my services be required, I had no fear of, nor objection to, performing whatever aid was in my power toward the relief of the sick. On approaching headquarters, Mr. Arnold met Major Stone coming to my quarters to inquire whether I would consent to attend the sick of the Post until the arrival of a regular surgeon.

When informed that I had offered my services, the Major seemed much pleased and had me forthwith detailed. Fortune favored me, and it so happened that during the intervals, amounting to nearly three weeks, that I had the exclusive care of the sick, not one died. Time will not permit me further digression. I shall pass over many incidents of interest connected with hospital management, difficulties I had to overcome in breaking up the prior arrangement of sending away the sick in open boats over a rough sea two miles and a half distant and also in obtaining an opposite order from the commander to send to one of the islands near by as many of the well soldiers as could be spared from the garrison. This latter measure, though I had advised it on the day I took charge of the hospital, was not carried out until the arrival of Dr. D. W. Whitehurst of Key West, Florida; a noble, kind-hearted gentleman, who superseded me on the 9th of September.

The first case of yellow fever at the Dry Tortugas, in the epidemic of which I now speak, occurred on the 18th of August, 1867, in Company K, which was located in the casemates on the south side of the Fort immediately over the unfinished moat, which at low tide gave rise to quite offensive odors. To this circumstance the surgeon of the Post attributed the cause of the disease, and at his request the company was removed and the portholes ordered to be closed, to prevent the supposed deadly miasma from entering the Fort.

Having the honor at this time of being a member of the carpenter's shop, it fell to my lot to aid in the work of barricading against the unseen foe, and it was during this patriotic service the 22nd of August, that I made my first note of the epidemic. The places occupied by the beds of the four men, one on the 18th, one on the 20th, and two on the 21st, that had gone to the hospital sick with yellow fever, were all contiguous. The Fort was hexagonal in shape with a bastion at each corner, and the company, after its removal, was placed on the east side, the bastion forming the center with several casemates above and below boarded up separating it from Company L on the north and the prisoners on the south, and in the most eligible position for the spread of the poison, owing to the prevalence of the wind, which from early in April up to this period had blown continuously from the southeast, varying only a few degrees.

There was a lull or temporary suspension of the activity of the poison on the 22d and 23d. For two days the company remained without any new cases, but on the 24th day one man was taken from the same company on stretchers, being unable to walk. The fever then rapidly extended right and left until it reached Company L, which was nearest the point where it arose this second time, and later the prisoners' quarters, which were more remote, were attacked. To show and to prove to you that the germs, or cause, spreads by continuity of matter, and not with the disease, the first two cases that occurred in Company L, and the first two cases among the prisoners, were immediately next the boarded partition that separated them from Company K, where the fever was raging, having followed along the rows of beds, up to this line of division, and then passed through the open spaces between the plank, which were loosely nailed.

There were at this time two hospitals, the Post Hospital within the Fort, and Sand Key Hospital on an adjacent island about two miles and a half distant, which latter was fitted up as soon as the fever began to assume an epidemical form. The sick that occurred during the night and following day were immediately taken to the Post Hospital, and from thence at 4 o'clock P. M. they were carried in boats by the surgeon, on his accustomed visit, to Sandy Key Hospital. Notwithstanding the fact that most of the sick walked from their beds to the Post Hospital, and no effort or pains on the part of the surgeon to isolate the disease were taken, owing to the belief in its miasmatic character, the germs or cause had not up to this time, September 12, viz: 25 days, reached either of the hospitals, if we may judge from the circumstance that not one of the many nurses, who waited upon the sick day and night and even slept in the same room, were stricken down with the fever.

The disease after extending into Company L, and to the prisoners' quarters, next made its appearance into Company I, located in the inner barracks, a building about three hundred feet long, thirty feet wide, and four stories high on the east side, running north and parallel with the Fort, and immediately in front of Company K and Company I, and distant about sixty feet.

I was called into this company on the morning of September 8, and found Sergeant Sheridan and a private that slept in the next bed ill with the fever. Sergeant Sheridan and the first sergeant of Company K were great friends, and when off duty were constantly in each other's quarters. Sheridan generally wore a heavy cloak during the showers of rain that were frequent at this period, and I feel satisfied that the poison was carried by the ferment set up in the cloak, or mechanically, by adhering formites, though it is possible for it to have been wafted across from Company K, the two beds in Company I being near the window facing that company. Then the fever gradually worked its way along through the whole company without a skip in regular succession as they slept.

At the northern extremity of the barracks two rooms were set apart, thirty feet square, as the Post Hospital. On the 7th we were necessitated by the increasing number of sick to provide other hospital quarters, and for convenience four casemates opposite on the ground tier, under Company L, were boarded up as a temporary hospital, with our kitchen and dispensary inter- mediate. On the 8th our hospital supply of beds and bedding gave out, and on the 9th we were compelled to bring the bed along with the patient into the hospital. Two days after the admission of the infected beds, our nurses began falling sick, three being attacked during the day and night of the 11th of September. Then the three laundresses, families who did the washing for the hospitals and separate quarters on the west side of the Fort, sixty or seventy yards apart, were all simultaneously attacked upon the first issue of soiled clothing - after our hospital became infected.

Then again, upon the breaking up of the Sand Key Hospital, and the return of the nurses to the Fort, they were all speedily stricken down with the fever upon their being placed on similar duty. These nurses had remained free from all disease up to their return to the Fort, although the majority of the cases whom they nursed at Sand Key died with the fever.

But the most remarkable spread of the disease occurred on the night of the 16th of September in Company M, which was quartered in the casemates immediately above the hospital and Company L, and notwithstanding the proximity up to this date, twenty-nine days since the epidemic began, had remained entirely exempt from the fever, owing no doubt to the fact that it laid behind the bastion, which, with the prevailing southeast wind, produced a downward or opposing current. However, on the morning of the above date, about nine o'clock, a small rain cloud common to that locality, arose to the south of the fort, which came up rapidly with a heavy wind, lasting about twenty minutes, and which blew directly from the hospital and Company L, toward Company M, and the night following every man went to bed in his usual health, yet between eleven and one o'clock nearly one-half of the company, or thirty men, were attacked with the most malignant form of the disease - beginning at the point nearest the hospitals and extending thirty beds without missing or skipping a single occupant.

It had been my custom to remain at the hospital every night until eleven o'clock to see that every patient received the medicine prescribed and was quiet. On this occasion I had not retired more than fifteen minutes before I was sent for by the sergeant of Company M to come to his quarters, that several of his men were sick. Feeling much fatigued, I did not attend the summons, but referred the messenger to Dr. Whitehurst and the steward of the hospital. At one o'clock the sergeant himself came down to my room and begged me for God's sake to get up, that one-half of his company were attacked with the fever, and that he did not know what to do with them, as the hospitals were already full. I went along with the sergeant, and found his statement fully correct, and the wildest alarm and confusion prevailing.

As the hospitals were already crowded, we concluded, for convenience, to enclose the six casemates nearest the regular hospitals, which was speedily executed with canvas, and in less than two hours all moved back and were quiet under comfortable treatment. The next night or two after, the balance of the company, in the order of their beds, were attacked with the disease without an exception.

The disease did not extend among the officers at headquarters until it had at first reached the negro prisoners, several of whom were employed by the officers as servants, and who were in the daily habit of carrying to and fro their blankets. The humble individual who now addresses you was not attacked until the 4th of October, forty-seven days after the beginning of the epidemic, though constantly at the bedside of the sick, and in the midst of the infected hospitals and quarters. One evening, at our usual supper hour, feeling much depressed and exhausted from the unaccustomed duties I went over to my mess, where I was besieged with many questions concerning the sick, and notwithstanding the solemnity of the occasion, a hearty laugh was frequently indulged at the expense of our ready wit, Edward Spangler.

The debilitating effects of the climate, added to the condition consequent upon the excitement, very much depressed me, and after finishing my bowl of coffee and slice of bread, I fell upon my rude cot to spend a few minutes of repose. The customary sea breeze at this hour had sprung up, and I was shortly lulled into sweet sleep. My faithful and ever solicitous roommate, Edward Spangler, who on former occasions had manifested so much concern when the least indisposition was complained of, seemed to anticipate my every want, was not unguarded at this time. As soon as he found me quiet, he closed the door and turned back several intruders, stating that the Doctor was feeling unwell, and had laid down to rest himself. In the course of an hour, he said, he will be through his nap, when he will return to the hospital, where all who desire can see him. Spangler made money by trafficking with the soldiers, and we are mainly indebted to him for something extra to the crude, unwholesome, and sometimes condemned Government ration that was issued to us. He was not generally select in his epithets toward those whom he disliked, yet if he saw them in suffering, it excited the liveliest sympathy, and he would do anything that laid in his power for their relief. At a later period he, in conjunction with Mr. Arnold, watched over me in my illness as attentively as if their own brother, and I owe my life to the unremitting care which they bestowed.

The reader, I am in hopes, will excuse this little digression from the subject - a tribute of thanks is due, and I know no more fitting place to give it expression. I may perhaps be doing injustice by omitting another name equally deserving of my esteem, Michael O'Loughlin. He, unfortunate young man, away from his family and friends, by whom he was most tenderly loved, fell a victim to the pestilence in spite of every effort on our part to save him. He had passed the first stage of the disease and was apparently convalescent, but, contrary to my earnest advice, he got out of bed a short time after I left in the morning, and was walking about the room looking over some periodicals the greater part of the day. In the evening, about five o'clock, a sudden collapse of the vital powers took place, which in thirty-six hours after terminated his life. He seemed all at once conscious of his impending fate, and the first warning I had of his condition was his exclamation, "Doctor, Doctor, you must tell my mother all!" He called then Edward Spangler, who was present, and extending his hand he said, "Good-by, Ned." These were his last words of consciousness. He fell back instantly into a profound stupor and for several minutes seemed lifeless; but by gently changing his position from side to side, and the use of stimulating and cold applications, we succeeded in restoring him to partial strength and recollection.

I never met with one more kind and forbearing, possessing a warm friendly disposition and a fine comprehensive intellect. I enjoyed greater ease in conversational intercourse with him than any of my prison associates. He was taken sick whilst my kind friend, Dr. D. W. Whitehurst of Key West, Florida, had charge of the Post; from him he received prompt medical attention from the beginning of his illness to his death.

The news had spread around through the garrison of the neat and comfortable appearance of the hospital and the improved condition of the sick, which had the effect to gain for me a reputation, and the confidence of the soldiers - all I could desire to insure success. It was not long before I discovered I could do more with nine cases out of ten by a few consoling and inspiring words, than with all the medicine known to me in the materia medica.

Edman Spangler wrote home about the yellow fever epidemic. His letter appeared in the September 22, 1867 issue of the New York Times:

Fort Jefferson Fla., Sept, 6, 1867.

I am well at present, but don't know how long it will last, for we have had the yellow fever here, and there are two or three dying each day, and I am busy working in the carpenters' shop, making coffins day and night, and don't know when my time will come. They don't last longer than a few hours. I will enclose a few moss pictures for you, and I will send you a barrel of coral if I don't get the yellow fever and die; but there are ten chances to one if I ever see you again. It is very desperate here. The doctor of the post is very sick with it, and there is no doctor here but Dr. Mudd, and he volunteered his services, and has made a good hit of it. We have lost no cases with him yet. - With love to all, Edward Spangler

Spangler was one of the few at Fort Jefferson who never contracted yellow fever during the epidemic. Sam Arnold contracted yellow fever, but lived to tell about it. His lengthy account of the epidemic may be found in the Source Documents section.

In his 1926 Saturday Evening Post article, author George Allan England reported the following excerpt from a letter written by the wife of a Fort Jefferson officer:

> The whole island became one immense hospital. The silence was oppressive beyond description. There were no soldiers for drill or parade, and the gloom was indescribable. Five hundred at one time would scarcely cover the list of sick.... Those able to move about looked like ghosts. The mercury was 104 in the hospital.... We seemed in some horrible nightmare. It was terrible beyond description to be hemmed in by those high, literally red-hot brick walls, with so much suffering. I could see the beds brought out, hoping for a breath of air to fan the burning brow and fever-parched lips. There was nothing to brighten the cloud of despair that encompassed the island.

By the end of October, the yellow fever epidemic had begun to abate. The last case occurred on November 14th. Dr. Thomas, the new physician who had replaced Dr. Whitehurst, came down with the fever himself. Dr. Mudd, although not fully recovered, resumed caring for the remaining sick. When it was all over, 270 of the 400 people at the fort had caught yellow fever, and 38 had died, including Michael O'Laughlen.

Alfred O'Donoghue wrote in the February 1869 issue of Galaxy magazine:

> During the prevalence of the yellow fever at the fort last year, when the garrison suffered terribly, Dr. Samuel Mudd, sent hither for complicity in the assassination of President Lincoln, was at one time our only physician. It is simple justice and gratitude to acknowledge the skillful and self-sacrificing service he rendered. I may add that nothing can be more exemplary than the conduct of the three political prisoners now on the island (Michael O'Loughlin having died of yellow fever last year). They perform the work assigned them without complaint, and with apparent cheerfulness; if the iron sometimes enter their souls, or the bitterness of their situation be felt, it is never exhibited. This, at least, if not much more, must in justice to them be told.

O'Donoghue and the other surviving Fort Jefferson soldiers signed a petition asking the government to release Dr. Mudd in recognition of his services in saving so many lives during the course of the epidemic. While the petition failed to secure Dr. Mudd's immediate release, it played a part in President Johnson's later pardon a little over a year later.

Here is the text of the petition[79], written by Edmund L. Zalinski, 1st Lieutenant, 5th U.S. Artillery, and signed by 300 soldiers:

> It is with sincere pleasure that we acknowledge the great services rendered by Dr. S. A. Mudd (prisoner) during the prevalence of yellow fever at the Fort. When the very worthy surgeon of the Post, Dr. J. Sim Smith, fell one of the first victims of the fatal epidemic, and the greatest dismay and alarm naturally prevailed on all sides, deprived as the garrison was of the assistance of any medical officer, Dr. Mudd, influenced by the most praiseworthy and humane motives, spontaneously and unsolicited came forward to devote all his energies and professional knowledge to the aid of the sick and dying. He inspired the hopeless with courage, and by his

---

[79] U.S. National Archives, College Park, Md., RG 204, Samuel A. Mudd Pardon File B-596.

constant presence in the midst of danger and infection, regardless of his own life, tranquillized the fearful and desponding.

By his prudence and foresight, the hospital upon an adjacent island, to which at first the sick were removed in an open boat, was discontinued. Those attacked with the malady were on the spot put under vigorous treatment. A protracted exposure on the open sea was avoided, and many now strong doubtless owe their lives to the care and treatment they received at his hands. He properly considered the nature and character of the infection and concluded that it could not be eradicated by the mere removal of the sick, entailing, as it did, the loss of valuable time necessary for the application of the proper remedies, exposure of those attacked and adding to the general fear and despondency. The entire different system of treatment and hospital arrangement was resorted to with the happiest effect.

Dr. Mudd's treatment and the change which he recommended met with the hearty approval and warm commendation of the regularly appointed surgeons, with whom, in a later stage of the epidemic, he was associated. Many here who have experienced his kind and judicious treatment, can never repay him the debt of obligation they owe him. We do, therefore, in consideration of the invaluable services rendered by him during this calamitous and fatal epidemic, earnestly recommend him to the well-merited clemency of the Government, and solicit his immediate release from here, and restoration to liberty and the bosom of his family.

Edmund L. Zalinski, 1st Lieutenant, 5th U.S. Artillery

President Johnson ignored the petition for Dr. Mudd's release. He was still under political siege in Washington. In his 1869 pardon, a year and a half after the epidemic, Johnson mentioned Dr. Mudd's work during the epidemic, but it was only one of several reasons given for the pardon.

Part 4 - Home Again

Dr. Mudd is Pardoned

On February 24, 1868, the U.S. House of Representatives approved by a vote of 126 to 47 an impeachment resolution accusing President Andrew Johnson of violating the Tenure of Office Act by removing Secretary of War Edwin M. Stanton from office.

Johnson's political enemies used this charge as a stand-in for all the Johnson post-war reconstruction policies they opposed, including his pardon of many former high-ranking Confederate officials. In all, by the end of his term in office, Johnson gave over 13,000 pardons, including one for Jefferson Davis, the president of the Confederacy. On May 16, 1868 Johnson survived the Senate impeachment trial by a single vote.

Dr. Mudd, Arnold, and Spangler had not been forgotten in prison. From the first days of their imprisonment, their families and friends had worked diligently for their release. Mrs. Mudd wrote several letters to President Johnson and went to see him often, begging for her husband's release. In her last public statement, in the Baltimore News newspaper of February 11, 1909, she said: "I called on President Johnson a great many times. He always treated me courteously, but impressed me always as one shrinking from some impending disaster. He conveyed to me always the idea that he wanted to release my husband, but said more than once 'the pressure on me is too great'".

General Thomas Ewing, who was Dr. Mudd's attorney during the conspiracy trial, continued to provide legal and moral support to Dr. and Mrs. Mudd during the years of his imprisonment.

Others continued their direct appeals to President Johnson for Dr. Mudd's pardon. On January 31, 1869, a month before he would leave office, President Johnson received a high-powered delegation of men from Maryland.[80] The delegation consisted of Maryland Governor Oden Bowie, three justices of the Maryland Court of Appeals - Chief Justice James Bartol, Justice John Robinson, and Justice Richard Grayson - and two Maryland congressmen - Hiram McCullough and Frederick Stone. As you will recall, Mr. Stone had been one of Dr. Mudd's defense counsels during the conspiracy trial. The six men asked Johnson to pardon Dr. Mudd before he left office. They also asked him to pardon Samuel Arnold and Edman Spangler. Everyone considered Spangler to be innocent, but he seemed to be comparatively friendless. Johnson said he would seriously think about it.

A week later, February 8, 1869, President Johnson summoned Mrs. Mudd to the White House and personally handed her Dr. Mudd's pardon. He apologized for not keeping his earlier promises to release Dr. Mudd, but now that his political enemies could no longer harm him, he was setting Dr. Mudd free.

Following the pardon, the War Department ordered the Commanding Officer of Fort Jefferson to release Dr. Mudd. The order was carried out on March 8, 1869, and Dr. Mudd's long ordeal was over. He had been in Government custody just six weeks shy of four years, from April 21, 1865 when he was arrested at his farm, until March 8, 1869 when he was released from custody at Fort Jefferson. He was still a young man, just 35 years old, but must have felt much older.

---

[80] Maryland, Baltimore. *The Dry Tortugas Prisoners - Visit of Gov. Bowie and Others to the President in Their Behalf.* Baltimore Sun, March 1, 1869.

Although free, Dr. Mudd had to wait three days for a ship that would carry him away from Fort Jefferson. On March 11th, he finally left Fort Jefferson on the Navy schooner Matchless for Key West. In Key West, Dr. Mudd secured passage on the steamship Liberty as it sailed up from Havana on its way to Baltimore.

The Liberty had just finished a six month overhaul which included upgrading all the passenger accommodations. This included new painting and carpeting throughout, and installation of a splendid new piano from the Baltimore piano factory of Knabe & Co. in the main salon.[81] The contrast between the prison cell where he had lived for the past four years and the luxurious accommodations aboard the Liberty must have overwhelmed Dr. Mudd.

The Liberty arrived in Baltimore at 4 o'clock in the morning on Thursday, March 18, 1869.[82] With no one to meet him at the dock at that time of the morning, Dr. Mudd left the ship and secured a room at Barnum's City Hotel, where he rested and waited for morning to arrive. When it did, he left Barnum's and went to his brother-in-law Jeremiah Dyer's house, where he was finally reunited with his wife after almost four years.

Later in the day, Dr. Mudd was visited by several prominent Marylanders who had worked for his release, including the Governor of Maryland, Oden Bowie. On Saturday, March 20, 1869, Dr. Mudd and his wife arrived back home at their farm, where there was a joyful reunion with his four children.

Dr. Mudd's mother Sarah Ann Mudd was no longer alive, having died shortly before his release from prison. His father Henry Mudd lived until 1877, but in ever-declining health.

Spangler and Arnold are Pardoned

On the evening of March 2, 1869, three weeks after he pardoned Dr. Mudd, President Johnson pardoned Edman Spangler and Samuel Arnold. The next day, March 3rd, Arnold's father, who lived in Baltimore, called at the White House where he received his son's pardon from the hands of President Johnson. The next day, March 4th, Ulysses S. Grant was sworn in as the 18th President of the United States.

Historians generally agree that Spangler had nothing to do with the assassination of Lincoln. However, he was philosophical about his sentence. Spangler is quoted by Emily Holder, the wife of a Fort Jefferson assistant surgeon, as saying:

> They made a mistake in sending me down here. I had nothing to do with Booth or the assassination of President Lincoln; but I suppose I have done enough in my life to deserve this, so I make the best of it.[83]

Arnold and Spangler were released from confinement at Fort Jefferson on March 21, 1869. Sam Arnold's father went to Fort Jefferson to bring his son back home. Sam, his father, and Spangler traveled back to Baltimore together on the steamship Cuba.

---

[81] Maryland, Baltimore. *The Steamship Liberty.* Baltimore Sun. February 11, 1869.

[82] Maryland, Baltimore. *Arrival of the Steamship Liberty.* Baltimore Sun, March 19, 1869.

[83] Holder, Emily, *At the Dry Tortugas During the War: A Lady's Journal.* Californian Illustrated Magazine. September 1892. Page 557.

The Baltimore Sun of April 7, 1869 reported their arrival this way:

Local Matters. Return of Arnold and Spangler, the Dry Tortugas Prisoners. - Samuel B. Arnold and Edman Spangler, the prisoners recently released from the Dry Tortugas, under pardon of President Johnson, the former having been sentenced for life and the latter for six years, by the military commission that tried the assassination conspirators, reached this city yesterday. They came passengers on the steamship Cuba, from Key West. Arnold appears in rather delicate health, but Spangler is well, and both seem in good spirits. They are set free now, after three years and eight months in durance vile.

After their trial and sentence, they reached the Dry Tortugas with Dr. Mudd, their late fellow-prisoner, and O'Laughlin, who died during imprisonment, on the 24th of July, 1865, and were released on the 22nd of March 1869. Both Arnold and Spangler reply readily to the queries concerning their imprisonment and the treatment they received from the different commanders of the post.

During the season of the fearful rage of the yellow fever in 1867 at the fort, they state that after nearly all the troops had been attacked and either recovered or died, Dr. Mudd, who had so faithfully and advantageously labored among the sick, was taken down with the disease, and there being no medical man left fit for duty, was nursed solely by themselves, his only remaining companion, O'Laughlin, having previously died. During its prevalence there were thirty-seven deaths in that limited community, two of whom were prisoners and the balance officers and soldiers. They speak highly of the late Major Stone, who commanded at the time. His wife having died of the epidemic of which he had recovered, he carried his little child over to Key West, with the intention of sending it to his relatives in the North, and shortly after reaching there he was taken with a relapse and died. Their treatment depended much on the commander of the post, but after the season of yellow fever they fared much better than previously.

They received a telegram on the 9th of March, informing them of their pardon, and Spangler says it appeared to him that from that time until the 21st, when Arnold's father reached there with the pardons, he gained in flesh every hour. Arnold was employed as a clerk at headquarters and Spangler as a carpenter, and both at times were compelled to work very hard.

After their release they left the Tortugas in a government sailing vessel and went over to Key West, where they remained several days, awaiting the arrival of the Cuba, and were treated in the kindest manner by the citizens.

On the terrible ordeal of the trial, under the circumstances by which they were surrounded, it is not to be supposed they would delight to dwell. Spangler says that from the torture he endured he was mostly unconscious of the proceedings in the case, and often knew nothing of what was going on around him. When the padded hood was placed upon his head in prison, covering over his eyes and tightened about his neck and chest, with manacles already on both hands and feet, he was told it was by order of Secretary Stanton, the subordinate thus excusing himself for his action. After arriving at the fort, and up to the time of his release, Spangler avers that the sense of his entire innocence only made his chains more galling, whilst at the same time it often kept him from utter despair. Both Arnold and Spangler speak of the kindness and attention they received on board the Cuba from Capt. Dukehart, his officers and passengers, who generally were disposed to make them comfortable.

The Fall and Redemption of Dr. Samuel A. Mudd

Home again, Arnold lived quietly out of the public eye for more than 30 years. In 1898, he returned to Fort Jefferson and took photographs of his old prison.[84] Unfortunately, these photographs have not survived. In 1902, Arnold wrote a series of newspaper articles for the Baltimore American describing his imprisonment at Fort Jefferson. Arnold died four years later on September 21, 1906. He is buried at Green Mount Cemetery in Baltimore, Maryland.

Michael O'Laughlen, who died of yellow fever at Fort Jefferson, is also buried at Green Mount Cemetery.

With Arnold's death in 1906, the only main figure in the Lincoln assassination story still alive was John H. Surratt. He died ten years later. April 21, 1916, at the age of seventy-two. Surratt is buried in the New Cathedral Cemetery in Baltimore, Maryland.

Edman Spangler at the Mudd Farm

When Edman Spangler left Fort Jefferson, he went to work at the Holliday Street Theatre in Baltimore for his old boss John T. Ford, the former owner of Ford's Theater where Lincoln was shot. When the Holliday Street Theatre burned down in 1873, Spangler traveled to the Mudd farm, where Dr. Mudd and his wife welcomed him as the friend whom Dr. Mudd credited with saving his life while suffering with yellow fever. Spangler lived with the Mudd family for about eighteen months, earning his keep by doing carpentry, gardening, and other farm chores.

Edman Spangler died in the Mudd farm house on February 7, 1875, in the upstairs bedroom next to the one in which John Wilkes Booth had stayed ten years earlier.

Nettie Mudd, in her book on the life of her father, said of Ned Spangler:

> He was a quiet, genial man, greatly respected by the members of our family and the people of the neighborhood. His greatest pleasure seemed to be found in extending kindnesses to others, and particularly children, of whom he was very fond.

The furniture and children's toys Spangler made while staying with the Mudd family may be seen today in the Dr. Samuel A. Mudd House Museum in Waldorf, Maryland.

Not long after Spangler's death, Dr. Mudd found a handwritten manuscript in Spangler's toolbox, containing Spangler's account of what he saw at Ford's Theater when Lincoln was assassinated[85]. Here is Spangler's statement:

> I was born in York County, Pennsylvania, and am about forty-three years of age, I am a house carpenter by trade, and became acquainted with J. Wilkes Booth when a boy. I worked for his father in building a cottage in Harford County, Maryland, in 1854.
>
> Since A. D. 1853, I have done carpenter work for the different theaters in the cities of Baltimore and Washington, to wit: The Holliday Street Theater and the Front Street Theater of Baltimore, and Ford's Theater in the City of Washington. I have acted also as scene shifter in all the above

---

[84] Baltimore Sun, July 11, 1934. Page 22. See also letter from Nettie Mudd to Samuel Arnold, June 28, 1906, in John T. Ford Papers, Maryland Historical Society, Baltimore, Maryland.

[85] Mudd, Nettie, *The Life of Dr. Samuel A. Mudd*, Fourth Edition. Page 322.

named theaters, and had a favorable opportunity to become acquainted with the different actors. I have acted as scene shifter in Ford's Theater, ever since it was first opened up, to the night of the assassination of President Lincoln.

During the winter of A.D. 1862 and 1863, J. Wilkes Booth played a star engagement at Ford's Theater for two weeks. At that time I saw him and conversed with him quite frequently. After completing his engagement he left Washington and I did not see him again until the winters of A.D. 1864 and 1865. I then saw him at various times in and about Ford's Theater.

Booth had free access to the theater at all times, and made himself very familiar with all persons connected with it. He had a stable in the rear of the theater where he kept his horses. A boy, Joseph Burroughs, commonly called 'Peanut John,' took care of them whenever Booth was absent from the city. I looked after his horses, which I did at his request, and saw that they were properly cared for. Booth promised to pay me for my trouble, but he never did. I frequently had the horses exercised, during Booth's absence from the city, by 'Peanut John,' walking them up and down the alley. 'Peanut John' kept the key to the stable in the theater, hanging upon a nail behind the small door, which opened into the alley at the rear of the theater.

Booth usually rode out on horseback every afternoon and evening, but seldom remained out later than eight or nine o'clock. He always went and returned alone. I never knew of his riding out on horseback and staying out all night, or of any person coming to the stable with him, or calling there for him. He had two horses at the stable, only a short time. He brought them there some time in the month of December. A man called George and myself repaired and fixed the stable for him. I usually saddled the horse for him when 'Peanut John' was absent. About the first of March Booth brought another horse and a buggy and harness to the stable, but in what manner I do not know; after that he used to ride out with his horse and buggy, and I frequently harnessed them up for him. I never saw any person ride out with him or return with him from these rides.

On the Monday evening previous to the assassination, Booth requested me to sell the horse, harness, and buggy, as he said he should leave the city soon. I took them the next morning to the horse market, and had them put up at auction, with the instruction not to sell unless they would net two hundred and sixty dollars; this was in accordance with Booth's orders to me. As no person bid sufficient to make them net that amount, they were not sold, and I took them back to the stable. I informed Booth of the result that same evening in front of the theater. He replied that he must then try and have them sold at private sale, and asked me if I would help him. I replied, 'Yes.' This was about six o'clock in the evening, and the conversation took place in the presence of John F. Sleichman and others. The next day I sold them for two hundred and sixty dollars. The purchaser accompanied me to the theater. Booth was not in, and the money was paid to James J. Gifford, who receipted for it. I did not see Booth to speak to him, after the sale, until the evening of the assassination.

Upon the afternoon of April 14 I was told by 'Peanut John' that the President and General Grant were coming to the theater that night, and that I must take out the partition in the President's box. It was my business to do all such work. I was assisted in doing it by Rittespaugh and 'Peanut John.'

In the evening, between five and six o'clock, Booth came into the theater and asked me for a halter. I was very busy at work at the time on the stage preparatory to the evening performance, and Rittespaugh went upstairs and brought one down. I went out to the stable with Booth and put the halter upon the horse. I commenced to take off the saddle when Booth said, 'Never mind, I do not want it off, but let it and the bridle remain.' He afterward took the saddle off himself, locked the stable, and went back to the theater.

Booth, Maddox, 'Peanut John,' and myself immediately went out of the theater to the adjoining restaurant next door, and took a drink at Booth's expense. I then went immediately back to the theatre, and Rittespaugh and myself went to supper. I did not see Booth again until between nine and ten o'clock. About that time Deboney called to me, and said Booth wanted me to hold his horse as soon as I could be spared. I went to the back door and Booth was standing in the alley holding a horse by the bridle rein, and requested me to hold it. I took the rein, but told him I could not remain, as Gifford was gone, and that all of the responsibility rested on me. Booth then passed into the theater. I called to Deboney to send "Peanut John" to hold the horse. He came, and took the horse, and I went back to my proper place.

In about a half hour afterward I heard a shot fired, and immediately saw a man run across the stage. I saw him as he passed by the center door of the scenery, behind which I then stood; this door is usually termed the center chamber door. I did not recognize the man as he crossed the stage as being Booth. I then heard some one say that the President was shot. Immediately all was confusion. I shoved the scenes back as quickly as possible in order to clear the stage, as many were rushing upon it. I was very much frightened, as I heard persons halloo, "Burn the theater!" I did not see Booth pass out; my situation was such that I could not see any person pass out of the back door. The back door has a spring attached to it, and would not shut of its own accord. I usually slept in the theater, but I did not upon the night of the assassination; I was fearful the theater would be burned, and I slept in a carpenter's shop adjoining.

I never heard Booth express himself in favor of the rebellion, or opposed to the Government, or converse upon political subjects; and I have no recollection of his mentioning the name of President Lincoln in any connection whatever. I know nothing of the mortise hole said to be in the wall behind the door of the President's box, or of any wooden bar to fasten or hold the door being there, or of the lock being out of order. I did not notice any hole in the door. Gifford usually attended to the carpentering in the front part of the theater, while I did the work about the stage. Mr. Gifford was the boss carpenter, and I was under him.

Edman Spangler is buried just two miles from Dr. Mudd's farm, at St. Peter's Cemetery, Waldorf, Maryland.

The Final Years

When Dr. Mudd returned home, well-wishing friends and strangers, and inquiring newspaper reporters besieged him. Dr. Mudd was very reluctant to talk to the press because he felt they had misquoted him in the past. He gave one interview to a New York Herald reporter, but immediately regretted it. The reporter's story contained several factual errors, and Dr. Mudd complained that it misrepresented his work at Fort Jefferson during the yellow fever epidemic.

On the whole though, he must have been gratified to find that he continued to enjoy the respect and friendship of his friends and neighbors. Dr. Mudd resumed his medical practice, slowly brought the family farm back to productivity, and became active once again in the life of his community. In 1874, he was elected Master (chief officer) of the local farmers association, Bryantown Grange 47.[86] In 1876, seven years after he returned home, he was elected Vice President of the local Democratic Tilden-Hendricks presidential election committee.[87] Tilden lost that year to Republican Rutherford B. Hayes in a hotly disputed election. The next year Dr. Mudd ran as a Democratic candidate for the Maryland House of Delegates, but was defeated by the popular Republican William D. Mitchell.[88]

Before he went to prison, Dr. and Mrs. Mudd had four children – Andrew, Lillian, Thomas, and Samuel. After prison, they had five more – Henry, Stella, Edward, Rose de Lima, and Mary Eleanor, known as 'Nettie.' Henry, named after Dr. Mudd's father, was born a year after Dr. Mudd returned home from prison, but died when only eight months old.

The 1870 census showed twenty people living at the Mudd farm. This included Dr. Mudd (35), Mrs. Mudd (34), their children Andrew (11), Lillian (10), Thomas (8), Samuel (6), and baby Henry , Mary G. Simons, (49), Mrs. Mudd's sister Betty Dyer (42), their long-time farm worker John Best (70), two domestic servants, Lettie Hall (17) and Louisa Cristie (14), farm laborer William Moore (18), and the Washington family, Frank Washington (32), wife Betty (30), and their children, Edward (13), J.R. (9), Sidney (7), Catherine (5), and William (2).

Betty Washington's husband Frank had been a slave on Dr. Mudd's farm before emancipation, and remained there afterwards as a paid plowman. His wife Betty, who had been a slave to Mrs. Adelaide Middleton, joined her husband on the Mudd farm after emancipation, working as the family cook. Frank and Betty Washington both testified in Dr. Mudd's defense at the conspiracy trial. Betty testified: "Dr. Mudd treated me very well. I have no fault to find with him."[89]

Dr. Mudd continued to study and write about yellow fever after his pardon. An article he wrote on yellow fever was printed in the Baltimore Sun newspaper on June 25, 1873. In the article, Dr. Mudd points out that there is "a wonderful diversity of opinion" about the cause and treatment of yellow fever. It would be almost two decades after he died in 1883 that researchers would discover that yellow fever was transmitted by infected mosquitoes. After that, yellow fever was controllable by mosquito eradication programs, and eventually by a yellow fever vaccine.

The five year period from 1873 to 1878 encompassed the third longest economic depression in U.S. history. Bankruptcies and insolvencies were widespread. In rural areas, the downward pressure on prices reduced farm income and created great hardship. Dr. Mudd and his family were not exempt from this hardship.

In February 1878, Congressman Eli Jones Henkle submitted HR 3418, a "Bill for the Relief of Dr. Samuel A. Mudd" during the 2nd session of the 45th Congress, U.S. House of Representatives. Congressman Henkle represented the 5th District of Maryland where Dr. Mudd lived.

---

[86] Port Tobacco Times, March 6, 1874.

[87] Port Tobacco Times, October 6, 1876.

[88] Port Tobacco Times, November 2, 1877.

[89] Pitman, *The Assassination of President Lincoln and the Trial of the Conspirators.* Testimony of Betty Washington. Page 194.

Following the 1867 yellow fever epidemic at Fort Jefferson, the Government paid Dr. Daniel Whitehurst, the civilian doctor whom Dr. Mudd worked under during the epidemic, the sum of $300 for services rendered during the epidemic. $300 at that time is equivalent to about $6,000 today. In HR 3418, Congressman Henkle requested compensation for Dr. Mudd of $3,000, which is about $60,000 today, or ten times what the Government paid Dr. Whitehurst..

The bill said:

H.R. 3418

In the House of Representatives
February 25, 1878

Read twice, referred to the Committee of Claims, and ordered to be printed.

Mr. Henkle, on leave, introduced the following bill:

A Bill

For the relief of Doctor Samuel A. Mudd, of Maryland.

Be it enacted by the Senate and House of Representatives of the United States of America in Congress assembled, that the Secretary of the Treasury be, and is hereby, authorized and directed to pay to Doctor Samuel A. Mudd, of Maryland, or his legally authorized attorney, the sum of three thousand dollars for services rendered to the United States as surgeon and assistant surgeon during the epidemic of yellow fever at Fort Jefferson, Florida, in the year eighteen hundred and sixty-seven.

Dr. Mudd and his congressman must have known that the likelihood of Congress providing the requested relief was extremely remote, so they were probably not surprised that the bill died in committee.

Also in 1878, despite their own hardships. Dr. and Mrs. Mudd temporarily took in a seven-year-old orphan named John Burke.[90] Burke was one of 300 abandoned children sent to Maryland families from the New York City Foundling Asylum run by the Catholic Sisters of Charity. A large number of orphans and abandoned children was one of the legacies of the Civil War. Other local families also took in children. The Burke boy was permanently settled with farmer Ben Jenkins.[91]

This was not the first time that Dr. and Mrs. Mudd took in orphan children. Former slave Mary Simms testified at the conspiracy trial that "two little orphan children" lived with Dr. and Mrs. Mudd in 1864, the year before the Lincoln assassination.[92]

---

[90] Mudd, Richard D., *The Mudd Family of the United States.* Volume 1. Second Edition. 1971. Page 470.

[91] Maryland, Charles County, 8th Election District, Enumeration District 45, Supervisor's District 3. Pages 1-2. 1880 U.S. Census. Population Schedule. Digital images. Ancestry.com.

[92] *Investigation And Trial Papers Relating To The Assassination Of President Lincoln*, 1865. Testimony of Mary Simms (NARA microfilm publication M-599), National Archives, Washington, D.C.

Although the rural economy began to recover as the depression of 1873 - 1878 ended, Dr. Mudd's financial problems continued. On April 28, 1880, the Port Tobacco Times and Charles County Advertiser reported that Dr. Mudd's barn and its contents, including his tobacco crop, were destroyed by fire. The paper reported:

Heavy Loss by Fire

On Saturday last, a barn belonging to Dr. S.A. Mudd, near Bryantown, was entirely destroyed by fire, together with its contents, between 6000 and 8000 pounds of tobacco, two horses, a wagon and a lot of farm implements. It seems that some hands had been engaged in clearing a piece of new land on the doctor's farm about a quarter of a mile from the barn, fire being used for the purpose of burning the brush and other growth. The fire it appears was neglected and communicated to the barn, which was totally destroyed in a very few minutes. We understand that there was no insurance upon the barn or any portion of its contents. Thus we have been called upon to chronicle two very heavy losses from fire by citizens of our county within the last few weeks.

Nettie Mudd told the story of her father's trial, imprisonment, and return home in her 1906 book *The Life of Dr. Samuel A. Mudd*. Nettie was born nine years after her father returned home. The details of her father's life was provided to her by her mother. Dr. Mudd died on Nettie's fifth birthday, January 10, 1883. This is Nettie's account of her father's pardon and life after returning home:

My father regained his liberty on the 8th day of March, 1869, having endured imprisonment for a period of four years, lacking about six weeks. Two days prior to the issue of the above order from the War Department, on the 13th of February, President Johnson wrote a note to my mother and sent it to her home by a special messenger, requesting her to come to Washington and receive my father's pardon. She left for Washington immediately, but being detained on the way, did not reach the city till the following morning. Once there, she repaired, in company with Dr. J. H. Blanford, my father's brother-in-law, to the White House. In a few moments President Johnson sent for my mother to come into the executive office. There he delivered to her the papers for the release of my father. My mother asked him if the papers would go safely through the mails. His reply, before he had signed the papers, was: "Mrs. Mudd, I will put the President's seal on them. I have complied with my promise to release your husband before I left the White House. I no longer hold myself responsible. Should these papers go amiss you may never hear from them again, as they may be put away in some pigeon-hole or corner. I guess, Mrs. Mudd, you think this is tardy justice in carrying out my promise made to you two years ago. The situation was such, however, that I could not act as I wanted to do.

After he had signed and sealed the papers, he handed them to my mother, who took them, thanked him and left. She had intended going to the Dry Tortugas and delivering in person the release to her long-afflicted husband. This, however, she was not permitted to do, as when she reached Baltimore, intending to take the steamer from that port for the Dry Tortugas, she found that the boat had departed a few hours before her arrival, and that another would not sail for two or three weeks. She therefore sent the papers by express to her brother in New Orleans, Thomas 0. Dyer, who paid a Mr. Loutrel three hundred dollars to deliver them to my father at Fort Jefferson.

On the 20th day of March, 1869, sixteen days after President Johnson's term of office had expired, my father arrived home, frail, weak and sick, never again to be strong during the thirteen years he survived. It is needless for me to try to picture the feelings and incidents of his home-coming. Pleasure and pain were intermingled—pleasure to him to be once more in his old home surrounded by his loved ones, and pleasure to them to have him back once more; pain to them to see him so broken in health and strength, and pain to him to find his savings all gone and his family almost destitute.

Again we find him, after a brief period for rest, engaged in the struggle to regain in a measure his lost means and position. This he never accomplished. He found himself surrounded by exacting duties, yet handicapped by innumerable disadvantages. There were no laborers to cultivate the farm; the fences had fallen down or been destroyed by the Federal soldiery, and the fields were unprotected against intrusive cattle; buildings were out of repair, and money almost unobtainable. His hardships in prison, however, had in a measure taught him to be patient. Gradually things became brighter. When the warm glow of summer passed into harvest time, he was encouraged by the fact that a generous yield of earth's products rewarded him for his labor. He only partially regained his practice. While he was confined in prison many of the families he had attended employed other physicians. Many of these families sought my father's services on his return, but some did not. Apart from this, the people of the neighborhood had become comparatively poor by reason of their losses occasioned by the war. A great deal of his attention and skill was therefore given gratuitously.

During the four years they were together in prison Edward Spangler became very much attached to my father. As a consequence, a short time after Spangler's release, he came to our home early one morning, and his greeting to my mother, after my father had introduced him, was: 'Mrs. Mudd, I came down last night, and asked some one to tell me the way here. I followed the road, but when I arrived I was afraid of your dogs, and I roosted in a tree.' He had come to stay.

He occupied himself chiefly in helping our old gardener, Mr. Best, and in doing small jobs of carpenter's work in the neighborhood. My father gave him five acres of land in a wood containing a bubbling spring, about five hundred yards from our dwelling. Here Spangler contemplated erecting a building and establishing for himself a home. This purpose, however, was never to be realized. About eighteen months after he came he contracted a severe illness, the result of having been caught in a heavy rain, which thoroughly saturated his clothing. His sickness resulted in his death—rheumatism of the heart being the immediate cause.

He was a quiet, genial man, greatly respected by the members of our family and the people of the neighborhood. His greatest pleasure seemed to be found in extending kindnesses to others, and particularly to children, of whom he was very fond. Not long after his death my father, in searching for a tool in Spangler's tool chest, found a manuscript, in Spangler's own handwriting, and presumably written while he was in prison. This manuscript contained Spangler's statement of his connection with the great 'conspiracy.'

My father died from pneumonia, January 10, 1883, after an illness of nine days. He contracted the disease while visiting the sick in the neighborhood in the nighttime and in inclement weather. He was buried in Saint Mary's cemetery, attached to the Bryantown church, where he had first met Booth. He was in the fiftieth year of his age at the time of his death.

The Death of Dr. Mudd

Nettie was only 5 years old when her father died, but her sister Stella was eleven, and remembered more details of her father's death. In a 1950 letter, an elderly Stella (now Sister Rosamunda) wrote[93] to Dr. Richard D. Mudd, the son of Stella's brother Thomas:

About a year before his death, he was not well and I was left to keep him company. While busy elsewhere he walked the floor. I thought he was saying 'misery me' - it was the Misererie. New Year's Day he went to Mass, visited a very sick patient after Mass - had pneumonia - died Jan. 10th. The day before his death he said to my mother 'Don't wait till it is too late, send for the priest, I know I am going to die.' The priest came, did not think need urgent and had to meet train, so did administer sacraments. The priest of Bryantown parish paid father a visit that day, heard his confession. Tom, your father, went for Father Southgate that night in snow and bitter cold. Father S. came, gave last rites - said prayers for dying and he was gone to God. I was present at death bed. Father said to my Mother - 'It is not hard to die. I am just waiting for call of the Old Master.' Mother said to him 'How can you talk like that and leave me with a house full of children?' He replied 'God knows best' (his last words) and died.

Dr. Mudd was just 49 years old when he died. He is buried in the cemetery at St. Mary's Catholic Church in Bryantown, the same church where he first met John Wilkes Booth.

The Port Tobacco Times and Charles County Advertiser ran the following obituary for Dr. Mudd on January 19, 1883:

Death of Dr. Samuel A. Mudd

Dr. Samuel A. Mudd died at his residence near Bryantown in this county on Wednesday of last week after a short illness of pneumonia. So short had been his illness that no information of it had been received here, and being, as he was, in the prime of manly vigor, the sudden intelligence of his death received here on Friday was as great a surprise as it was an unfeigned and universal regret.

In the death of Dr. Mudd, Charles County has lost one of its most honored citizens, the profession a learned and useful member, while his family must endure the loss of a kind, loving and painstaking husband and father. He was ever ready to lend his aid and assistance to the poor and needy, and around the bed of pain and suffering his generous nature was ever ready to extend comfort and solace, with his means and the talents with which God had endowed him.

In the death of Dr. Mudd has passed from earth the last of those who were associated in the assassination of the lamented President Lincoln. As free from any guilty connection with conspirators in this crime, which will ever darken the pages of history, as an unborn babe, he nevertheless, upon bare suspicion was made to suffer from the brutal treatment of an enraged and ungovernable people. Awed by the circumstances of finding the assassin of the President in his house, he having imposed upon his generous nature by false statements as to the origin of his accident, his crime was simply not admitting the service rendered to Booth in setting his leg. Under the excitement prevailing at the time, Dr. Mudd denied any knowledge of Booth, or that he

---

[93] Tom Mudd, Mudd and Related Families, FHL Microfilm 1426475. Family History Library, Salt Lake City, UT.

had been at his house. He was afraid to admit service rendered even under the misapprehension that the accident occurred by a fall from his horse while traveling through the county, as he had been told by Booth, would certainly secure his arrest and incarceration, his courage forsook him and he denied his having been with him, when upon search of his house the boot leg was found which had been cut from the broken limb with "J. Wilkes" written within it. To then tell the whole truth availed him nothing. He was tried for conspiracy in the assassination, convicted and sentenced to the Dry Tortugas for life, when after some three years he was pardoned by President Johnson. It is an injustice to the memory of a generous, warmhearted man to associate him with the guilty Booth. His only crime being rendering medical aid to Booth in his suffering, he not knowing Booth to be guilty of any crime, but laboring under the false impression he had sustained his accident in an innocent fall from his horse.

He was in his 48th year at the time of his death. He leaves a widow and six children to mourn his great loss.

Comment

"Oh what a tangled web we weave, when first we practice to deceive"
- Sir Walter Scott, Marmion, Canto vi. Stanza 17 -

Dr. Samuel A. Mudd was his own worst enemy. Instead of being truthful with investigators, he lied about recognizing that the man with the broken leg was John Wilkes Booth, lied about when he first learned of the assassination, and lied about his meeting with Booth in Washington. Had he been truthful with investigators, it is very likely he would not have been prosecuted. In fact, he may have received a portion of the reward money offered for Booth's capture and become somewhat of a hero.

Mrs. Mudd was equally culpable in trying to deceive investigators. It was she, not Dr. Mudd, who thought of claiming that Booth was wearing a false beard. It is likely she escaped arrest only because she had four small children to take care of.

Despite the fact that Dr. Mudd admitted to several people that he recognized Booth at his farm, and that trial testimony showed he knew Booth had assassinated the President before Booth left the farm, Dr. Mudd continued to proclaim his innocence to the end of his life, and even beyond. In an article he wrote before he died, and published in the Baltimore Sun a month after he died, Dr. Mudd said "my only offense consisted of setting the leg of a man whom I did not at the time know to be a fugitive from justice." (See the Source Documents section for the complete text.)

Why didn't Dr. Mudd turn Booth over to the authorities? Many have speculated, but no one really knows. As in many things, the simplest answer may be closest to the truth. It may simply be that upon learning of the assassination while at Bryantown, Dr. Mudd panicked. He may have thought that his relationship with Booth would make him appear to be an accomplice. After all, Booth had slept at Dr. Mudd's home, had later had a meeting with Dr. Mudd in Washington, and had come to Dr. Mudd's farm immediately after the assassination. Probably fearing that he would be unjustly tied to Booth, Dr. Mudd denied that he knew the man with the broken leg was Booth, denied learning of Lincoln's assassination until after Booth had left his farm, and denied the Washington meeting with Booth. All three denials were untrue.

Dr. Mudd paid a heavy price for not being forthright with Government investigators. He spent nearly four years in a hard military prison located on an isolated speck of desert island in the Gulf of Mexico, more than a thousand miles from family and friends.

But whatever his faults may have been, Dr. Mudd ultimately redeemed himself by his selfless actions during the hellish yellow fever epidemic at Fort Jefferson in the late summer and early fall of 1867. He didn't have to volunteer to help the suffering soldiers who were his daily guards, but he did. He could have stayed away from the sick soldiers to avoid becoming infected himself, but he didn't. He put his life on the line to help them, and almost lost his life in the process.

Many soldiers survived the epidemic only because of Dr. Mudd's tireless work. When the epidemic had run its course, 300 soldiers at Fort Jefferson signed a petition testifying to his bravery and asking President Johnson to pardon him. The petition said in part:

He inspired the hopeless with courage, and by his constant presence in the midst of danger and infection, regardless of his own life, tranquilized the fearful and desponding.

Most people would think their life had been worthwhile if they had an epitaph such as this.

Source Documents

10-17-1852: Sam Mudd's Expulsion from Georgetown College

Source: Letter from Fr. Callaghan to Fr. George, Georgetown University Lauinger Library, Special Collections Division, Washington, D.C.

Georgetown College, Oct. 31st, 1852

Rev. & Dear Father George,

... The most exciting thing that we have had lately was a disturbance among the boys. It is entirely settled now, so that I can give you a full account of it...

Last Friday week a boy a refused a punishment which Mr. Tehan had given him for going out of studies without permission. Fr. Maguire therefore gave him his choice to submit to the punishment or leave the College. He chose the latter. When the boys heard of the affair, they murmured about it, and complained of the regulation that prefects have about going out of studies. They held a sort of indignation meeting, and decided that the boy ought to be excused from his punishment, and the rule abolished. They tried an appeal to Fr. Maguire and to Mr. Tehan, but to no purpose. When the bell rang for free studies at 12 ¾ (this was Friday noon) none of them went. Mr. Clark, who kept those studies, went up to the study room, and finding no one there, walked down as cooly and naturally as he does everything else. At the time for regular studies, he rang the bell, but none of the boys moved. Their resolution held for about five minutes, and at length one started, and another, and finally they all went. The middle studies were undisturbed. All was quiet from that time till the recreation after school which was spent in indignation, like the one after dinner. In night studies there was a good deal of stamping in the beginning. Mr. Brady kept these studies. He bore with the noise for a little while, and then said a few calm words to them which had the effect of producing quiet for the rest of the studies. The next day some of the larger ones apologized in the name of all to Mr. Brady, explaining to him that the indignation was only against Mr. Tehan. He answered them bluntly that he required no special regard from them, he entirely approved Mr. Tehan's course, and would do the same thing himself if he were in Mr. Tehan's place. The next morning Mr. Tehan kept studies, and then the grand row took place. At the beginning of studies they saluted him with a hip, and when he said the prayers, they answered with a howl. He did nothing but 'keep cool' which was all that he could do, and was not a very easy task, for during the whole studies they kept up a regular beating on their desks to a tune prepared for the occasion. During both of the studies the prefects were on the watch and secured the names of many and especially of six who took a principal part in the meetings and the noise. A great many in the house thought the best plan would be to expel those six immediately and publicly, but Fr. Maguire judged it more prudent to wait a little. It is probable that if the ring leaders had been expelled immediately, a great many of the others would have followed them.

When they came down to breakfast after studies, they were all in the humors of uproar. Fr. Maguire met them in the refectory, and addressed them in a quiet but decided manner. He mentioned to them that six of their leaders had been noted, and that he would deal with them as he thought they deserved. The effect of his words was that the noisy doings were stopped, and those who were conscious of having been notable, were put on their good behavior, hoping to save themselves.

Fr. Maguire wrote immediately to the parents of the six, and requested them to come and take their children home. This was on Saturday. The next Tuesday five of the parents or guardians came, and the boys were despatched at very short notice. The way of proceeding was this. The parent or guardian came. The whole matter was explained to them, the prefects were called in to testify, the boys clothes were packed, and he went away in the carriage that had brought his father or guardian.

Those sent the first day were Samuel Mudd from Maryland, Coleman from Cincinnati (the boy who came to Holy Cross with Fr. Blox 4 summers ago), Rogers from Baltimore, Ned Campbell and Mooney from N. York. The boys were pretty well sobered down by these dismissals and those who had done anything were quaking, for fear their turn should come next. Tuesday night, one of them went to Fr. Maguire, and asked to go of his own accord. He was allowed to go of course. The next day the sixth one, Miller of N. York went. His father is a lawyer in New York with whom John Devlin is in partnership. Devlin came for the boy, with a message from his father, that before leaving the College, his son should apologize to Fr. Maguire for his conduct. The next day, Thursday, the boys were made perfectly quiet by being told that those who were to be dismissed had all been dealt with, that if any remaining in the college were dissatisfied, they might apply to the President and he would permit them to go home, that if they made any further trouble, they were watched, and would be immediately sent home. Now that their fears are removed, they are quite orderly. The whole affair has been advantageous to the College. Some of those who would have been most troublesome during the year have been got rid of (the prefects say the selection could not have been better made). The parents are satisfied, and the disorderly fellows that remain know that they are watched, and know what they may expect if they commit themselves...

Truly yours in Christ,

J.G. Callaghan, S.J.

03-05-1856: Dr. Samuel Mudd's 1856 Graduation Thesis

Source: University of Maryland, Health Sciences and Human Services Library, Baltimore, Maryland.

The University of Maryland's Medical Department in the 1850s was, and still is today, one of the country's leading medical schools. The instruction Dr. Mudd received was the best available to medical science at the time. However, medical science then did not have the knowledge we do today of bacterial infection, or the antibiotics to treat such infections. Dr. Mudd's graduation thesis on dysentery provides a fascinating insight into the state of medical knowledge in the mid 1800's. Almost none of it would be applicable today.

Dr. Mudd's graduation thesis was handwritten. All spelling, grammar, and punctuation in the document below is exactly as written by Dr. Mudd.

An Inaugural Dissertation on Dysentery Submitted for Examination of the Provost, Regents and Faculty of Physic of the University of Maryland for the Degree of Doctor of Medicine by Samuel Alex. Mudd.

Dysentery

Dysentery - a disease which is common to nearly every clime - is found to prevail with unrelenting severity during some seasons - bidding defiance to the most active medical treatment and skill; at others mild and under the control of simple medical agents and care. It is a disease which visits impartially the man of wealth as well as the man of poverty - the man of authority - as well as the subject. It, like the avenging Angel of the Almighty Being, has been the instrument to humble the pride of nations. Armies have been attacked and thousands, like the leaves of the forest on the approach of the first autumnal frost, have faded, withered and fallen to the dust. The fireside has been made desolate, the orphan's cry has been heard to utter the sweet but sad accents of grief, Where is my mama? Where is my papa? The wife's brow is bedewed with a tear at the loss of her kind and grief soothing husband, or the tender offspring of her bosom, and the husband made wretched and weary of living, on account of its too cruel visitation, but enough of unimportant and tedious detail.

The characteristic symptoms of dysentery are first, griping pains in the abdomen, followed sometimes and very often by diarrhoea, which soon develop itself into frequent discharges of mucus and blood - with spasmodic action of the muscles engaged in defecation straining and tenesmus. The disease however just as commonly burst forth without the least complication. The first intimation the patient has of his situation is probably by one or two shooting pains across the abdomen, with a desire to stool, which after a somewhat fruitless attempt, nothing but a little mucus, he returns and in a short time is called again and again with about the same result, with the exception probably of a little addition of blood. Sometimes hard lumps of feces called scybala are thrown out combined with the mucus or blood, which seems to be the exciting cause - or more likely there seems to be a retention of the natural feces, which are occasionally expelled in small hard lumps, with their surfaces lubricated with the prevailing mucous evacuations. This mucus packets within the folds of the intestine, near the anus, which the first efforts at defecation throws out and all further attempts and desires for expulsion are in vain. This was the case with several patients that came under my observation and attention whilst a resident of the Baltimore Infirmary. The rectum from irritation produced by inflamation contracts upon itself involuntarily and spasmodically, and the only way apparently that the contents of the alimentary canal gain exit is by its gravitation.

Dysentery consists in inflamation of the mucous membrane of the colon and rectum. It may be either acute or chronic, both of which may occur independently of the other.

The acute form in its incipiency may be ushered in suddenly with active hemorrhagic discharges from the bowels as a diarrhoea, with tormina and tenesmus followed by inflamation of the above named intestines. It sometimes manifests itself in a periodic form - occurring at regular intervals with griping pains etc., and the stools may consist either of bloody mucous or serous - this variety is called the intermitting form of the disease or the disease may come on superadded, the derangement of the functions of the liver, spleen and stomach, especially those that reside in malarious districts, which has been termed the bilious or remittent type. Of these I shall hereafter speak.

The most marked symptoms in the acute form are uneasiness in the abdomen, griping pains, with tormina and tenesmus, hot and tender abdomen over the courses of the colon and rectum. The stools are bloody, mucous, foetid, dark coloured, and contain lumps of a pultaceous character, that is, when they contain faecal matter. At other times there is a great desire to stool, and when the patient is in the act, he is seized with great pains - and a vain attempt to pass more than half an ounce of bloody mucus, of a gelatinous nature, without the least trace of faecal matter.

Dysentery may set in with or without precursory symptoms. In the former case, it is preceded by general uneasiness, lassitude, impairment of the appetite, dull or transient pains in the abdomen, costiveness or diarrhoea, and other evidences of moderate intestinal irritation. Sometimes the local symptoms make their appearance before the general, and in mild cases may run its course without fever. Then again the local and febrile phenomena commence simultaneously - the patient being attacked with a shivering of the frame almost as soon as he complains of pain and tenesmus. Again the fever often precedes, and occasionally for a considerable period any evidences of disorder of the bowels.

The disease prevails from a very slight affection, implicating but a very small extent of the colon and rectum, passing off in two or three days, but sometimes owing to a peculiarity of the constitution, or to some great malignancy of the poison, the system receives a shock which the powers of life are scarcely able to react. Or after the disease has gone on for sometime, unaided by medical treatment or neglect, all the powers of the frame will sink down into a typhoid or collapse condition, or a general depression of the vital forces - livid lips, the eyes sunken, circumscribed by a bluish tint, with delirium, hiccough and finally death terminates his mortal existance. Such cases occur but seldom; principally observed by large and experienced practitioners to prevail during epidemic. I have seen but one case in which all these symptoms were developed. The patient from the beginning was attended by two eminent and talented physicians, who did all that the case seemed to require but to no avail - the system never recovered from the first shock.

The nature of the stools in the beginning, consist somewhat of a transparent whitish mucus, or of mucus streaked with blood and a little faecal matter, which may be altered by bile, small portions of false membranes and coagulated lymph. It is this decay of animal matter combined with vitiated secretions, or secretions undergoing decomposition no doubt that gives this peculiar disagreeable fetor to the discharges. Though this does not occur generally until the disease has gone on for two or three days, at which time in severe or moderately severe cases, there is nearly entire suspension of the natural stool. The inflammation if not checked will gradually and sometimes rapidly extend along the courses of the colon and rectum, the extent of which may be pretty accurately ascertained by percussion or pressure over those parts. If there is much tenderness over the epigastrium and right side we may conclude that the whole of the large intestines are involved or the inflamation has reached the transverse and ascending colon.

There is also tympanitis very often of the abdomen, principally over the regions of the colon - owing to the accumulation of flatus. When this takes place, there is more or less high fevers, the pulse full hard and quick, the skin dry and hot, the tongue coated with a whitish fur, and the stomach, liver, kidneys, bladder, urethra sharing in the general disorder - producing emesis, strangury, and painful micturation, and in females the vagina sympathises.

As a general rule the disease takes a healthy turn about the eighth or ninth day - danger in ordinary cases is increased from neglect or when the disease continues for a week or ten days without any moderation - the symptoms before spoken of are apt to become developed, and if the patient does not perish immediately, the chronic form with all its sequences are very likely to supervene, and from its constant drain upon the system the patient sikns or complete recovery may take place, but in agravated cases most commonly end fatally. In the latter stage of the disease, the discharges become very offensive and resembles the washings of fresh meat. I recollect seeing a patient troubled with a chronic mucoid discharge, which he said lasted for five years, scarcely without any intermission, and were increased whenever he was imprudent or indulged in his usual diet. which consisted principally of milk and mush, tea, toasted bread soaked in water, chicken and broth, soups, etc.

Chronic Dysentery - commonly follows the acute form - when it occurs independently it is generally associated or complicated with chronic enteritis. It sometimes though rarely proceeds from fistula in ano and hemorrhoidal - tumours - the inflammation being extended.

The principal symptoms in this form consist in the stools being less frequent, more feculent, mingled with mucus, tormina generally only when pressure is made and less tenesmus than in the acute. There is scarcely any perceptable difference in the skin, pulse, and indeed general health of the patient in chronic dysentery and chronic enteritis. After the disease has continued for a time, signs of hectic fever, or the various hydropic affections are very likely to come on in consequence of the system becoming prostrated through the excessive evacuations, depraved nutrition, secretions, deposits, etc. The membranes are also very apt to become thickened and the patient sooner or later falls a victim.

The Bilious form - in regard to the bilious form, there is nearly always functional disorder of the organs - the liver may fail to secrete, or it may over secrete the natural healthy supply of bile, but most commonly there is supression. The bilious secretions may precede, supervene or coexist with the disease, as a general rule however, they are present in the beginning, and arise very probably from the same cause that lights up the inflamation in the intestines. But in the simple and mild cases, where apparently, and no doubt the disease sometimes is produced by indegestible articles of food, or from the irritation that follows active diarrhoea from the bowels the derangement of the functions of the liver and stomach seems to depend upon sympathy. The symptoms that most commonly mark this form of the disease is epigastric oppression, vomiting, yellowness of the skin and conjunctiva, the tongue coated with a yellow brown surface with its borders red, and diminished secretions of bile and urine. The fevers are higher and a greater tendency to delirium.

The remittent character of the disease prevails chiefly in malarious districts, and is known by the marks of remittent fever being blended with it. There is constant fever with exacerbations and remissions, the tongue coated with a whitish fur generally and dry, the skin dry and hot. The stomach is more irritable than in any of the other forms - vomiting is more constant and the ejectment of bilious matter more common.

Sometimes the disease from the beginning assume the typhoid character, with sinking of all the powers of the frame and when apparently on the brink of eternity, the system reacts and convalescence takes place. Then again death may be the result, though it most usually run a regular course and terminates favourably under judicious treatment.

The intermitting form is very common in some sections of the country and like its kindred affection, remittent fever, prevails in malarious districts. It is a very interesting malady, and consist in a perfect intermission, occurring at regular intervals with all the symptoms in the acute form, lasting two or three hours, when they subside with a langour, the consequence of the paroxism. These paroxisms may be either of the quotidian, tertian, or quartan variety. There is a disease very much resembling this viz intermitting diarrhoea, and it is sometimes very difficult to discriminate between the two, the evacuations in both being somewhat serous, though there is one great mark or distinction. In the intermitting diarrhoea, there is no straining and tenesmus, and often but little tormina; but in the dysentery there is all or nearly all of the signs of the real disease in the acute stage present, viz straining, tenesmus, tormina, bloody and mucous stools, etc.

The causes of the disease are various, but for the most part, especially that which gives rise to the epidemic character, is unknown and unaccountable. Dysentery prevail epidemically or sporadically - epidemically where a whole district or section of country is simultaneously affected - sporadically where the disease arises from imprudence, or where a single individual is attacked. The contagiousness of the disease is doubted, and thus far the opion of the profession tends to the negative.

It has been observed by numerous authors, that persons exposed to all states of the atmosphere, subject to great variations of temperature, of heat, cold, wet and dry - persons traveling a long distance in hot and moist weather, or labouring people are apt to contract the disease. Those that are subjected to the same epidemic influences as give rise to remittent and intermittent fevers, are said to be more susceptable than those that are remote from its cause.

One of the most common reputed causes for its production on the Western shore of Maryland is the imprudence in eating unripe and acid fruits, such as apples, cherries, grapes etc. In eighteen hundred and fifty-three, nearly every family in my district, eight or ten miles around probably suffered from this malady and nine cases in ten the patients had indulged in eating cherries - there being quite an abundant crop that year.

Another and what appears to be more of an exciting than a productive cause is the sitting down upon wet and cold ground, thus armies and travellers, being often necessitated to sleep out with scanty insufficient clothing and food have been attacked by dysentery and thousands have fallen victim to its rage. Again, it exists epidemically without giving the least perceptable cause for its prevalence, and I have known men who were considered scrupulously exact in regard to their diet and habits to be seized with the disease, with as much violence, as those with some reputed cause might be adduced. Then again on the other hand I have known persons who have indulged in every species of luxury, such as eating all kinds of unripe fruits, drinking to excess all kinds of liquors, and exposing themselves to all kinds of harsh and inclement weather, to escape its influence. Drinking of cold water by workmen in warm weather seems to be one of the means by which the distemper is lighted into action; and I have known six out of twelve in the harvest field to be seized, where no other cause could be ascertained, with the exception probably of a little whiskey, which the farmers during those occasions are in the habit of furnishing to labourers.

The eating of indigestible articles of food also seems to be one of the sources by which the disease is set up, but during its prevalence, or where the nature of the malady is epidemic many simple and foolish causes of its production are mentioned, but it appears as often without as with a cause.

The treatment of acute dysentery - In mild cases where the patient only suffers from frequent evacuations, with but little tormina and tenesmus, unattended with fever, and where the contents of the abdomen expelled consists the greater part fecal matter - little or no treatment is required - rest, low diet generally in such cases being sufficient to effect a cure, though we should never rely on this, for very often the mildest cases are prolonged and even prove fatal in consequence of paying too little regard to the state of the patient. Very often when the disease commences with symptoms of diarrhoea it may in many cases be cut short by a simple glass of brandy, or any common astringent, combined with rest and resisting the inclination to stool as much as possible.

But in the more severe forms, where the tormina and tenesmus gain the ascendancy of the will, where the stools are of a mucous purulent and bloody character, where the skin is hot and dry, the tongue coated and associated with these, fever - active medical treatment must be pursued or adopted. If the patient be of a plestoric, robust habit, general bleeding in most instances has a marked tendency to put a stop to, or to decrease the violence of the malady. After this I have observed in those cases that have come under my charge - that small doses of chloride of mercury, combined with opium and ipecacuanha, act very beneficially by calming the irritation, improving the condition of the skin and secretions - together with its antiphlogistic prpoerty - check the inflammation. This is equally applicable in cases after or in the absence of bleeding. It is well in most cases to continue this prescription for twenty four or forty eight hours, giving it at intervals of every four hours, watching its effects, and suspending its employment, when symptoms arise contraindicating its use. The dose in such examples might be given in proportions of proto chlorid. hydrarg. ipecac. of each three to five grains and opium one. Ipecacuanha is said by some to act remedially by lessening the peristaltic motion of the intestines with its revulsive agency.

Another very excellent remedy, after the employment of mercury of in cases where it is not required is the acetas plumbi and opium in equal parts made into pill - one or two or more through the day according to the effects they produce, or as the case may seem to require. To be sure this ought to be the rule and the duty of every prudent physician. It is hard to say what should be the treatment without the case is presented to our view. We always minister to the symptoms and not to the name of the disease, for otherwise gross errors and sad consequences would be the result. There is no agent in the Materia Medica that deserves more praise than the judicious employment of mercury. I have seen well marked cases that have been cured where no other medicine has been used, with the exception of an ounce or two of ol. recini.

Equal to, or next in efficacy is opium. Without this agent our attempts in many cases at cure would be fruitless. We have no other remedy in which there is connected so many important requisites towards the restoration to health in this disease. It seems in every stage to be applicable, and but a few in which it is contraindicated. Yet in those which it appears unfit, it sometimes produces opposite effects - as in cases of hot and dry skin, tongue and fauces, the very effect in the healthy subject it produces, this symptom is very often and frequently entirely relieved by the action of this article.

A very good domestic astringent, which in many parts of the country is very convenient, is made by taking equal parts or quantities of red oak bark, pine tops or branches and ground olive. I have seen this used by persons with the approbation of the physician with the best results, also the common running brier root, made by boiling one or two ounces of the root with a pint of water, which is generally called brier root tea; in order to make it more palatable, it may be slightly sweetened, and the patient may take one, two or three ounces at a time during the day as an ordinary drink.

In the more advanced stage of the disease, where there exists a pretty considerable erethism, anxiety about the praecordia nausea and vomiting, the countenance pale and anemic, the tongue red, the abdomen tumid, distended with flatus and painful to the touch - discharges, foetid, consisting chiefly of blood and mucus.

The best mode of procedure in this instance would be cups or leeches over the abdomen, along the courses of the colon, or inflamation. In the latter stage of dysentery, the best agent known to relieve the distended and tumid abdomen is the oleum Lerebinthinae. This I have seen used often in drachm doses with the greatest satisfaction to the patient and physician.

Opiates internally by way of the mouth, or injection per rectum, demulcent drinks; and when the system is very feeble and prostrated, the diet should be nutritious, and to subserve this purpose, beef tea answers our intention the best.

The action of opium sometimes in this and similar effections varies from its general. It often acts as a purgative secondary by destroying the spasm and irritation consequent upon the inflamation, thus allowing the retained faeces to pass without obstruction, or the opium relieving the strangulation, thus allows the purgatives to act.

We treat all the various forms upon the same general principal - to check inflamation where it is present, to build up the system when the powers of life are declining by nutritious diets and stimulants, to relieve congestion and promote the secretory and excretory functions of the organs, and lastly, but not least, after we have done all to the best of our knowledge to relieve, leave the balance for nature to accomplish.

In the bilious forms we cannot do well without mercury, the liver very often being much deranged in its functions - we will in some cases have to be quite persistent in its use, then again it may be of no utility. In those cases where there is an over secretion and excretion - that is it may not be primarily of any service, but secondarily by correcting the morbid condition in other parts of the body.

In the remittent and intermittent types, Lumia, combined when the patient is aenemic with some of the ferruginous tonics and gentle purgation is all that is necessary to eradicate the disease.

In the chronic stage the best mode of treatment depends upon our attention to diet and regimen - for without this precaution, it is vain to expect a cure. In this stage the patient sooner or later becomes aenemic, thus indicating the replacing properties of the iron, which may be given in doses from a half to a grain of the sulfate two or three times a day. A very good combination of articles to prevent the hemorrhage from the bowels and supply the colouring material in the asthenic and aenemic, consist in Creta. praep., Ferri. Ferrocyan., Ext. haematoxylon, Opii grs.iij, cinna., vj grs., sach alba si, made into eight powders, of which one may be taken every three or four hours. If the case be a bad one, there may be used in conjunction of acetas plumbi grains ten and opium one or two, administered once or twice a day, according to the symptoms and effects.

We may also follow, when the disease is determined and obstinate the acetate of lead and opium pill every two, three, or four hours and if it does not succeed in arresting the symptoms, the nitras argenti pill or sulphate of copper in quantities varying from a half to a grain and a half at the same intervals, and if signs of ulceration come on the two latter named substances may injected per rectum in larger doses.

Prognosis. When the disease is about to end in convalescence, all the symptoms become more mild. The tormina and tenesmus diminishes, the stools become more fecal, larger and less frequent, or there is a general subsidence of all the marks of the disease, and nothing for the most part left, except a moderate diarrhoea, which passes off in the course of a few days. The patient sometimes though not often - after all signs of the disease has gone off - complain of cramps, which come on once or twice a week suddenly, and during their continuance causes great suffering.

But on the contrary, if there should supervene, tympanitis, high fevers with quick and weak pulse, following this, a cold clammy sweat, with coldness of the extremities, the features sunken and depressed, with a purplish hue of the skin, especially about the eyes, mouth and the tips of the fingers - attended with hiccough delerium, subsultus tendinum etc., we conclude that these are omens which portend an unfavorable termination.

Danger in this disease as in all others, is proportionate to the extent of the inflamation. If we ascertain on pressure that the whole of the colon is involved, our attention should be directed with watchful anxiety, and unless means be adopted to check the inflamation and the irritation thus produced - in a large majority of cases the powers of life will sink and the disease end fatally. In Sporadic dysentery - where the patient is well attended to, there is not so much to dread - nearly always yielding to the influence of medical agents and means. But in the epidemic character, we should never be too sanguine for I have known mild cases to occur in young subjects with constitutions strong and robust, and have been in the care of the best physicians, who persued the regular treatment with all its activity, without success.

Anatomical Characters - The lining membrane or the mucous coat of the lower and sometimes of the whole extent of the colon and rectum shows marks of inflamatory action after death. It has been observed where the irritation has been transmitted from the large to the small intestines, the solitary or Brunners glands found in the curvatures of the stomach and duodenum have been found considerably engorged and distended with evident signs of inflamation. There is also a condition existing very much resembling the lesions produced by typhoid fever, the mesentery and the glands of Peyer presenting nearly the same aspect. Ulceration in this disease is more common than any other, except probably that of typhoid fever - the appearance of which presents a smooth surface, or edge coated very often with the membranes that are frequently ejected during the evacuations, such as false membranes, coagulated lymph, etc. There again there have been instances cited where actual mortification and sloughing in the parts have taken place.

Thickening of the coats of the intestines also is produced, and I remember seeing a post mortem examination of a case resulting from this disease in which there was stricture of the colon - the opening so small that the little finger could scarcely be introduced - it was bound down by a thick, firm muscular band.

Various other lesions resulting from a scrupulous taint of the system, stinty diet, depraved nutrition, residing in badly ventilated departments, exposure, etc. have been noticed as producing a dissimilar anatomical lesion. In climates within the trophics the liver is frequently found diseased with hepatic abscesses etc.

In conclusion, let me remark - that in appreciating the moral and scientific lessons and instructions in the art of medicine - delivered by those who have given us practical and theoretical illustrations in the guide of the knife, when it was required, and its utter repugnance when no good could be effected - by those who have taught us practically the true method of searching out disease, and when we have found it, to administer the indicated soothing or healing agent - by those who have marked out the path to the most vital organs, that in case of accident or from a morbid action going on in the system, it may be in our power to apply the ligature or the barrier to death by those who have Instructed us in the nature and action physiologically of articles contained in the Materia Medica, as observed by practitioners from their experience in the healing art, and from experiments on the lower order of animal beings, and finally - by those who have acquainted us with the means whereby we can detect fraud and the hypocricy of the assassin when under the cloak of medical agents,

I can only express my sincere thanks, and only hope that the knowledge derived from your wise teachings may prove a credit to the institution in your behalf and my future reward. Wishing that this badly gotten up preamble may meet with your approbation, I respectfully conclude with bright anticipations of being numbered with the profession.

Yours, etc.
Saml. A Mudd

01-13-1862: Dr. Mudd's Letter to Orestes A. Brownson

Source: Mudd, Nettie, *The Life of Dr. Samuel A. Mudd*, 1906. Fourth Edition, Page 351.

Dr. Mudd subscribed to a Catholic journal called Brownson's Quarterly Review. When the editor, Orestes A. Brownson, began to write during the Civil War that slavery should be abolished in order to preserve the Union, Dr. Mudd wrote to Mr. Brownson to cancel his subscription. Dr. Mudd's January 13, 1862 letter said:

Bryantown, Chas. Co., Md. Jan 13th, 1862

O.A. Brownson
Dear Sir:

I sometimes since received a bill from your publisher in New York—whom I wrote stating my reasons for withdrawing my subscription to your once able review for non payment of the present account. I now repeat in substance what I then wrote to the publisher—viz. that I had not been a subscriber since 1859—the Rev. Father Vizinanzi was then agent—The Review continued to be rec'd in 1860. I inquired of Father Vizinanzi whether he had erased my name from his list of subscribers? He told me he had. When the first Vol. 1860 was rec'd I considered it a mistake or negligence on the part of the Agent—but learning to the contrary I considered it a gratuity or inducement for further subscription—so I did not trouble myself until the reception of a bill from the Publisher in New York—to which I replied immediately that I was no subscriber and ordered it to be discontinued. It was sent again in 1861 until receiving a bill, which I again a second time responded to, and stated that many of the Vols. I had refused to take from the office—and at his request and expense, those that I had and those in the Post Office would be returned. This is the third time I have been troubled on your account, and I am in hopes you will not bother me again, unless you can show clearly that I am truly indebted to you.

"It is hard to kiss the hand that smites." Through you our country beloved by its people and the wonder of the world, has rec'd. an irreparable injury. Your encouragement to the Revolutionist and men of no religion of Europe—Your condemnation of the National party or parties, and influence given to Sectionalism and the fear of rendering yourself unpopular in the North—has had a great weight in bringing about the present deplorable state of our Country—You have even advocated revolution here, in order to be consistent with your language upon European affairs, forgetting that there is no rule without an exception, and the principles of the Constitution.

The present Civil War now raging, was not brought about entirely by fear on the part of the South, that their property in Slaves was endangered, but more by an unwillingness to yield up rights guaranteed by the Constitution of the United States—the privilege of framing laws and enjoying all immunities not reserved by the General Constitution. The South could not give up State rights —The North found Slavery unprofitable, therefore, abolished it, without any interference by the South—and all we have asked is the exercise of the same power and right. Under the system of State Rights, under the Constitution of the United States—Every Abolitionist is a disunionist. Republicanism we view in the same light on account of its exclusiveness and Sectionalism. We do not object to Republicanism or Abolitionism being a State organization or party, (provided they are passive) because the right the power is accorded under the Constitution. But we are bitterly opposed to its being brought into National Politics or its principles rendering fit, an officer to execute or legislate for our Common Country. A majority of the people of the North believe

Slavery to be Sinful, thereby they attempt to force down our throats, their religious Conviction, which is Anti-Catholic and uncharitable.

The North on account of its pride, shortsightedness, hypocricy and much phylanthropy—has caused the destruction of one of the most glorious nations upon the face of the earth. The South even those termed Seceders and leaders of Secession desire union! Yes Union!—It is the longing of my heart, that the same old Star Spangled should continue to wave over the land of the free and the home of the Brave. But Alas! we know not in what manner it can be brought about. One thing seems certain to us all, the Union can never be restored by war, and the North must be very blind not to know and see it. The Success of the Federal arms does not justify a further prosecution of the war, thus far they have not gained a single victory; they have not gained one foot of territory, other than the enemy by his prudence and defensive attitude granted—with exception of a few batteries on the barren sea coast. The South has already manifested more energy, industry, prudence and Yankeeism than the North—They have erected foundries, manufactories of various sorts, and in a few months will be enabled to live well, with sealed ports.

She is possessed of every ingredient to make her self-sustaining and powerful—all she wants is a little more time, and if the war should be protracted, all the better for her future, because her resources will be brought out. Her iron, lead and other mines, which she is rich in will be worked and cause her not to look abroad for supplies.

The people of the South are differently constituted from those of the North—attributable to education and climate. As an example they are more sensitive—their sense of honor is much more keen and they would sooner run the risk of death, than live with an injured reputation. It is seldom you hear of a duel in the North, where parties are challenged to mortal combat to settle their grievances, but you find instead a recourse to law—a few dollars satisfying the dishonored. I say this in no disparagement, but merely to show the dissimilarity of the two people. The South also possess in a high degree—the virtues of forbearance, endurance and magnanimity. The war as it has progressed goes to prove and you will find these characteristics still more noticeable as it advances. The people of the North are Puritanical, long faced or Methodistic and hypocritical— they deal in Sympathetic language to hide their deception—their actions are Pharisaical, covert, stealthy, and cowardly. They are law abiding so long as it bears them out in their selfish interest, and praisers and scatterers and followers of the Bible so long as it does not conflict with their passions. They make good cow drivers, pickpockets and gamblers. With these traits of character in your leading politicians and preachers—it is impossible that confidence can be inspired in the South. Their words and actions for reasons alleged above are all met with mistrust by their Southern brethren. Your people have so degenerated, that were it not for the foreign element— which you possess—there would be only war on parchment, as it is, there is just enough of true Yankee to make the rest good for nothing, but an expense to the Nation. They fight very hard when there is no danger of being hurt and for the want of some visible exemplification of the destruction of shell and shot, they turn their pieces upon each other, resulting in the death of many, which fortunately is more gain than loss to the Federal Government.

The Union would be better maintained and restored, if the battles could always take place among each of this vast Army of 700,000 and end in its own total destruction, because the cause being removed—the patient the Government, would be soon convalescent—unless the system is so much depressed, there is not left sufficient vital power to bring about a healthy reaction.

I regret sincerely to see such a lack of Patriotism in the Present Administration and in the representatives of the North. They seem to be dreamy and mystified—they rush headlong regardless of law and its consequences and skulk like sheep-stealing dogs, when another nation stands up in open contravention. I confidently assert, that if there was any other man at the head of the Government of true conservative and constitutional principles, the Revolution would immediately cease so far as the South is concerned.

It's my opinion that you and Bishop Hughes have put yourselves upon the same footing as the rest of the demagogues and Preachers of your Section such as Beecher, Cheeves, Smith, Phillips and Etc. You have destroyed all the good you have accomplished and the church instead of prospering will lose ground in your midst so soon as the government settles down once more into a peace. They will see clearly, the folly of those would be leaders political and religious, and it's not the least improbable that many will have to seek an asylum in a foreign land.

You will please excuse this hasty and roughly scribbled epistle—it is not my intention to rob you of that jewel—honesty of intention. You know full well, that slavery being a State institution recognized by every administration and confirmed by many acts of Congress, can only be abrogated by State will. The South has stood a high protective tariff for many years, without a murmur, (excepting S. Carolina) and for what? Namely to support a few manufacturing interests in the North. The North has grown rich by the products of slave labor, pride and self esteem was its consequence; he considers himself the most exalted of God's creation, and deigns to establish principles of humanity for the rest of mankind. Christ, our Saviour found slavery at his coming and yet he made no command against its practice. Therefore I think it is a great presumption in man to supply the omissions which God in his infinity thought proper to make.

My remarks are more directed to the Non-Catholic portion of the North but I fear from your leaning and that of Bishop Hughes, you will bring about an unkind feeling between members of our church—especially against their Superiors, North and South.

I would like, had I the time to give you some practical illustrations of the two systems of labor in a medical, religious and temporal point of view, as it is manifest to me, but I must now conclude by wishing you prosperity in all your undertakings when directed for the honor and glory of God.

Most respectfully, Samuel A. Mudd, M.D.

0. A. BROWNSON D. D. LL.D.

04-22-1865: Dr. Mudd's Statement to Colonel Henry H. Wells

Source: *Investigation And Trial Papers Relating To The Assassination Of President Lincoln*, 1865. (NARA microfilm publication M-599). National Archives, Washington, D.C. Note: The statement was drafted on April 21st and signed on April 22nd.

Following his arrest by Lieutenant Alexander Lovett, Dr. Mudd provided the following signed and sworn statement to Colonel Henry H. Wells in Bryantown.

Note Dr. Mudd's statement that "I have never seen Booth since that time to my knowledge until last Saturday morning." This falsehood, and his refusal to retract it even after trial testimony showed it was false, was probably the tipping point that led the Military Commission to convict him.

Bryantown, Md   April 21, 1865

Dr. S.A. Mudd, residing four miles north of Bryantown, Maryland, being duly sworn deposes and says:

Last Saturday morning, April 15th, about four o'clock, two men called at my house and knocked very loudly. I was aroused by the noise, and as it was such an unusual thing for persons to knock so loudly, I took the precaution of asking who were there before opening the door. After they had knocked twice more, I opened the door, but before doing so they told me they were two strangers on their way to Washington, that one of their horses had fallen by which one of the men had broken his leg. On opening the door, I found two men, one on a horse led by the other man, who had tied his horse to a tree near by. I aided the man in getting off of his horse and into the house, and laid him on a sofa in my parlor. After getting a light, I assisted him in getting upstairs where there were two beds, one of which he took. He seemed to be very much injured in the back, and complained very much of it. I did not see his face at all. He seemed to be tremulous and not inclined to talk, and had his cloak thrown around his head and seemed inclined to sleep, as I thought in order to ease himself, and every now and then he would groan pretty heavily.

I had no proper paste-board for making splints, and went and got an old band-box and made one of it; and as he wanted it done hastily, I hurried more than I otherwise would. He wanted me to fix it up any way, as he said he wanted to get back, or get home and have it done by a regular physician. I then took a piece of the band-box and split it in half, doubled it at right angles, and took some paste and pasted it into a splint. On examination, I found there was a straight fracture of the tibia about two inches above the ankle. My examination was quite short, and I did not find the adjoining bone fractured in any way. I do not regard it a peculiarly painful or dangerous wound; there was nothing resembling a compound fracture. I do not suppose I was more than three-quarters of an hour in making the examination of the wound and applying the splint. He continued still to suffer, and complained of severe pain in the back, especially when being moved. In my opinion, pain in the back may originate from riding; I judge that in this case it originated from the fall and also from riding, as he seemed to be prostrated. He sometimes breathed very shortly and as if exhausted.

He was a man, I should suppose about five feet ten inches high, and appeared to be pretty well made, but he had a heavy shawl on all the time. I suppose he would weigh 150 or 160 pounds. His hair was black, and seemed to be somewhat inclined to curl; it was worn long. He had a pretty full forehead and his skin was fair. He was very pale when I saw him, and appeared as if accustomed to in-door rather than out-door life. I do not know how to describe his skin exactly but I should think he might be classed as dark, and his paleness might be attributed to receiving this injury. I did not observe his hand to see whether it was small or large. I have been shown the photograph of J. Wilkes Booth and I should not think that this was the man from any resemblance to the photograph, but from other causes I have every reason to believe that he is the man whose leg I dressed as above stated.

In order to examine and operate upon his leg, I had occasion to cut his boot longitudinally in front of the instep. It seems that when he left my house, this boot was left behind. Yesterday morning my attention was called to this boot, which is a long top-boot. On making an examination of it, I find written on the inside in apparently a German hand, what I take to be "Henry Luz, Maker. 445 Broadway, J. Wilkes." I did not notice the writing in this boot until my attention was called to it by Lieutenant Lovett. [Boot produced and identified by deponent as the one taken from the leg of the wounded man.]

I have seen J. Wilkes Booth. I was introduced to him by Mr. J.C. Thompson, a son-in-law of Dr. William Queen, in November or December last. Mr. Thompson resides with his father-in-law, and his place is about five miles southwesterly from Bryantown, near the lower edge of what is known as Zechiah Swamp. Mr. Thompson told me at the time that Booth was looking out for lands in this neighborhood or in this county, he said he was not very particular where, if he could get such a lot as he wanted, whether it was in Charles, Prince Georges, or Saint Mary's county; and Booth inquired if I knew any parties in this neighborhood who had any fine horses for sale. I told him there was a neighbor of mine who had some very fine traveling horses, and he said he thought if he could purchase one reasonable he would do so, and would ride up to Washington on him instead of riding in the stage. The next evening he rode to my house and staid with me that night, and the next morning he purchased a rather old horse, but a very fine mover, of Mr. George Gardiner, Sr., who resides but a short distance from my house. I would know the horse if I should see him again. He is a darkish bay horse, not bright bay, with tolerably large head, and had a defect in one eye. Booth gave eighty dollars for the horse. I have never seen Booth since that time to my knowledge until last Saturday morning.

When I assisted the wounded man into my house on Saturday morning last, the other party with him, who appeared to be very youthful, took charge of the horse and said he would keep it and the other one until they could be put in the stable. As soon as I could I woke my colored man Frank Washington, and sent him out to put the horses in the stable, and the young man came into the house. After setting the wounded man's leg the best I could for the time, I think I walked around to my farm-yard and gave some directions, and when I returned breakfast was ready; and as this young man was up and knocking about, I asked him to come to breakfast. He did so, but the other man remained upstairs in bed. I did not know who this young man was, but he remarked that he had seen me. He appeared to be a very fast young man and was very talkative. He was about five feet two or three inches high. I would not be positive as to his height. He had a smooth face and appeared as if he had never shaved; his hair was black, and I should consider his complexion dark. I did not notice his eyes very particularly. He wore a dark-colored business coat. I have seen the photograph of Harold, but I do not recognize it as that of the young man. He seemed to be well acquainted throughout the whole country, and I asked his name; he gave it as Henson, and that of the wounded man as Tyser or Tyson. I did not hear either of them address the other by the first name.

The only thing that excited my suspicion, on reflecting upon these circumstances, was that after breakfast, when I was about to leave for my farm-work, this young man asked me if I had a razor about the house that his friend desired to take a shave, as perhaps he would feel better. I had noticed that the wounded man had whiskers and a moustache when he came into the house. After dinner, I went to see the patient and although he kept his face partly turned away from me I noticed that he had lost his moustache, but still retained his whiskers. I did not pay sufficient attention to his beard to determine whether it was false or natural.

This young man asked me if I could fix up clumsily some crutches for his friend to hobble along with, and I went down to the old Englishman I had there who had a saw and auger, and he and I made a rude pair of crutches out of a piece of plank and sent them to him. This young man mentioned the names of several parties in this neighborhood whom we knew; among others, several here in Bryantown. He mentioned being in the store of William Moore; he did not say when. I think he said he knew Bean, who kept store here; and he knew very well Len Roby, Rufus Roby, & Major James Thomas, Sr. He inquired the way from my house to Bryantown, although he represented in the morning that they had come from Bryantown. He said he knew parson Wilmer, who lives at a place called Piney Church; he said also that they had met two persons, a lady and a gentleman, walking somewhere near Bryantown that morning, and inquired of them the way to my house, and that they also met a negro, but did not state where; & that they also inquired of him the way to my place.

I saw only one of the horses which these men rode to my house. She was a bay mare, moderately long tail, dark mane and tail. I won't be certain whether she had a star in the forehead or not; she appeared to be a mettlesome, high-spirited animal. I saw her after dinner, between twelve and one o'clock, when this young man and I rode over to my father's place in order to see if we could get a carriage for the wounded man; but I found that the carriages were all out of repair except one and we could not get that one. He then concluded to go to Bryantown for a conveyance to get his friend over as far as his friend's Mr. Wilmer's. I then went down to Mr. Hardy's, and was in conversation fully an hour when I returned home leisurely, and found the two men were just in the act of leaving. The young man inquired of me the nearest way to Mr. Wilmer's. I told them there were two ways; one was by the public road leading by Beantown; the other led across the swamp directly across from me, by which they could save a mile; both are easterly. This road from my house is directly across in a strait line; it is not a public way, but by taking down a fence you can get through. They concluded to take this latter route, and I gave them the necessary directions. I did not see them leave my house. The man on crutches had left the house when I got back, and he was some fifty to seventy yards from me when this young man came to me and began to inquire of me the direction. I do not know how or where Booth got a conveyance away from my house; he did not go in a carriage; but he undoubtedly went on horseback.

When they came there in the morning this young man said that one of the horses would not stand without tying and asked that both of them should be put in the stable. He held one of the horses until I returned into the house with the wounded man, when I called a colored boy named Frank Washington and sent him round to take the horses to the stable. I have also a white man named Thomas Davis, who has charge of my horses, and I judge that he saw the horses which were in the stable during Saturday.

I judge that between four and five o'clock on Saturday afternoon they left my house. I do not know where they went; I have not been spoken to by any one for professional advice in their behalf since that time, and have not seen either of them since.

It is about four miles across from my house to Parson Wilmer's, and by the public road it is about five miles. I suppose they could go in about an hour or an hour and a half by walking their horses.

I suppose in a day or two swelling would take place in the wounded man's leg; there was very little tumefaction in the wound, and I could discover crepitation very distinctly. It would be necessary to dress it again in two or three days if it were left in a recumbent posture, but if moved at a moderate rate, I do not know as it would aggravate it very much unless it was struck by something. I do not know much about wounds of that sort; a military surgeon would know more about those things.

Saml A Mudd

Subscribed and sworn before me this 22nd day of April 1865

H H Wells
Col. & P.M. Genl Def. S of P

05-16-1865: Testimony of Lieutenant Lovett and Detectives

Source: Benn Pitman, *The Assassination of President Lincoln and the Trial of the Conspirators*. New York, N.Y.. Moore, Wilstach, and Baldwin. 1865. Page 87.

Lieutenant Alexander Lovett
For the prosecution - May 16

On the day after the assassination of the President, I went with others in pursuit of the murderers. We went by way of Surrattsville to the house of Dr. Samuel A. Mudd, which is about thirty miles from Washington, and about one-quarter of a mile or so off the road that runs from Bryantown, arriving there on Tuesday, the 18th of April. Dr. Mudd, whom I recognize among the accused, did not at first seemed inclined to give us any satisfaction; afterward he went on to state that on Saturday morning, at daybreak, two strangers had come to his place; one of them rapped at the door, the other remained on his horse. Mudd went down and opened the door, and with the aid of the young man who had knocked at the door helped the other, who had his leg broken, off his horse, took him into the house and set his leg.

On asking him who the man with the broken leg was, he said he did not know; he was a stranger to him. The other, he said, was a young man, about seventeen or eighteen years of age. Mudd said that one of them called for a razor, which he furnished, together with soap and water, and the wounded man shaved off his moustache. One of our men remarked that this was suspicious, and Dr. Mudd said it did look suspicious. I last him if he had any other beard. He said, "Yes, he had a long pair of whiskers." He said the men remained there but for a short time, and I understood him that they left in the course of the morning. He said that the wounded man went off on crutches that he (Mudd) had had made for him. He said the other led the horse of the injured man, and he (Mudd) showed them the way across the swamp. He told me that he had heard, at church, on Sunday morning, that the President had been assassinated, but did not mention by whom. We were at his house probably an hour, and to the last he represented that those men were entire strangers to him.

It was generally understood at this time that Booth was the man who assassinated the President; even the darkeys knew it; and I was told by them that Booth had been there, and that he had his leg broken.

On Friday, the 21st of April, I went to Dr. Mudd's again, for the purpose of arresting him. When he found we were going to search the house, he said something to his wife, and she went up stairs and brought down a boot. Mudd said he had cut it off the man's leg, in order to set the leg. I turned down the top of the boot and saw the name "J. Wilkes" written in it.

I called Mudd's attention to it, and he said he had not taken notice of it before. Some of the men said the name of Booth was scratched out, but I said that the name of Booth had never been written.

[A long riding boot, for the left foot, slit up in front for about eight inches, was exhibited to the witness.]

That is the boot.

(The boot was offered in evidence.)

At the second interview, he still insisted that the men were strangers to him. I made the remark to him that his wife said she has seen the whiskers detached from the face, and I suppose he was satisfied then, for he subsequently said it was Booth. After we left his house, one of the men showed him Booth's photograph, and Mudd remarked that it did not look like Booth, except a little across the eyes. Shortly after that, he said he had an introduction to Booth in November or December last, at church, from a man named Johnson or Thompson. On being questioned, he said he had been along with Booth in the country, looking up some land, and was with him when he bought a horse of Esquire Gardiner, last fall.

Although I was in citizen's clothes at the time, and addressed no threats to him, Dr. Mudd appeared to be much frightened and anxious. When asked what arms the men had, Dr. Mudd stated that the injured man had a pair of revolvers, but he said nothing about the other having a carbine, or either of them having a knife; his manner was very reserved and evasive.

Cross-examined by Mr. Ewing

At the time that Dr. Mudd was describing to me the "two strangers" that had been to his house, I did not tell him of my tracking Booth from Washington; I did not mentioned Booth's name at all; it was not my business to tell him whom I was after.

On my second visit, Dr. Mudd was out, and his wife sent after him; I walked down and met him. I was accompanied by special officers Simon Gavacan, Joshua Lloyd, and William Williams. After we entered the house, I demanded the razor that the man had used. It was not until after we had been in the house some minutes, and one of the men said we should have to search the house, that Dr. Mudd told us the boot had been found, and his wife brought it to us.

I asked him if that might not be a false whisker; he said he did not know. I asked this because Mrs. Mudd has said that the whisker became detached when he got to the foot of the stairs. The Doctor never told me that he had Booth up stairs; he told me he was on the sofa or lounge.

Mudd stated, at our first interview, that the men remained but a short time; afterward his wife told me that they had staid to about 3 or 4 o'clock, on Saturday afternoon. I asked Mudd if the men had much money about them. He said they had considerable greenbacks; and, in this connection, although I did not ask him if he had been paid for setting the man's leg, he said it was customary to make a charge to strangers in such a case. When Dr. Mudd said he had shown the men the way across the swamps, I understood him to refer to the swamps a thousand yards in the rear of his own house. He told us that the men went to the Rev. Dr. Wilmer's, or inquired for Parson Wilmer's; that he took them to the swamps; that they were on their way to Allen's Fresh; but I paid no attention to this at the time, as I considered it was a blind to throw us off the track. We, however, afterward searched Mr. Wilmer's, a thing I did not like to do, as I knew the man by reputation, and was satisfied it was unnecessary. We tracked the men as far we could. We went into the swamp and scoured it all over; I went through a half a dozen times; it was not a very nice job though. I first heard from Lieutenant Dana that two men had been at Mudd's house. I afterward heard from Dr. George Mudd that a party of two had been at Dr. Samuel Mudd's.

Cross-examined by Mr. Stone

When we first went to Dr. Samuel Mudd's house, we were accompanied by Dr. George Mudd, whom we had taken from Bryantown along with us. Our first conversation was with the Doctor's wife. When we asked Dr. Mudd whether two strangers had been there, he seemed very much excited, and got as pale as a sheet of paper, and blue about the lips, like a man that was frightened at something he had done. Dr. George Mudd was present when I asked if two strangers had been there. He had spoken to Dr. Samuel Mudd previous to that. He admitted that two strangers had been there, and gave a description of them.

In my first interview with Mudd on the Tuesday, I did not mention the name of Booth at all; and it was not till I had arrested him, when on horseback, that he told me he was introduced to Booth last fall, by a man named Johnson or Thompson.

Lieutenant David D. Dana
For the prosecution - May 20

On Saturday, the day after the assassination of the President, I sent a guard of four men ahead of me to Bryantown, and they arrived about half an hour before me. I arrived there about 1 o'clock. I communicated the intelligence of the assassination, and the name of the assassin, to the citizens; it spread through the village in a quarter of an hour. Some of the citizens asked me if I knew for a certainty it was J. Wilkes Booth, and I told them yes, as near as a person could know any thing.

William Williams
For the prosecution - May 17

On Monday, the 17th of April, in company with some cavalry, I proceeded to Surrattsville. On the next day, Tuesday, I arrived at Dr. Mudd's. He was not at home, and his wife sent for him. I asked if any strangers had been that way, and he said there had not. Some of the officers then talked with him. I think he stated that he first heard of the assassination of the President at church, on the Sunday morning. He seemed to be uneasy, and unwilling to give us any information without being asked directly.

On Friday, the 21st, we went there again for the purpose of arresting Dr. Mudd. He was not at home, but his wife sent for him. I asked him concerning the two men who had been at his house, one of them having a broken leg. He then said that they had been there. I asked him if those men were not Booth and Herold. He said they were not. He said he knew Booth, having been introduced to him last fall by a man by the name of Thompson, I believe.

After we had arrested him, and were on our way to Bryantown, I showed him Booth's picture, and asked him if that looked like the man who had his leg broken. After looking at the picture a little while, he said it did not; he did not remember the features; after awhile, however, he said it looked something like Booth across the eyes.

At our second visit to Dr. Mudd's house, I informed Mrs. Mudd that we had to search the house. She then said ---

Mr. Ewing. You need not state what Mrs. Mudd said.

The Judge Advocate. Anything that was said in Dr. Mudd's presence is admissible.

The witness continued. This was said, I believe, in Dr. Mudd's presence. She said that the man with the broken leg had left his boot in the bed. She then went and brought the boot down. It was a long riding boot, with "J. Wilkes" and the maker's name, "Broadway, N. Y.," written inside. The boot was cut some ten inches from the instep.

Dr. Mudd said that the men had arrived before daybreak, and that they went away on foot between 3 and 4 o'clock on the afternoon of Saturday. He had set the man's leg, and had had crutches made for him by one of his men.

Cross-examined by Mr. Stone

Lieutenant Lovett was present at this conversation. I believe it was on Friday that Dr. Mudd said that the first knowledge he had of the assassination was received at church on the Sunday before. I asked him the question on Friday, if "two strangers" had been there. He said that there had been. Two men had come there at daybreak; one, a smooth-faced young man, apparently seventeen or eighteen years of age, and that he had set the leg of one of them. They had come to his door and knocked, and he had looked out of the window up stairs, and asked them who they were. I believe he said their reply was that they were friends and wanted to come in. Dr. Mudd then came down stairs, and, with the assistance of the young man, got the wounded man off his horse into the parlor, and examined his leg on the sofa. The wounded man had a moustache, he said, and pretty long chin-whiskers. I asked him if he thought the whiskers were natural. He said he could not tell. The injured man had a shawl round his shoulders. Doctor Mudd said that on leaving they asked him the road to Parson Wilmer's, and that he had shown them the way down to the swamp. I did not pay much attention to their going to Parson Wilmer's at first, because I thought it was to throw us off the track; but we followed the road as far as we could, after which we divided ourselves, and went all through the different swamp roads. The road is not much frequented. We found horses' tracks, but not such as satisfied me that they were the tracks of these men, and we heard nothing of them on the road. We got to the Rev. Mr. Wilmer's, I think, on the Wednesday evening. We were acting under the orders of Major O'Beirne, and Lieutenant Lovett had charge of our squad.

Simon Gavacan
For the prosecution - May 17

I was at Dr. Mudd's house on the fore-noon of Tuesday, the 18th of April, in pursuit of the murderers of the President. We inquired if two men passed there on the Saturday morning after the assassination, and Dr. Mudd said no. Then we inquired more particularly if two men had been there, one having his leg fractured. He said yes. In answer to our questions, he told us the they had come about 4, or half past 4, on Saturday morning, and rapped at his door; that he was a little alarmed at the noise, but came down and let them in; that he and the other person assisted the man with the broken leg into the house, and that he attended to the fractured leg as well as he could, though he had not much facilities for doing so. I believe he said the wounded person staid on the sofa for awhile, and after that was taken up stairs, and remained there until between 3 and 5 o'clock in the afternoon of Saturday. He said that he went out with the other man to find a buggy to take away the wounded man, but could not get one. I understood him to say that on leaving his house they first inquired the road to Allen's Fresh, and also to the Rev. Dr. Wilmer's, and that he took them part of the way to show them the road. He told us he did not know the persons at all.

On Friday, the 21st, we went to Dr. Mudd's again, for the purpose of arresting him and searching his house. He was not in, but his wife sent for him. When he came, we told him that we would have to search his house. His wife then went up stairs and brought down a boot and a razor. Inside the leg of the boot we found the words, "J. Wilkes". We asked him if he thought that was Booth, and he said he thought not. He said the man had whiskers on, but that he thought he shaved off his moustache up stairs. When we inquired of him if knew Booth, he said that he was introduced to him last fall by a man named Thompson, but he thought the man who had been there was not Booth.

Cross-examined by Mr. Ewing

Our conversation with Dr. Mudd lasted probably an hour. He was asked questions by all of us. Lieutenant Lovett was there all the time. When Mrs. Mudd brought down the boot and razor, we thought we had satisfactory evidence that Booth and Herold had been there, and did not search the house further. I believe there was a photograph of Booth shown to Dr. Mudd on Tuesday, and he said he did not recognize it, but said there was something about the forehead or the eyes that resembled one of the parties.

Joshua Lloyd
For the prosecution. - May 16

I was engaged with others in the pursuit of the murderers of the President in the direction of Surrattsville. We got to Dr. Mudd's on Tuesday, the 18th. I asked him if he had not heard of the President being assassinated; he said yes. I then asked him if he has seen any of the parties - Booth, Herald, or Surratt; he said he had never seen them.

On Friday, the 21st, at the second interview, he said two men came there about 4 o'clock on the Saturday morning, and remained there until about 4 in the afternoon. They came on horseback; one of them had a broken leg, and when they left his house one was riding and other walking, leading his horse.

As we were sitting in the parlor, Mrs. Mudd seemed very much worried, so did the Doctor, and he seemed to be very much excited. At this interview Lieutenant Lovett and Mr. Williams did most of the talking; I was not well. Dr. Mudd said that he had been in company with Booth; that he had been introduced to him by a man named Thompson, I think he said, at church. He offered no explanation of his previous denial. When the men left, he said they went up the hill toward Parson Wilmer's, and I think he said he showed them the road. I understood him to say that the man's leg was broken by the fall of the horse.

Cross-examined by Mr. Stone

It was late on to Tuesday evening when we were there. Each time that we went to his house Dr. Mudd was out, but not far away, for he was not long in returning with the messenger sent for him. At the first interview, I asked him if any strangers had passed that way, and then if Booth and Herold had passed; I describe them to him, and the horses they rode, and he denied either that any strangers or Booth and Herold had passed. The interview only lasted a few minutes.

Booth's portrait was shown to Dr. Mudd. He told us that Booth had been down there last fall, when he was introduced to him by Mr. Thompson. I think he said Booth was there to buy some property.

Before he came to the house, Mrs. Mudd brought us the boot, and when the Doctor saw that we had the boot, he admitted that Booth had been there. Dr. Mudd then brought the razor down himself, and gave it to Lieutenant Lovett.

06-16-1865: Mrs. Mudd's First Affidavit

Source: Thomas Ewing Papers, Library of Congress, Washington, D.C.

Dr. Mudd's attorney, General Thomas Ewing, had Mrs. Mudd prepare an affidavit describing Booth's visit to the Mudd farm in case it could somehow be useful. This June 16, 1865 affidavit wasn't admitted as evidence, and the trial ended without the Court seeing it.

After the trial, General Ewing had Mrs. Mudd prepare an updated affidavit which he sent to President Johnson, asking that Dr. Mudd's sentence be set aside. He didn't. This July 6, 1865 second affidavit and General Ewing's transmittal letter to President Johnson are included next in this Source Documents section.

Mrs. Mudd's first affidavit said:

I, Sarah F. Mudd, wife of Dr. Samuel A. Mudd, do hereby certify that when my husband returned from Bryantown on Saturday evening the 15th of April, the two men since ascertained to be Booth and Herald, were leaving the house.

I was standing in the passage when they came down stairs and noticed that the whiskers of the lame man were false from their becoming partially detached on one side. And that about night Dr. and I were speaking about those men, I then told him about the whiskers becoming detached. He then told me he did not like the actions of those men who had been at the house, that the lame man had shaved off his moustache and they both seemed to be under more excitement than the breaking of a leg would cause. He then remarked he would return immediately to Bryantown and give this information to the authorities of the fact of those parties having been there. I became alarmed and earnestly entreated him not to go. I recalled the fate of Capt. Watkins and reminded him of the report that Boyle and his associates were infesting the neighborhood and begged him not to expose his life by openly giving information on the parties who had left his house. He warned me of the danger he would be incurring by deferring to give the information. I told him it would be as well to wait until morning as it was then quite dark, and give the information indirectly. I suggested to him to tell Dr. Mudd or some one living in the village of Bryantown and let them tell the authorities. He seemed unwilling to yield but finally gave up to my fears and entreaties.

I know that my husband had no knowledge or suspicion that the man with a broken leg was Booth until after the man had gone, that since his arrest I have never ceased to regret my interposing in his purpose of that evening and have openly blamed myself as the cause of his trouble. He has suffered on account of not having given immediate information and that I dissuaded him from giving information purely in consideration of his personal danger and in the belief it would be as well to get some one to do it for him.

Sarah F. Mudd

07-06-1865: Mrs. Mudd's Second Affidavit

Source: Thomas Ewing Papers, Library of Congress, Washington, D.C.

See the previous document for Mrs. Mudd's first affidavit.

When the conspiracy trial ended, General Ewing had Mrs. Mudd prepare an updated affidavit, and sent it to President Johnson, asking that Dr. Mudd's sentence be set aside. He didn't, and on July 15th, Dr. Mudd and his three companions were informed of their sentences. Mrs. Mudd's second affidavit of July 6, 1865 is presented below. Her first affidavit of June 16, 1865, and General Ewing's July 10, 1865 letter to President Johnson, are also included in this Source Documents section.

I, Sarah F. Mudd, wife of Dr. Mudd, on oath do say,

That I saw John Wilkes Booth when he was in Charles County last fall. He came Sunday evening after supper, staid all night, and next day my husband went with him to Gardiner's where Booth bought the horse - Booth did not return from Gardiner's with my husband - and was never at my husband's house, or so far as I know in the neighborhood before or after until the 15th of April - nor did I ever hear of my husband having met him elsewhere, or being in any way directly or indirectly in communication with him.

The two men came to the house on the 15th of April just before daybreak. After my husband had set the leg he went to bed again, and slept till about 9 o'clock when he breakfasted and went to the field where the hands were working. He returned between 11 and 12 and went to the crippled man's room for a few minutes and then went back to the field to get a pair of crutches made. He returned at dinner, when Herold (who called himself Hanson, or Harrison) asked if he could not get a carriage or buggy to take his friend (who was called Tyson) away. The Doctor said his father had a carriage which might be got, and he would go with him and see about it. I then told the Doctor that I wanted some calico, soda, needles, and matches, and asked him to go on to Bryantown to get them. He said he would, and I am sure that is all he went to Bryantown for.

The Doctor and Herold had not been gone over a half an hour, when Herold returned and said he could not get father's carriage and that Doctor had gone into Bryantown and he was going to take his friend off horseback. While Herold was gone, I went to the room where the crippled man was. He had heavy whiskers on - and looked pale, thin and haggard. I staid about five minutes and talked with him. He said his leg was broken a mile and a half from our house by the fall of his horse, and that he had been thrown against a stone which injured his back.

About an hour after Herold got back, they left. As Booth came down to go I was in the hall and saw his whiskers become detached and he pushed them back. Herold came down with him, and went to the front gate where his horse had been standing after his return from Bryantown, and rode him around the house to the stable. Booth went on his crutches through the back yard towards the stable, and just as he was getting to the stable the Doctor rode up from Bryantown to the front gate. The stable is 300 yards from the house. The Doctor dismounted at the front gate and came into the house. He did not see either Booth or Herold on his return near enough to speak to either of them. He came into the house, and went to the fire, and took a book and commenced reading. He did not leave the room until supper time - an hour and a half after they had gone.

Before supper he told me of the report in Bryantown that the President was killed and Mr. Seward and his son. After supper I was speaking of the two men and told him of the crippled man's whiskers becoming detached. He said that that looked suspicious; and that he had also shaved off his moustache and seemed more excited than the mere fracture of the limb would cause him to be. He then sent for his horse to go to Bryantown and tell the military authorities about these two men. I begged him not to go himself - but to wait till Church next day and tell Dr. George Mudd or some one else living in Bryantown all the circumstances, and have him tell the officers at Bryantown about it. He was very unwilling to delay and warned me of the danger from failure to tell of these men at once. I told him that if he went himself Boyle who was reported to be one of the assassins and who killed Capt. Watkins last fall in that country might have him assassinated for it, and that it would be just as well for the authorities to hear it next day because the crippled man could not escape.

Up to this time I had not the least suspicion that the crippled man was Booth - and I am sure no one would have recognized him as being the same man who was at our house last fall - for he was very much thinner, and looked so pale and haggard, and changed with his heavy whiskers, as to alter entirely his appearance. I am certain that my husband did not recognize him, or suspect him to be Booth even after I told him of the false whiskers. I am sure too that Herold was a total stranger to the Doctor, as he was to me.

Something was said at the trial about the boot, but it was not shown when it was found. I found it on Thursday under the bed, when I was cleaning the room. And next day my husband told Lt. Lovett about it as soon as he saw him and before a word had been said between them as Mr. Hardy testifies.

On Tuesday when the officers came to the house I sent for the Doctor to the field and before he came told the officers everything in presence of Dr. George Mudd. They said from my description the smaller man was certainly Herold. When my husband came to the house and before he saw the officers I told him that I had given them a full statement. He said "That was right". Then Dr. George Mudd before he introduced my husband told him that he had bought the officers there in compliance with his request on Sunday, for further information about the two suspected men who had been at our house.

The description given by my husband to Herold of the short route to Parson Wilmer's was given before they started to Bryantown. I saw my husband point out the route to him - they both were then standing in the yard from which the by road could be seen. This was in the early part of the day, while the young man was talking of taking his friend off horseback. The carriage was not spoken of until dinner. I do further certify that Dr. Mudd was not from home but three nights from the 23rd of December until the 21st of April, one of which was in January when he went with me to a party at Mr. George Gardiner's. On the 23rd of March he came up to Washington with Mr. Lewellyn Gardiner to attend a sale of Government horses and mistook the day. On the third occasion, which was the 10th of April, he came up to Dr. Blanford's with his brother Henry, remained all night, went to Giesborough the next day in company with Dr. Blanford and his brother Henry and did not come into Washington. If my husband knows John Surratt at all, it is nothing more than a passing acquaintance - having seen him at his hotel at Surrattsville. I saw John Surratt once at Surrattsville. I have never seen him at our house and never know of his having stopped there.

It was said in the Argument of the Judge Advocate that Booth and Herold were secreted in the woods near our house after they left. If they were secreted there, neither I nor my husband knew it. My husband was not out of the yard that evening or the next day until he went to church, and we both supposed the men had gone to Parson Wilmer's.

As to my husband having recognized Booth while he was at our house, I repeat that he did not recognize or suspect the stranger to be Booth; had he done so he certainly would have mentioned it to me, but he did not. Moreover, he did not notice the crippled man specially, nor seem to be interested in learning where he came from or where he was going.

Sarah F. Mudd

Sworn and Subscribed before me this 6th day of July 1865 B.W. Ferguson J.P.

07-10-1865: General Ewing's Request to President Johnson

Source: Samuel A. Mudd Pardon File B-596, U.S. National Archives, College Park, Md. RG 204

Dr. Mudd's attorney, General Thomas Ewing, had Mrs. Mudd prepare an affidavit describing Booth's visit to the Mudd farm in case it could somehow be useful. It wasn't admitted as evidence, and the trial ended without the Court seeing it.

After the trial, General Ewing had Mrs. Mudd prepare an updated affidavit, and sent it to President Johnson on July 10, 1865, requesting that Dr. Mudd's sentence be set aside. General Ewing's transmittal letter is presented below.

President Johnson did not set Dr. Mudd's sentence aside, and on July 15th, Dr. Mudd and his three companions were informed of their sentences. Mrs. Mudd's first affidavit of June 16, 1865, and her second affidavit of July 6, 1865 are also included in this Source Documents section.

At the end of General Ewing's request to President Johnson below, note the P.S. concerning an alleged confession of George Atzerodt. He says "Since writing the foregoing, I have seen an alleged confession by Atzerodt, in which he is reported as saying that two weeks before the assassination Booth told him that 'he had sent provisions and liquors to Dr. Mudd's to be used by the conspirators on the route to Richmond with the President, and that he was acquainted with him, and had letters to him...'"

Some writers cite Atzerodt's alleged confession as evidence that Dr. Mudd was part of Booth's original plot to kidnap President Lincoln. Most historians, however, put no credence in the document since Atzerodt was desperately trying to save his life by telling the Government investigators whatever he thought they wanted to hear.

Washington, D.C.
No. 12 North "A" Street
July 10th 1865
His Excellency Andrew Johnson
President of the United States

Sir,

I enclose herewith the affidavit of Sarah F. Mudd, wife of Dr. Samuel A. Mudd who has recently been tried before a Military Commission on the charge of conspiracy to assassinate the President and other Chief Officers of the Government, and also the affidavits of Dr. J. H. Blanford, Mrs. Elizabeth A. Dyer and Sylvester Mudd in corroboration of her statements - to all of which I ask your Excellency's most earnest attention, in connection with the record in that case.

Mrs. Mudd's affidavit, if accepted as truthful, shows:

1st That the testimony of Norton as to the accused having entered his room at the National on the 3rd of March enquiring for Booth is false - and that Evans' statement in corroboration of Norton that Mudd came to Washington on either the 1st, 2nd or 3rd of March is also false.

Her statement would not have been taken to refute the evidence of these witnesses (because it was fully and overwhelmingly refuted on the trial by the evidence of Thomas Davis, J. H.

Blanford, Frank Washington, Betty Washington, Mary, Fannie, Emily and Henry L. Mudd, and John Davis) were it not for the fact that the Special Judge Advocate insisted on the truth of the statements of Evans and Norton, who were strangers to Mudd, against the flatly contradictory evidence of these nine witnesses, who all knew him intimately. And it is not unfair to presume that the Court were greatly influenced by its legal advices all on questions of the weight of evidence, as they were controlled by them on all other questions arising in the trial.

2d   Mrs. Mudd's affidavit also shows that her husband was not here between the 23rd of December and the 23rd of March - and therefore the statement of Weichmann as to the interview between Booth, Surratt and Mudd at the National, which that witness swears occurred about the middle of January, is not entitled to credence. On this point she corroborates the evidence of Betty Washington, Thomas Davis, Henry L. Mudd Jr., Mary Mudd and Frank Washington - whose evidence the Special Judge Advocate also declared in his argument could not outweigh the statements of the one witness Weichmann, who was a stranger to the accused - while the five witnesses contradicting him knew the accused intimately.

3d Her affidavit also shows that on Tuesday after the assassination her husband could not have denied to Williams and Gavacan (the detectives) that the two strangers had been at his house, as they swear he did. In this she is corroborated by Dr. George Mudd - and also by Lieut. Lovett who was quoted by the Special Judge Advocate in his argument as having sworn to the denial, whereas in fact he swears to the opposite.

4th Her affidavit also shows that on Friday after the assassination the accused spoke of Booth's boot having been found, voluntarily, and not as claimed only after a threat was made to search the house. In this she is corroborated by Hardy.

5th   Her affidavit also shows that the boot was not discovered until Thursday - so that her husband practiced no concealment in not producing it Tuesday.

6th It also shows that she saw and conversed with Booth when he was at her husband's house last fall - and again saw and talked with them while her husband was gone to Bryantown on Saturday the 15th April - and that he was then so thin, pale and haggard, and so thoroughly disguised by his false whiskers, that she did not expect at all that he was the same man she met and talked with last fall. This point is of great importance because the Special Judge Advocate assumed it was proved beyond all question that the accused recognized the crippled man as Booth - while there is no evidence to show that he did, except the bare fact that he had met him in the fall or winter before; added to Colonel Wells' statement which is only of an indistinct impression as to what he inferred from Mudd's statements, while all other witnesses say the accused denied having recognized Booth while at his house. Mrs. Mudd says also that she is certain her husband did not recognize or suspect the crippled man to be Booth at any time that day.

On this point of recognition the accused was not able to offer any direct evidence of a single witness - because none whose saw him last fall saw him that Saturday again.

This was, perhaps, a controlling point with the Court against the accused - and therefor Mrs. Mudd's statement as to her own failure to recognize or suspect the crippled man to be Booth is of vital importance.

7th   Mrs. Mudd's affidavit also shows that Herald could not have gone to Bryantown with her husband, as the Judge Advocate claims, (8 miles) as he was gone not over half an hour. In this she is corroborated by Primus Johnson and others (see page 25 of argument).

8th   It also shows that he pointed out the short route through the swamp (to Parson Wilmer's) to Herold before going to Bryantown and before he learned of the assassination. And that when he returned home, Booth and Herold had left the house and he never spoke to them after he heard of the assassination. In this she is corroborated by her husband's admissions in evidence, and by Betty Washington. See Col. Wells statement also; and pages 35 & 36 of argument, and evidence of there cited.

The Special Judge Advocate claimed that the evidence showed that after the accused returned from Bryantown, where he heard of the assassination, and that a man named Booth was one of the assassins, he aided the escape and concealment of Booth and Herald. The Court doubtless accepted that fact as proved on the Judge Advocate's assertion and on the statement of the detective Gavacan as to Mudd's statement on the subject to him. (See page 27 of argument.) Gavacan's statement as to Mudd's denial on Tuesday that the two men had been at his house at all was clearly shown false (see pages 29 & 30 argument). And I think that evidence on this point as to Mudd's having gone with Booth and Herold part of the way was also fairly overthrown (pages 27 & 28 argument). But the Special Judge Advocate had the ear of the Court, and was with it throughout its deliberations on this case, I am informed - and I have no doubt the Court therefore accepted as true the falsehood that Mudd said he helped the men off after he returned from Bryantown. That act of pointing the route to Wilmer's was the only act shown to have been done by Mudd which could have implicated him had he from the first known the crime and the criminal. Mrs. Mudd's affidavit shows that that act was done before her husband knew of the assassination, or suspected the crippled man to be Booth. And that after he knew of the assassination he did not see Booth or Herold. (See pages 35 & 36 argument)

9th   Her affidavit also shows that her husband's suspicions towards those men were not aroused until she told him, an hour after they had gone, that the whiskers of the crippled man were false. And that he then ordered his horse to go to Bryantown to tell the authorities about them, and was only prevented doing so by her fears and entreaties. And that in consequence of her advice only he delayed until next day and sent the information through Dr. George Mudd. This delay was dwelt on by the Special Judge Advocate as proof of his complicity with the assassins, and had, I think, great weight with the Court.

10th   The Special Judge Advocate asserted that it was shown that he accused secreted Booth and Herold in the woods Saturday night. There is not a word of evidence justifying that assertion - and Mrs. Mudd's affidavit shows it to be utterly erroneous.

11th   Some evidence was offered by the Prosecution (Mary and Milo Simms) going to show that John H. Surratt frequented the house of the accused last year and year before, which, though fully disproved, (see argument pages 14, 15 & 16) was yet insisted on by the Assistant Judge Advocate as true. Mrs. Mudd says she had seen John H. Surratt at his mother's house, at Surrattsville Hotel, before the war - but that she never saw him at the house of the accused or heard of his having been there.

In connection with this letter and its enclosures I ask the attention of your Excellency to my letter to you of the 3rd instant, in which I pointed out in the argument of the Special Judge Advocate eleven material errors in his statement of the evidence against Dr. Mudd, which errors I was not permitted by the Court to call to its attention. In addition to these errors in statements of fact his argument was full of erroneous inferences and inconsequent deductions.

As one of the legal advisers of the Court in its discussions and deliberations on the evidence he was in position to give effect to his conclusions in the finding and sentence which followed, and doubtless did much to lead them into the errors, into which he himself had fallen. I venture to say that the recorded evidence, aside from the affidavits herewith offered, does not support the finding of the Court - and that not only was there not sufficient proof to exclude reasonable doubt of guilt, but that there was not such proof as made guilt more probable that innocence.

But by these affidavits, if they be accepted as true, all doubt is removed, and the innocence of Dr. Mudd is established beyond question. For, if the interview described by Weichmann did occur, it was on the 23rd of December, and was followed by no further intercourse between the accused and Booth or Surratt either written or oral. If can not be claimed that the conspiracy was entered into then, at Booth's first introduction to Surratt and in presence of Weichmann, who was a stranger to Mudd and Booth, and known to Surratt as an employee of the War Department. Besides, the evidence shows that the conspiracy to capture the President - as Booth first professed its object to his accomplices - was got up late in January or in February. If Dr. Mudd had on the 23rd of December had such a scheme proposed to him, and if he had assented to it, no one can doubt that he would have subsequently met the conspirators or some of them. But it is shown he did not see Booth or Surratt after the 23rd of December, and did not even call on either when he was here on the 23rd of March, and at Giesboro on the 11th of April. Admit, what I think the recorded evidence and Mrs. Mudd's statement clearly show, that Dr. Mudd did not have any intercourse whatever with Booth or Surratt after the 23rd of December - before the assassination - and it follows beyond dispute that he was not informed of or assenting to the conspiracy.

If this be so, his entire innocence then follows from the evidence, and these affidavits.

For even though he recognized Booth while at his house, which he constantly asserted and still asserts he did not, and which Mrs. Mudd's failure to recognize him makes most probable, yet no one can suppose that Booth on reaching his house disclosed his horrid crime. In fact the open manner of Mudd in going out with Herold to get his father's carriage, and keeping the men without the slightest effort at concealment, or appearance of concern, at his house, makes it to my mind certain that he did not suspect their guilt before he got to Bryantown. When he got back to his house the men had gone, and he saw them no more - they taking the route he has shown Herold in the forenoon. When his wife told him of the false whiskers of the crippled man, his suspicions were aroused, and his first impulse was that of an innocent man and a good citizen - to go at once to Bryantown and tell of these men to the authorities. Her fears and and entreaties led him to delay sending word to them until next day, when he did it fully and truthfully.

I feel confident that the recorded evidence on an examination will not be found to sustain the finding and sentence of the Court in whole or in part - and that had the case been tried in a Civil Court no jury would have hesitated to rendered a verdict of acquittal. And I feel safe in appealing to the Judge Advocate General, who was probably present at the deliberations of the Court, to sustain me in the assertion that but for the evidence, 1st: as to Mudd's seeking Booth at the National Hotel on the 3rd of March; and 2nd: as to his having seen and assisted Booth and Herold after his return from Bryantown on the 15th of April; and 3rd: as to his unexplained delay until the 16th to communicate his information to the authorities, the Commission itself would have entirely acquitted him. On these three vital points Mrs. Mudd's testimony, if it could have been received by the Court, would have wholly relieved her husband of suspicion; and procured his acquittal. I appeal to your Excellency to receive it now, and give at the weight and effect it would probably have had if received by the Court. It would be not unworthy of Executive consideration if the prisoner had been tried and convicted by a Civil Tribunal with the benefit of every safeguard of liberty provided by law. But as he was tried before the tribunal where many of these safeguards were relaxed, inapplicable or ineffective - and especially as he was borne down by more false testimony than ever took the life of an innocent man in a Court of Justice - I can not be mistaken in believing that you will hear and give effect to the sworn statements of her, who (though she be the wife of the prisoner) knows more of the vital issues of the cause that all other witnesses together; and of whose perfect truth no one, who knows or talks with her, can doubt.

On this corroborated testimony of Mrs. Mudd, I respectfully ask on behalf of the prisoner, his wife, and children, a remission of his sentence.

I am, Sir, Very Respectfully,
Your Obedient Servant

Thomas Ewing Jr.
Atty

P.S.

Since writing the foregoing, I have seen an alleged confession by Atzerodt, in which he is reported as saying that two weeks before the assassination Booth told him that "he had sent provisions and liquors to Dr. Mudd's to be used by the conspirators on the route to Richmond with the President, and that he was acquainted with him, and had letters to him." If such a statement was in fact made by Atzerodt, the statement by Booth as to his having sent anything to the house of the prisoner we can show was utterly false. The statement on its face shows that Mudd was not then a conspirator; for if he were, why should Booth mention the letters? Would he not have told Atzerodt that he was a conspirator with them? I am informed by Mr. Stone, who was counsel for Herold, that he said he tried to dissuade Booth from going so far out of his route - but that Booth said he must get his leg set and dressed. And that they did not while there intimate to Mudd what had been done. If Herold's confession is in the hands of the Judge Advocate, I ask that it be considered with this application for remission of sentence.

Thomas Ewing Jr.
Attorney

07-27-1865: Navy Paymaster William Keeler's Two Letters

First letter:

Source: Keeler, William Frederick, *Aboard the U.S.S. Florida: 1863-65.*

Dr. Mudd, Edman Spangler, Michael O'Laughlin, and Samuel Arnold were taken to Fort Jefferson aboard the U.S.S. Florida. William F. Keeler, the Navy Paymaster aboard the Florida, described the Florida's trip in the following letter to his wife Anna.

U.S. Steamer Florida
Key West, Florida
July 27th, 1865

Dear Anna,

We left New York, as I have previously informed you in a brief note, on Sunday 16th. We had been ordered to be ready for Sea a number of days previously & had been given to understand that we were going to go to Port Royal to tow one of the monitors to Philadelphia.

When the final sailing orders came we were taking on naval stores for Port Royal & carpenters and painters were at work repairing damages caused by the falling of a large derrick across us & which came very near sending us to the bottom. Mechanics were hurried ashore leaving their work half done, the remainder of the stores were soon on board & we were off.

It seems however that the orders for Port Royal &c were only for a blind & to conceal the real purpose in sending us off. Just as we were leaving the dock a telegram from Washington was received ordering us to call at Hampton Roads.

We reached there the next day about noon & dropped an anchor opposite Fortress Monroe, the familiar scenery on all sides reminding me of the eventful occurrences at the outbreak of the war. Of course we were all ignorant of the cause of our being sent there & many speculation were ventured as to the why and wherefore. We had not long to wait however for a steamer which we saw coming down the bay as we came into the harbor, came up and anchored near us.

Brig. Gen [Levi Axtell] Dodd with a portion of his staff came on board in a small boat and were soon followed by Dr. [Samuel A.] Mudd, [Samuel] Arnold, McLaughlan [Michael O'Laughlin] & [Edward] Spangler, the unhung ones of the President's assassins & a guard of 30 of the veteran reserves in charge.

The mystery was now solved and our real destination was found to be the Dry Tortugas. The prisoners were brought on board in irons and closely guarded, nothing about them to attract particular attention though their crime had given them a notoriety which made them objects of curiosity to all on board. They had been gazed at I suppose till they ceased to regard it as anything strange & seated themselves quite composedly in some chairs which had been placed for them on the quarter deck.

None of us were allowed any communication with the shore. We were under way again before sundown & were probably many miles at sea before the curious public knew but what the murderers were safely housed as four weeks past in the old capital prison. They were taken from Washington in the middle of the night, none but the President & his Cabinet being aware of the transaction except the guard who accompanied them. The prisoners had seen in the papers that they were to be sent to the Albany penitentiary & supposed they were put on board of us for the purpose of being conveyed to New York. It was not till they had been on board for forty-eight hours that they began to mistrust their real destination. They appeared a good deal dejected when they learned that truth.

The Dr. wanted to know "how long a person would probably live at the Tortugas." Like most criminals they all claimed that they had been found guilty upon false evidence. Dr. Mudd had a good deal to say about the trial, pointing out the evidence where it clashed as he thought, giving the character of various witnesses, calling attention to points which he thought had been overlooked or had not received sufficient attention from the court. He had had that evidence in his case, pro & con, published in book form and produced a copy of which he commended to our careful perusal.

He is about 30 years of age though he looks much older, he leaves a wife & four children. He is said to be a sharp shrewd man but I saw nothing about him to indicate it - he has a sort of cunning, foxy, look as if possessed of plenty of low cunning & a desire for concealment.

The officers in charge of them & who have had a good opportunity of knowing say that "Mrs. Surratt & him furnished the brains for the party" - & they think that he should have accompanied her to the gallows, that her fate was just & merited they have no doubt & that she had any claims, as a woman, one executive clemency, they deny.

Spangler is a course, rough, uneducated, unprincipled man. His bull neck, bullet head & brutish features mark a villain, but without sufficient nerve & steadiness to carry out the villainy his heart would prompt. He appears to take his punishment (six years) quite stoically & appears at times quite light hearted. He protests with any amount of profanity his entire innocence of the charge but he admits that he has committed crime enough of other kinds to merit the punishment so that his sentence is not undeserved.

The other two are young men, quiet & still, saying but little except when spoken to - men of no more than ordinary information and intelligence. With the exception of Dr. Mudd who may have the ability to plan I cannot conceive how the execution of plans of such vast consequences to the rebels could have been entrusted to such kind of persons.

With Gen. Dodd was Capt. [George W.] Dutton, Dr. [John H.] Porter & thirty privates. The Assistant Judge Advocate General (Col. [Levi C.] Turner) also went down with us with instructions to look into the status of all the political prisoners at Tortugas & other places south & with power to liberate such as in his judgment he might deem advisable. We had a very pleasant company, the Gen. & Col. going into the cabin to mess & the Dr. & Capt. coming into the Ward Room.

The hand irons were taken off the prisoners after they came on board but the leg irons were kept on for the first two or three days, after that they were removed during the day but put on at night. The first two nights they were kept on the orlop deck below the Ward Room, but they complained so much of the heat & closeness they were allowed to spread their mattresses on the quarter deck but were closely guarded. They were fed the same as the sailors - the regular ration. I was in hopes they would send us Jeff Davis from Fortress Monroe, it needed him to make the assortment of scoundrels complete. They appeared much more contented & resigned than I should suppose persons leaving behind them everything that could make life desirable, to be shut out from the world the remainder of their lives, could be - that they realized their condition was shewn by a remark of the Dr.'s one day - that "if it were not for his dread of an hereafter he should jump overboard."

We arrived at Port Royal on Wednesday the 19th & left for the Dry Tortugas on the 21st. During our stay there [Port Royal] we lay at the docks of the naval station across the harbour from Hilton Head. General Dodd had a tug placed at his disposal during his stay & made a trip up to Beaufort, about 16 miles. Capt. Dutton and Dr. Porter accompanied him & I made one of the party by his invitation.

I could imagine the feelings of our prisoners as we approached Fort Jefferson, on the Dry Tortugas, on the morning of the 24th where they were to spend the remainder of their lives. The particular island is a small, low patch of white sand on the coral reef of about thirteen acres, seven of which are enclosed within the brick walls of the fort, a good portion of the remainder being covered with sheds, shops, stables &c pertaining to the fort & its occupants giving it, at a short distance, the appearance of a small village.

Not a particle of vegetation is visible on the island outside the fort. The only green thing in sight was a few scrubby oak bushes on another small patch of sand a half mile or so distant. Inside the fort, vegetation adapted to the dry, sandy, hot soil was nursed with the great deal of care, most of it transplanted from Key West, a tamarina, a few oaks, some banannas, mangroves, a number of varieties of the cactus (one of them producing the flower from which the night blooming cereus is extracted) were pointed out to me growing around the officers quarters.

A false impression seems to be entertained of this place at the north - that it is dreary & desolate in its appearance you can infer from what I have already said - nothing but the "wide blue sea" can be seen from it except of few small patches of low, barren, white sand scattered at irregular intervals along the coral reefs. The sea breeze continually blowing makes it cool & comfortable & the health must be good as a visit with the Surgeon to the hospital of the garrison of a full regiment (the 110th N.Y.) shewed but five patients & that of the 550 prisoners contained but 4. The Dr. told me that in his six years residence there he had had but six cases of yellow fever. His wife had just left for the north after a stay of three years.

The prisoners are kept employed when there is work to do, but, now there is nothing for them to do & they roam about the fort & beach at will, fishing, bathing, gathering corals, shells, mosses &c which they sell to those visiting the place or send abroad for sale, many of them realizing quite a handsome sum from the proceeds of these curiosities. They are kindly treated & seen to enjoy almost unrestricted liberty. Notwithstanding the sentence of "hard labor with ball and chain" with which many of them are sent there such punishment is not carried out & is only resorted to as a penalty for misbehavior after their arrival on the island.

Dr. Mudd is to be sent into the hospital as an assistant to the Surgeon, Arnold is to be employed as a clerk & Spangler will be kept to work in his trade. I have no doubt but what they are glad by this time that they were not sent to the penitentiary as was at first intended.

I got some beautiful corals which I will send home the first opportunity - hope I will be able to bring them myself.

The Capt. & some of our officers had another drunkenness spree here in which they were ably assisted by some of the officers from the fort. Such things are degrading to the officers and disgraceful to the Service & could it be shewn to the Department and it's true light would undoubtedly subject the offenders to dismissal, for drunkenness is strictly forbidden. There is but little use however in bringing such complaint against a commanding officer by an inferior, as it has been tried a number of times & by some species of legerdemain has resulted in the acquittal of the offender and the dismissal of the complaint, so that all we can do is to look quietly on & inwardly condemn them.

We left the next morning for Key West, about sixty-five miles, & arrived here [Key West] about noon & are now just passing out the harbor after a stay of two days.

We find Col. Turner a very pleasant companion. He has resided at Washington during the war in charge of the political prisoners, or rather superintending all proceedings in relation to them. He was well acquainted with Mr. Lincoln & is full of anecdotes of him as well as of other public characters in Washington. In a two or three hours' conversation with him last night he gave me an account of the secret history of the rebellion, how mails & letters were opened, detectives employed, & other secret measures taken to detect and ferret out the traitors in our midst. Many he says who are now esteemed loyal would tremble if they knew the record against them at Washington.

Capt. Dutton is from Boston, I cannot find that he is related to your family. He is full of fun & makes a good deal of sport for us in the Ward Room.

The Gen. is a quiet, modest, retiring man with a broad, good humored face ever ready to light up with a smile. All on board like him. He was promoted for gallantry at Petersburg. This is his first trip to sea & of course everything is new - the source of an endless variety of questions which are always asked with a good humored smile.

Monday evening, July 31st

"Home again!" I wish it were so. We have just taken on board a Sandy Hook pilot, which seems a step in that direction. Early tomorrow morning we shall be passing up the Narrows - the most delightful ride in the world. I wish you were on board to enjoy it with me. By eight o'clock we shall be at anchor off the Battery, there we will all be longing to know what the future has in store for us - whether the Florida goes out of commission & we go home or are to be sent off again - quien sabe?

Good night, with love & kisses to yourself and our little ones, if they can be still called such - nearly three years (long ones) since I have seen one of them - I suppose he can scarcely be called small now - how much I want to see him.

William

William Keeler's second letter:

Source: Samuel A. Mudd Pardon File B-596, RG 204, U.S. National Archives, College Park, Md

In 1869, when Keeler learned that Dr. Mudd was being considered for a pardon, he wrote the following letter:

La Salle, Ill.
Jany 21, 1869

Hon. B.C. Cook

Dear Sir

I learned by yesterday's Chicago Tribune that efforts are being made to procure the pardon of Dr. Mudd. The U.S. Steamer Florida, to which I was attached conveyed him and his associates from Hampton Roads to the Tortugas. In conversation with myself, & I think with others on our passage down he admitted what I believe the prosecution failed to prove at his trial - viz - that he knew who Booth was when he set his leg & of what crime he was guilty. I have thought it might be well to have these facts known if they are not.

Very truly yours

W.F. Keeler

08-03-1865: Washington Evening Star Article on Trip to Fort Jefferson

Source: Washington Evening Star, August 3, 1865

The following Washington Evening Star article reports on the trip of Dr. Samuel Mudd, Samuel Arnold, Edman Spangler, and Michael O'Laughlen to Fort Jefferson in the Dry Tortugas aboard the U.S.S. Florida. The August 4, 1865 edition of the New York Times carried an abbreviated version of this same story.

> The United States steamer Florida, Lieut. Commander Budd, which conveyed Dr. Mudd, Spangler, O'Laughlin, and Arnold to the Dry Tortugas, in charge of Gen. Dodd, arrived at New York on Tuesday, having left the prisoners at their destination on the 25th; and some of the officers who accompanied them have returned to the city.
>
> The prisoners, as we have stated before, left their quarters at the penitentiary (where they were tried) at two o'clock on the morning of July 18th, in the steamer State of Maine, and carried to Fortress Monroe, where they were transferred to the U. S. steamer Florida, Capt. Budd, on the afternoon of the same day, and proceeded to sea. They were in charge of Gen. Levi A. Dodd, who had been on duty at the penitentiary during the whole of their confinement, who was accompanied by Col. Turner, Assistant Judge Advocate General, who went out to examine into the mode of keeping and treating prisoners there, Brevet Capt. Potter, Surgeon U.S.A. who had medical supervision of the prisoners during their incarceration here, and Capt. Dutton, of the Veteran Reserve Corps, with a guard of 28 men.
>
> The prisoners, all of whom with the exception of Spangler, were sentenced to imprisonment and hard labor for life, and he for six years, had no idea of their destination, unless it was to Albany, until they reached Fortress Monroe, and then seeing the large quantity of rations placed on board, they began to suspect that they were bound to a more distant place than Albany. They were allowed to be together at times during the trip, and frequently engaged in a game of draughts, &c., during the day, but at night they were placed in separate state-rooms, closely guarded. The weather during the whole trip was pleasant, and but one on board (Mudd) was sea sick, and he on the first day at sea only. They were considerably depressed in spirits soon after starting, and when informed of their destination by Gen. Dodd after leaving Port Royal on the 21st, they became quite gloomy; but on reaching the Tortugas, and finding it an island of about 13 acres, enjoying a fine sea breeze and comparatively healthy, they expressed themselves as agreeably surprised, and became more buoyant in spirits. On landing and seeing comfortable quarters inside the fort, and a clump of coconut trees and other vegetation growing, and noticing the other prisoners confined there in good spirits, they soon became quite cheerful.
>
> There are about 550 prisoners confined at the Dry Tortugas at this time, who are well treated, and seemingly enjoy life as well as they could in confinement anywhere. At present there are but nine persons on the sick list, a fact which speaks well for the treatment of the prisoners. The 110th New York Volunteers, Col. Hamilton, has been on duty here for the past sixteen months.
>
> The Florida reached the Tortugas (about sixty miles from Key West) at noon on the 25th of July, and Gen. Dodd with his charge, immediately landed. Sam Arnold was immediately assigned to a desk as clerk in the engineers department, he being familiar with such work. Spangler at once noticed workmen shingling some of the buildings, and expressing a wish to take hand in his old business, was permitted to resume the hatchet and saw. Doctor S. A. Mudd arrived just in the nick of time, the Surgeon of the Post who has been there for six years past, stating that he

wished an assistant, Dr. Mudd was notified that he would in future be expected to follow the practice of medicine among the prisoners. O'Laughlin had not, when the Florida left on the morning of the 26th, had his work allotted to him, but would no doubt be assigned some suitable occupation.

On the trip Dr. Mudd acknowledged to Capt. Budd, Gen. Dodd and others, that he knew Booth when he came to his house with Herold on the morning after the assassination, but that he was afraid to tell of his having been there, fearing the life of himself and family would be endangered thereby. He knew that Booth would never be taken alive. He also acknowledged that he had been acquainted with Booth for some time, and that he was with Booth at the National Hotel on the evening referred to by Weichman; that he met Booth in the street and Booth said he wanted him (Mudd) to introduce him to John Surratt; that they started up 7th street on their way to Mrs. Surratts house, and on the way they met John Surratt and Weichman, and returned to Booth's room at the National, where he and John Surratt had some conversation of a private character. He said that the Military commission in his case had done their duty, and as far as they were concerned the sentence in his case was just; but some of the witnesses had sworn falsely and maliciously.

O'Laughlin acknowledged that the Court had done its duty, and said that he was in the plot to capture the President, but that after the ineffectual attempt in March, when the party hoped to have captured the coach containing the President, he thought that the entire project was given up, and it was as far as he was concerned. He denies positively that he had part or knowledge in the plot to assassinate the President, Gen. Grant, or anyone else.

Sam Arnold made about the same statement as he did before the trial, that he was in the plot to capture, but not to assassinate; that that had failed and he considered himself out of it, and never knew anything about the assassination, which he thought was gotten up by Booth only a few hours before executing it. He thought the Court could not have done otherwise than it did. He expressed his sorrow that he had been led into the plot to capture by Booth and others, and expressed himself thankful that the punishment was no worse.

Spangler talked considerably during the trip, but like the others, was despondent at times, in the uncertainty about their place of destination. While on the voyage he expressed some impatience at his own stupidity in not having recollected while on trial a circumstance in connection with Booth's escape from the stage, that would have told materially to his (Spangler's) advantage. Some of the testimony went to show that Spangler has slammed the door to after Booth's exit, in a way to hinder immediate pursuit. Spangler says it quite escaped his recollection that some time previous to the assassination a patent spring had been put on the door for the purpose of closing it when left carelessly open. He says, however, that he supposes the Court had done right, and if they gave them plenty of work and plenty to eat he was satisfied; although he was not guilty, and knew nothing of Booth's intentions. He says he did say to Booth "I would do all I can for you" but that was in reference to selling his (Booth's) horse and buggy, and that it was three days before the assassination. He says that some of the witnesses lied in their testimony, especially about his slapping anyone in the mouth and telling him to keep his mouth shut.

The officers in charge of the prisoners carried out their instructions fully, and before leaving they received the thanks of each of the prisoners for the kind treatment to them.

08-22-1865: The Dutton Report & Dr. Mudd's Rebuttal

Two sources:

Dutton Report: Pitman, Benn, *The Assassination of President Lincoln and the Trial of the Conspirators*. New York, N.Y.. Moore, Wilstach, and Baldwin. 1865. Page 421.

Dr. Mudd's Rebuttal: Mudd, Nettie, *The Life of Dr. Samuel A. Mudd*, 1906. Fourth Edition, Page 42.

Newspaper reporters were not allowed on the U.S.S. Florida when it transported Dr. Mudd and the others to Fort Jefferson. However, when the Florida returned to New York, reporters talked to the Army officers who had gone on the trip. The August 3, 1865 edition of the Washington Evening Star carried their story, the full text of which is included elsewhere in this Source Documents section. The New York Times carried an abbreviated version of the Star story the next day.

The Star story read in part:

> On the trip, Dr. Mudd acknowledged to Capt. Budd, Gen. Dodd and others, that he knew Booth when he came to his house with Herold on the morning after the assassination, but that he was afraid to tell of his having been there, fearing the life of himself and family would be endangered thereby. He knew that Booth would never be taken alive.

Judge Advocate General Joseph Holt was the lead prosecutor in the Lincoln assassination trial. When he read the newspaper story, he asked Captain George W. Dutton, who had been in charge of the guards aboard the Florida, to tell him if Dr. Mudd had actually said what the article claimed he said. Captain Dutton submitted the following affidavit confirming the accuracy of the Washington Evening Star article. His report was the last document added to Benn Pitman's official record of the assassination trial, *The Assassination of President Lincoln and the Trial of the Conspirators*.

Captain Dutton's report:

Camp Fry, Washington, D.C.
August 22,1865.

Brig. Gen. Joseph Holt,
Judge Advocate General, U. S. A.:

Sir - I am in receipt of your communication of this date, in which you request information as regards the truthfulness of certain statements and confessions reported to have been made by Dr. Mudd while under my charge, en route to the Dry Tortugas.

In reply, I have the honor to state that my duties required me to be constantly with the prisoners, and during a conversation with Dr. Mudd, on the 22nd of July, he confessed that he knew Booth when he came to his house with Herold, on the morning after the assassination of the President; that he had known Booth for some time but was afraid to tell of his having been at his house on the 15th of April fearing that his own and the lives of his family would be endangered thereby. He also confessed that he was with Booth at the National Hotel on the evening referred to by Weichmann in his testimony; and that he came to Washington on that occasion to meet Booth by appointment, who wished to be introduced to John Surratt; that when he and Booth were going to

Mrs. Surratt's house to see John Surratt, they met, on Seventh street, John Surratt, who was introduced to Booth, and they had a conversation of a private nature. I will here add that Dr. Mudd had with him a printed copy of the testimony pertaining to his trial, and I had, upon a number of occasions, referred to the same. I will also state that this confession was voluntary, and made without solicitation, threat or promise, and was made after the destination of the prisoners was communicated to them, which communication affected Dr. Mudd more than the rest; and he frequently exclaimed, 'Oh, there is now no hope for me.' 'Oh, I can not live in such a place.'

Please acknowledge receipt of this letter.
I am General, very respectfully,
Your obedient servant,
George W. Dutton
Capt. Co. C, 10th Reg't. V. R. C., com'dg. Guard.

Dr. Mudd's Rebuttal:[94]

When Dr. Mudd learned of Captain Dutton's report, he wrote a heated rebuttal, which included an admission of his December 23, 1864 meeting with Booth in Washington, but also included his continued denial that he recognized Booth at his farmhouse.

The official report on the Lincoln conspiracy trail included a copy of Captain Dutton's report, but not Dr. Mudd's rebuttal, so Dr. Mudd sent it to his wife, who then made it public, saying:

The following is a sworn statement written by my husband while he was a prisoner in Fort Jefferson and which he was not permitted by the authorities to have published. He sent it to me in a letter about the 1st of October, 1865. This statement was made to correct erroneous statements, which had appeared in the public press, allegedly quoting my husband.

Following is Dr. Mudd's rebuttal of Captain Dutton's report:

August 28, 1865

1st. That I confessed to having known Booth while in my house; was afraid to give information of the fact, fearing to endanger my life, or made use of any language in that connection - I positively and emphatically declare to be notoriously false.

2nd. That I was satisfied and willingly acquiesced in the wisdom and decision of the Military Commission who tried me, is again notoriously erroneous and false. On the contrary I charged it (the Commission) with irregularity, injustice, usurpation, and illegality. I confess to being animated at the time but have no recollection of having apologized.

3rd. I did confess to a casual or accidental meeting with Booth in front of one of the hotels on Pennsylvania Avenue, Washington, D. C. on the 23d of December 1864, and not on the 15th of January, 1865, as testified to by Weichman. Booth, on that occasion desired me to give him an introduction to Surratt, from whom he said he wished to obtain a knowledge of the country around

---

[94] Mudd, Nettie, *The Life of Dr. Samuel A. Mudd*, Fourth Edition. 1906. Page 42.

Washington, in order to be able to select a good locality for a country residence. He had the number, street, and name of John Surratt, written on a card, saying, to comply with his request would not detain me over five minutes. (At the time I was not aware that Surratt was a resident of Washington.) I declined at first, stating I was with a relative and friend from the country and was expecting some friends over from Baltimore, who intended going down with me to spend Christmas, and was by appointment expected to be at the Pennsylvania House by a certain hour - eight o'clock. We started down one street, and then up another, and had not gone far before we met Surratt and Weichman.

Introductions took place, and we turned back in the direction of the hotel. Arriving there, Booth insisted on our going to his room and taking something to drink with him, which I declined for reasons above mentioned; but finding that Weichman and Surratt were disposed to accept - I yielded, remarking, I could not remain many minutes. After arriving in the room, I took the first opportunity presented to apologize to Surratt for having introduced to him Booth - a man I knew so little concerning. This conversation took place in the passage in front of the room and was not over three minutes in duration. Whilst Surratt and myself were in the hall, Booth and Weichman were sitting on the sofa in a corner of the room looking over some Congressional documents. Surratt and myself returned and resumed our former seats (after taking drinks ordered), around a center table, which stood midway the room and distant seven or eight feet from Booth and Weichman. Booth remarked that he had been down in the country a few days before, and said he had not yet recovered from the fatigue. Afterward he said he had been down in Charles County and had made me an offer for the purchase of my land, which I confirmed by an affirmative answer; and he further remarked that on his way up he lost his way and rode several miles off the track. When he said this he left his seat and came over and took a seat immediately by Surratt; taking from his pocket an old letter, he began to draw lines, in order to ascertain from Surratt the location and description of the roads. I was a mere looker on. The conversation that took place could be distinctly heard to any part of the room by any one paying attention. There was nothing secret to my knowledge that took place, with the exception of the conversation of Surratt and myself, which I have before mentioned. I had no secret conversation with Booth, nor with Booth and Surratt together, as testified to by Weichman. I never volunteered any statement of Booth having made me an offer for the purchase of my land, but made an affirmative response only to what Booth said in that connection.

Booth's visit in November 1864, to Charles County was for the purpose, as expressed by himself, to purchase land and horses; he was inquisitive concerning the political sentiments of the people, inquiring about the contraband trade that existed between the North and South, and wished to be informed about the roads bordering on the Potomac, which I declined doing. He spoke of his being an actor and having two other brothers, who also were actors. He spoke of Junius Brutus as being a good Republican. He said they were largely engaged in the oil business, and gave me a lengthy description of the theory of oil and the process of boring, etc. He said he had a younger brother in California. These and many minor matters spoken of caused me to suspect him to be a Government detective and to advise Surratt regarding him.

We were together in Booth's room about fifteen minutes, after which, at my invitation, they walked up to the Pennsylvania House, where the conversation that ensued between Weichman and myself as testified to by him is in the main correct - only that he, of the two, appeared the better Southern man, and undertook to give me facts from his office to substantiate his statements and opinions. This was but a short time after the defeat of Hood in Tennessee. The papers stated that over nine thousand prisoners had been taken, and that the whole of Hood's army was demoralized and falling back, and there was every prospect of his whole army being either captured or destroyed. To this Weichman replied that only four thousand prisoners had been ordered to be provided for by the Commissary-General, and that he was far from believing the defeat of Hood so disastrous. I spoke with sincerity, and said it was a blow from which the South never would be able to recover; and that the whole South then laid at the mercy of Sherman. Weichman seemed, whilst on the stand, to be disposed to give what he believed a truthful statement. I am in hopes the above will refresh his memory, and he will do me the justice, though late, to correct his erroneous testimony.

To recapitulate - I made use of no such statement as reported by the "Washington Correspondent of the New York Times," only in the sense and meaning as testified to by Dr. George D. Mudd, and as either misunderstood or misrepresented by Colonel Wells and others before the Commission.

I never saw Mrs. Surratt in my life to my knowledge previous to the assassination, and then only through her veil. I never saw Arnold, O'Loughlin, Atzerodt, Payne alias Powel, or Spangler - or ever heard their names mentioned previous to the assassination of the President. I never saw or heard of Booth after the 23d of December 1864, until after the assassination, and then he was in disguise. I did not know Booth whilst in my house, nor did I know Herold; neither of whom made himself known to me. And I further declare they did not make known to me their true destination before I left the house. They inquired the way to many places and desired particularly to go to the Rev. Mr. Wilmer's. I gave a full description of the two parties (whom I represented as suspicious) to Lieutenant Lovett and three other officers, on the Tuesday after the assassination.

I gave a description of one horse - the other I never took any notice of, and do not know to this day the color or appearance. Neither Booth's nor Herold's name was mentioned in connection with the assassination, nor was there any name mentioned on the Tuesday after the assassination, nor was there any name mentioned in connection with the assassination, nor was there any photograph exhibited of any one implicated in the infamous deed. I was merely called upon to give a description of the men and horses and the places they inquired. The evidence of the four detectives - Lovett, Gavacan, Lloyd, and Williams - conflict (unintentionally) vitally on this point; they evidently prove and disprove the fact as they have done in every instance affecting my interest, or upon points in which my welfare was at issue. Some swore that the photograph of Booth was exhibited on Tuesday, which was false. I do not advert to the false testimony; it is evident to the reader, and bears the impress of foul play and persecution somewhere - it may be owing to the thirst after the enormous reward offered by the Government, or a false idea for notoriety. Evans and Norton evidently swore falsely and perjured themselves. Daniel I. Thomas was bought by the detectives - likewise the negroes who swore against me. The court certainly must have seen that a great deal of the testimony was false and incompetent - upon this I charge them with injustice, etc.

Reverend Evans and Norton - I never saw nor heard their names in my life. I never knew, nor have I any knowledge whatsoever, of John Surratt ever visiting Richmond. I had not seen him previous to the 23d of December, 1864, for more than nine months. He was no visitor to my house.

The detectives, Lovett, Gavacan, Lloyd, and Williams, having failed to search my house or to make any inquiries whether the parties left anything behind on the Tuesday after the assassination, I myself did not think - consequently did not remind them. A day or two after their leaving, the boot that was cut from the injured man's leg by myself, was brought to our attention, and I resolved on sending it to the military authorities, but it escaped my memory and I was not reminded of its presence until the Friday after the assassination, when Lieutenant Lovett and the above parties, with a squad of cavalry, came again and asked for the razor the party shaved with. I was then reminded immediately of the boot and, without hesitation, I told them of it and the circumstances. I had never examined the inside of boot leg, consequently knew nothing about a name which was there contained. As soon as I handed the boot to Lieutenant Lovett, they examined and discovered the name "J. Wilkes"; they then handed me his photograph, and asked whether it bore any resemblance to the party, to which I said I would not be able to recognize that as the man (injured), but remarked that there was a resemblance about the eyes and hair. Herold's likeness was also handed me, and I could not see any resemblance, but I had described the horse upon which he rode, which, one of the detectives said, answered exactly to the one taken from one of the stables in Washington.

From the above facts and circumstances I was enabled to form a judgment, which I expressed without hesitation, and I said that I was convinced that the injured man was Booth, the same man who visited my house in November, 1864, and purchased a horse from my neighbor, George Gardiner. I said this because I thought my judgment in the matter was necessary to secure pursuit promptly of the assassins.

09-01-1865: Captain Prentice to General Townsend

Source: Provost Marshal, Fort Jefferson, Florida. Records Relating to Prisoners 1865-1870. Record Group 393, Entry 56, Volume 5. U.S. National Archives. Washington, D.C.

Immediately after Dr. Mudd and his companions were sent to Fort Jefferson, there were rumors of planned attempts to free them. In response, the authorities in Washington asked Fort Jefferson's commanding officer for assurances that any such attempt would not succeed. The commanding officer reported in the following letter that, despite personnel shortages, he was confident of his ability to hold the prisoners. But he also asked that a gunboat be sent immediately to help protect the fort from external attack.

> Fort Jefferson, Florida
> September 1st, 1865
>
> General,
>
> Your communication of August 17th enclosing copy of telegram from Gen. Baker and directing that such disposition be made of the four state prisoners Mudd, Arnold, O'Laughlin and Spangler as should render abortive any attempt at release, also requiring statement of "means adopted" etc. is received.
>
> In reply I have the honor to state that a similar notice was on the 24th received from Maj. Genl. Sheridan enclosing copy of telegram from the Secretary of War, dated Washington, August 17th 12:30 p.m.
>
> Such steps were immediately taken as deemed consistent with the numbers of the garrison, and a statement of the same, together with the strength of the garrison, number of prisoners etc. returned by the Captain bringing the despatches. In the first place, I will state that no prisoner is allowed outside the fort after sunset; the system of sentinels, patrols etc. Lieutenant Carpenter will explain, the patrols going over every part of the fort and once around the breakwater each hour during the night. A sufficient force is held constantly in readiness, close by the quarters of the guard, to man four heavy 10 inch guns. I inclose a copy of a General Order regulating the approach of vessels; a system of signals has also been established between the boarding party and the Guard. All prisoners are required to remain in their quarters after dusk when a patrol arrests anyone found outside. The detail for guard is 75 men each day, with two officers. The pieces of the guard are all loaded and when in post are primed, the guard remaining constantly at their post by the Parterre.
>
> The state prisoners are placed under precisely the same restrictions as the military. I inclose a consolidated Morning Report, which shows the full strength of the garrison to be 377. The large number upon daily duty is explained by the fact that all squads of prisoners and all workshops have to be under charge of soldiers. All are kept armed and could be turned out, but 275 enlisted man and six officers shows the whole number to meet a sudden emergency. The fact of our Lieut. Col., six company officers and more than one hundred enlisted man being on detached service within the Department of Florida has been reported to Maj. Genl. Sheridan. I feel very much embarrassed in consequence of the smallness of the Garrison and especially the small number of commissioned officers having upon my own hands the command of the Post, of my regiment, and

the charge of the prisoners. All the field and staff officers being absent, except the Regimental Quartermaster, Chaplin and one Assistant Surgeon, the latter being confined to his bed with fever.

The term of service of 37 recruits (one year's men) expired in August and that of 94 will expire during the present month. They will all be kept at duty, however, until some relief arrives. I am only anxious to do my duty, in which I am aided by the good offices of every officer present and feel confident of our ability to hold the prisoners, but I cannot help knowing that the affairs of the Post are in a bad condition which it is impossible for me to remedy. I would respectfully suggest as the best precaution that a reliable gunboat be sent here immediately for duty, there being no vessel of any character at the Post.

I am, Sir, Very Respectfully, Yr. Obdt. Svt.
(sd) W.R. Prentice
Capt. 161st N.Y. Vols. Comdg. Post

Brig. Gen. E.D. Townsend
Asst. Adj. Genl. U.S.A.

09-04-1865: Mrs. Mudd's Letter to Judge Advocate General Joseph Holt

Source: Joseph Holt Papers, Manuscript Division, Library of Congress, Washington, D.C.

Doctor Mudd had been in prison at Fort Jefferson for just a month and a half when his wife wrote this letter to Judge Advocate General Joseph Holt, who had been in charge of the proceedings of the Lincoln assassination trial.

Rock Hill, Sept 4th 1865

Judge Holt: Dear Sir,

When I called to see you in Washington on the 5th of July, I intended to speak to you as a child would to a father, and explain every circumstance just as they occurred in relation to the knowledge Dr. had of Booth and his visit to our house after he had committed the heinous crime, which threw sorrow and gloom over the American nation, and heaven knows I have had my share.

Your dignified and reserved manner somewhat awed me. I thought I could see through the reserve a kind heart, and you felt for me in my deep distress.

Under this belief I will venture to explain to you a few circumstances in Doctor's case and ask your sympathy and aid. When Booth and Herald came to our house on the morning of the 15th of April, Booth was disguised and gave the name of Tyson. Herald gave the name of Hanson or Harrison. Dr. did not recognize him as the man who came to our house last winter at the time he bought the horse of Mr. Gardiner. When Booth came to our house it was only an act of courtesy to a stranger, and kindness to Mr. Gardiner, who is a very old man and a great friend of Doctor's, that he went with him to the house of Mr. Gardiner's at the time he purchased the horse, Mr. Gardiner having several fine horses to sell at that time.

When Booth was down here last winter, he was looked upon with distrust; Dr. and everybody who saw him thought he was a Government detective.

When Doctor heard for a fact from his brother late on Saturday night of the 15th of April that the President had been killed, and he remembered those men who had been at our house acted rather strangely and I told him of the man's whiskers becoming detached, he got his horse and wanted to go to Bryantown and give immediate information of the fact. Through my fears and entreaties he delayed until next day, and sent word by Dr. George Mudd to Lt. Dana then in Bryantown. This information was given on Sunday morning but the men in pursuit did not come to our house until Tuesday evening. And when Doctor told them all he knew and pointed the direction Booth had taken they did not seem to believe him. Doctor told Lt. Lovett and those other detectives of Booth's visit to the country last winter. Also of Booth's purchasing a horse of Mr. Gardiner. He gave them all the information he could, and all of the aid he could towards their capture.

Those men misconstrued everything he told them and tortured it into criminality. And Doctor is now the innocent victim of a Nation's wrath. Had those men in pursuit of Booth acted upon Doctor's directions Booth would have been captured days before he was, and would have saved a great deal of trouble and money to the Government. But they lounged around our yards and farm professing to believe we had Booth concealed, and said they did not care whether they caught Booth or not, so they caught two or three of his accomplices as the President had offered $25 a person for them, and that would pay them well enough. Little did I think that Doctor was to be one of their victims.

Judge, I do not believe had demons been sent from the infernal regions they could not have sworn more falsely against Doctor than did Evans, Thomas, Norton, Weichmann and those negroes. The negroes are more excusable. They are ignorant and do not know the nature of an oath as well as a white man. And I feel sure they were bribed by those who expected to get the reward. If you will remember Evans said in his testimony he had to leave Prince Georges County on account of his loyalty. He was obliged to leave so I have heard for forgery and stealing a man's buggy, and any man that will cheat and steal will lie. Doctor never saw nor heard of Evans until he appeared against him, and Doctor's father has never seen him notwithstanding Evan's professed to know him well. Thomas is a low degraded creature, and would sell his soul for money. There is not a negro who knows him who would believe him under oath.

I know nothing about Norton and Weichmann except that their testimony is as false as falsehood itself. I do not believe there has ever been on record where so much false testimony has been taken against any one man as against Doctor.

I have thought of having those men brought before the grand jury and tried for perjury. I think we can bring proof enough against them to count. Judge, do you think this procedure would be of any benefit in Doctor's case? Please give me your advice and Almighty God will reward your charity.

I wish I could picture to your imagination all I have suffered in the past four months. I am sure the picture would move you to pity. When the trial was going on and day after day I saw in the papers false witness after false witness testify against my innocent husband. I felt that reason would forsake me and I suffered an agony which I hope no other mortal may ever suffer. I would have been glad to have died but Almighty God would not hear my prayer and take me. I have lived longer in the last four months than all of the rest of my life.

I will explain to you my helpless condition. I am in a country place. I have neither father, mother, or brother that I can call on for aid. Doctor's father has a large family. I cannot burden him. I have four little children, the oldest but seven years. The soldiers who were in pursuit of Booth destroyed all of our last year's crop, and prevented me from planting any this year by taking our farm hands and putting them in prison until it was too late to plant.

I only have a home to shelter me and my little babies and under present circumstances I cannot tell how long I will have that. I have never known want and have never had a wish but what has been gratified from my childhood, and now when I see poverty for myself and little children, I know not what to resort to. A dark and dreary, dreary life before me. I am only twenty seven years old and I am afraid I will have to live so long.

The separation from my husband who has been my companion from childhood is worse than death. Doctor and I had fondly hoped to raise our little children to be ornaments to society and to their country. What can I expect for them now, ignorance and poverty? Before Dr. was taken from me, I felt if one of our little children were to die, I would die too. Now I pray the Almighty to take them all. I can better se them all die young than see them undergo the hardship they will have to undergo if they live to be grown.

Judge, how I do wish you knew Doctor in social life. If you had, I know you would not for one moment suspect he could be guilty of the enormous crime with which he is charged. Every man who has ever known Doctor knows he is innocent. Doctor knew nothing in the world to capture or assassinate the President until after the deed was done. He had never seen but one of those men who were tried with him. He saw Herald who came to our house on the morning of the 15th of April. If it was a crime to set Booth's leg when he did not know he had committed any crime, and did not recognize the man, then and then only is he guilty.

Judge, I know and appreciate how far you are above me, so if I have written anything offensive it is through ignorance. I ask you to be a friend to the orphan, the widow and child of misfortune. I know you are all powerful in the case of my husband. Be assured of his innocence and you can convince others. Every word which I have written is as true as if it had to go to the throne of the Almighty for inspection. Pity me; write to me and tell me to come to you, that you will assist me. And I will come and explain every little circumstance and tell you all as a child would tell her troubles to a father. And as truthfully as I would at the bar of Divine justice. I will teach my little children to love and pray for you as long as they live.

Most respectfully and etc.
Sarah F. Mudd

(Judge Advocate General Holt)

09-16-1865: Lieutenant Carpenter to General Townsend

Source: Provost Marshal, Fort Jefferson, Florida. Records Relating to Prisoners 1865-1870. Record Group 393, Entry 56, Volume 5. U.S. National Archives. Washington, D.C.

Captain W. R. Prentice's September 1, 1865 Letter to General E. D. Townsend (see earlier document) responded to the concerns of the authorities in Washington about the ability of the military at Fort Jefferson to prevent any attempt to free Dr. Mudd and his companions. Lieutenant G.S. Carpenter, who carried the response back to Washington, was alarmed by the loose discipline he saw at Fort Jefferson, and gave his superiors the following unsolicited report of what he had seen.

Washington, September 16th 1865
Brvt. Brig. Gen. E.D. Townsend
Assistant Adjutant General

General,

I have the honor to submit the following report of matters at Fort Jefferson which came to my knowledge from personal observation or from conversations with the commanding officer at that Post during my late visit there as the bearer of despatches. I deem it my duty to submit this although not called for by your letter of instructions of the 16th inst.

Captain W.R. Prentiss, 161st N. Y. Vols. cmd'g his regiment relieved Colonel Hamilton, 110th New York of the command of the Post August 16th. Major Willis E. Craig of the same regiment at the same time relieved Colonel Hamilton of the command of the Sub Dist. of Key West and Tortugas, Headquarters at Key West. The Garrison at Key West numbers about 300 men while the prisoners number 495. The quarters of the prisoners are in the second tier of casemates commencing to the left of the Sally Port and occupying through the second face of the work from it while the quarters of the soldiery are next in this order, thus throwing the prisoners between the main guard at the Sally Port and the rest of the Garrison and in case of an emute giving the prisoners the chance to overpower the guard before the other troops could get under arms and come to their aid. In a small room built with rough boards on the floor of casemates occupied by the prisoners having two lightly laticed windows looking on a passage way for prisoners between it and the rear wall are placed in the racks about 40 muskets, with the locks removed, not under guard, which it would be but the work of a moment for the prisoners to seize unopposed. Drawn through a broken or uncompleted passage in the breakwater and near the Sally Port are moored in the moat three small barges nearly under the embrasures to casemates of prisoners. These I should judge by their situation would at least afford a temptation to prisoners giving access for an attack on the guard without the Sally Port. From 6 a.m. to 6 p.m. several squads of prisoners, each under charge of a single soldier may be and are continually employed outside the work on the wharfs or bar discharging vessels, shifting materials, ordinance stores and alike. The passing promiscuously of these parties, or individually without a guard, the employees of the Engineering Department (of whom there are about one hundred) and others through the Sally Port was so illy regulated that it was easy for a prisoner unauthorized to slip out to the shipping, lurk among the piles of material or buildings, seize one of the numerous sail or row boats about, and be off, under cover of night at least unobserved. There being no practiced artillerists in the Garrison, merely a squad of men drilled at odd hours by a non-commissioned officer in the manual of the piece; the fact that a vessel can by a skillful pilot be put clear around the fort very near the breakwater; and the absence of any steam vessel to give immediate notice in case of mutiny or rescue are considerations in favor of any concerted plan to release the prisoners by aid from without.

I could not learn that there were any regular hours for roll-call of prisoners, only that each soldier in charge of a squad of laborers was responsible for any absentee from his squad. The numbers that were in quarters lounging, card playing and the like at 10 a.m. and the appearance of a few rowing and fishing not under guard about the harbor gave evidence of an exceeding lax discipline over these convicts. Many prisoners were not in the dress I was told was prescribed for them. No surveillance whatever was exercised over their mail; the same facilities for communicating by letter was open to them as to any in the garrison.

Of the four state prisoners Mudd and Arnold have of late not been locked up at night. Mudd is on duty as nurse in the Hospital situate midway nearly of the Parade. Arnold is on duty as clerk to the Provost Marshal where he must have every facility for learning all regulations touching the guards, and the two others are employed as laborers and are locked in cells at night.

The commanding officer informed me that about the 20th inst. eight prisoners were missing whom it was supposed escaped by concealing themselves on the steamer T. A. Scott which left Fort Jefferson the evening before for New York under charge of Lieutenant Flood, 2nd Infty., statement of the case had been made to Major Craig, Commanding Sub District of Key West.

There were no permanent books of record for the Post, not even a morning-report-book, save at the Provost Marshal's office there was a descriptive book of prisoners. There however the papers pertaining to the case of each prisoner were separately filed with a numerical designation to which there was an index book for convenience of reference. The Post order book it was said had been taken away by the former commanding officer when he left the Post. No Post funds were turned over to Captain Prentice by his predecessor, nor were there any records pertaining to any such funds or of any Council of administration. About one hundred prisoners were under orders to be discharged but owing to the fact that there were no blanks on hand it was the commanding officer's intention to send these men to New Orleans to be discharged there as soon as transportation could be obtained. Complaints were made of the difficulty of obtaining supplies - that the Commissary stores on hand were of bad quality - that there was then no fresh beef and several cases of scurvy in the Hospital.

On the 5th inst. Major W.E. Craig, 161st New York was relieved of the command of the Sub. District by Colonel B. Townsend, 2nd U.S. Colored Infantry and left Key West that day for Fort Jefferson to assume the command of that Post. He, in conversation with reference to matters of Fort Jefferson, assured me that he was aware of the loose discipline there and should endeavor to remedy this and should see to it that the four state prisoners there were under strict surveillance.

I have the honor to be,

Very Respectfully
Your Obt, Servant

(S) G.S. Carpenter
1st Lieut. 18th U.S. Infty.

09-30-1865: Dr. Mudd's Description of His Escape Attempt

Source: Mudd, Nettie, *The Life of Dr. Samuel A. Mudd*, 1906. Fourth Edition, Page 123.

Included in Lieutenant Carpenter's report (see previous document) is an account of the recent escape from Fort Jefferson of eight prisoners who concealed themselves on the visiting steamer Thomas A. Scott bound for New York. This successful escape inspired Dr. Mudd to attempt the same thing on the Scott's return visit on July 25, 1865, just nine days after Lieutenant Carpenter wrote this letter to General Townsend. However, Dr. Mudd was caught hiding on the Thomas A. Scott, lost his privilege of working in the post hospital, and spent the next four months in the prison's dungeon.

In the following letter, Dr. Mudd describes his failed escape attempt to his brother-in-law, Jeremiah Dyer. Dr. Mudd's wife had two brothers, Jeremiah and Thomas, and two sisters, Betty and Mary Ellen. Sam and Sarah Frances were particularly close to Jeremiah, known as 'Jere', who lived just a half mile from the Mudd farm. Sam and Sarah Frances lived with Jere after their marriage while their new farm house was being built. In 1863, Jere moved to Baltimore. In 1865, he testified on Dr. Mudd's behalf at the Lincoln conspiracy trial. In 1867, Jere married Dr. Mudd's sister Mary Clare Mudd, known as 'M.C.'.

During Dr. Mudd's imprisonment, Jere Dyer provided a great deal of moral and other support to his sister, helping her with farm management and financial problems. He worked with lawyers and politicians to try to secure Dr. Mudd's release from prison. He corresponded regularly with Dr. Mudd to encourage him and keep him informed of events. The following letter is the first one that Dr. Mudd wrote to Jere from Fort Jefferson.

Fort Jefferson, Tortugas Island, Fla.,
September 30, 1865.

My dear Jere:

I wrote to you and Frank by the last steamer, but at the same time intended to arrive before it. Providence was against me. I was too well known and was apprehended five or ten minutes after being aboard the steamer. They were so much rejoiced at finding me, they did not care to look much farther; the consequence was, the boat went off and carried away four other prisoners, who no doubt will make good their escape. I suppose this attempt of mine to escape will furnish the dealers in newspapers matter for comment, and a renewal of the calumnious charges against me. Could the world know to what a degraded condition the prisoners of this place have been reduced recently, they, instead of censure, would give me credit for making the attempt. This place is now wholly guarded by negro troops with the exception of a few white officers. I was told by members of the 161st N.Y.V. Reg., that so soon as they departed, the prisoners would be denied many of their former privileges, and life would be very insecure in their hands. This has already proved true; a parcel of new rules and regulations have already been made and are being enforced, which sensibly decreases our former liberties.

For attempting to make my escape, I was put in the guard-house, with chains on hands and feet, and closely confined for two days. An order then came from the Major for me to be put to hard labor, wheeling sand. I was placed under a boss, who put me to cleaning old bricks. I worked hard all day, and came very near finishing one brick. The order also directs the Provost Marshal to have me closely confined on the arrival of every steamer and until she departs. I know not how long this state of things will continue. I have arrived at that state of mind at which I feel indifferent to what treatment I am subjected. The 161st N.Y. Reg. were very kind and generous to me, and I was as much induced by them to make the attempt to take French leave as my own inclination and judgment dictated. I am now thrown out of my former position, chief of dispensary, and not likely to be reinstated. I know not what degree of degradation they may have in store for me. I was forced, under the penalty of being shot, to inform on one of the crew who promised to secrete me aboard. They have him still in close confinement, and will likely try him before court martial for the offense. I have written a note to the Major and have seen the Provost Marshal, and have taken upon myself the whole blame and responsibility of the affair, yet they pay little or no attention, and the young fellow is still kept in close confinement.

I don't regret the loss of my position. Take away the honor attached, the labor was more confining than any other place or avocation on the island. At the same time it relieved me of the disagreeable necessity of witnessing men starve for the nutriment essential for a sick man, when it could be had with no trouble and but a little expense. Four prisoners have died during the short time I have been here; the last one died the morning I made my attempt to escape. Not a single soldier or citizen laborer has died or suffered with any serious sickness; thereby showing something wrong, something unfair, and a distinction made between the two classes of individuals. Every case of acute dysentery or diarrhea among the prisoners, either dies in the onset or lingers on and terminates in the chronic, which eventually kills.

We have a disease here which is termed bone fever, or mild yellow fever, which has attacked at least three-fourths of the inmates of the Fort. It lasts generally but two or three days; during the time, the patient imagines every bone will break from the enormous pain he suffers in his limbs. None has died with it.

I have not been a day sick or unwell, owing no doubt to the fact of my thoughts being concentrated upon home, my dear Frank, and the children. Little did I think I would ever become the veriest slave and lose the control of my own actions, but such, unfortunately, is too true, and God, I suppose, only knows whether these misfortunes will terminate with my frail existence, or that after being broken down with cares and afflictions of every kind, I be returned to my family a burden, more than a help and consoler. My only hope now is with you and the influence you can bring to bear. To be relieved from my present situation, I would be willing to live in poverty the balance of my days with Heaven my only hope of reward. If money be necessary, sell everything that I possess, and what might be allotted by poor Papa from his already exhausted means.

I feel that I am able now, and have resolution to make a decent living in any section of the world in which I am thrown by the Grace and Providence of the Almighty.

It strikes me that the Hon. Reverdy Johnson, Montgomery Blair, and many others whose principles and opinions are growing daily more popular - their influence could be easily brought to bear in my behalf. You fail to give me any idea of what was being done or any reasons for me to hope for relief by any certain time. You may have omitted this for prudential reasons. I have been too careless in my language among the evil disposed. They have never failed to misinterpret my language and meaning, and to omit everything having a tendency to exonerate me.

Knowing this, I shall be the keeper or guardian of my own thoughts and words for the future. I never knew how corrupt the world was before being visited by my recent calamities and troubles. They have shamefully lied and detracted everything I have said or done - a privilege for the future they shall never have.

No doubt they will get up a great sensation in regard to my attempted escape. Some thirty or forty have made their escape, or attempts to do so, since I have been here, and there never was anything thought of them. Since my unlucky attempt, everything seems to have been put in commotion, and most unfounded suspicions, rumors, etc., started.

My only object for leaving at the time I attempted, was to avoid the greater degradation, and insecurity of life, and at the same time be united again with my precious little family. I don't perceive why there is so much odium attached, as the authorities, by their harsh and cruel treatment, endeavor to make believe.

I will soon be returned to some duty more compatible with my qualifications. In the mean time, assure Frank and all that I am well and hearty, and as determined as ever. Write soon. Give my unbounded love to all at home, and believe me most truly and devotedly,

Yours, etc.,
S.A. MUDD

10-05-1865: Dr. Mudd's Letter to Jere Dyer

Source: Mudd, Nettie, *The Life of Dr. Samuel A. Mudd*, 1906. Fourth Edition, Page 127.

Dr. Mudd writes to his brother-in-law Jere Dyer that the consequences of his recent escape attempt will soon blow over, and that he will shortly return to his position in the prison hospital, or one equally respectable. He is very mistaken. Just a few days after writing this letter, Dr. Mudd, Sam Arnold, Mike O'Laughlin, Edman Spangler, and a fifth state prisoner, Colonel Grenfell, were placed in the prison's dungeon for four months. After release from the dungeon, Dr. Mudd was assigned to work with Edman Spangler in the fort's carpentry shop. The only time Dr. Mudd again worked in the post hospital was during the 1867 yellow fever epidemic.

Fort Jefferson, Dry Tortugas, Fla.,
October 5, 1865.

My dear Jere:

A vessel is about leaving port. I take advantage of it to drop you a few hasty lines. I forgot to mention, in the letters previously written, to inform you that none of the drafts, that I drew upon you, will be presented for payment. I was fortunate in being able to borrow twenty-five dollars; the check, so soon as I can obtain the money, will go to liquidate it. I shall endeavor to be as economical as possible, knowing to what straits my family has been already reduced. The only need I have for money is to purchase a few vegetables, and supply myself with tobacco. The only article of clothing I need is shirts. The Government furnishes flannel shirts, which I find very pleasant in damp weather, but very disagreeable and warm in dry sunshine.

If the friends of Arnold and O'Laughlin should send a box of clothing to them, you may put in a couple of brown linen, or check linen, shirts and a couple pairs cotton drawers. You may not bother yourself to this extent if you anticipate an early release. My clothing is sufficient to come home in. I will need no more money before the first of December, or latter part of November. It generally takes a letter ten or twelve days to reach this place, so anticipate the period, and send me twenty-five dollars in greenbacks. Address your letters to me, and not in care of anyone, and I will get them without fail. Write me soon and let me know whether my attempted escape caused much comment in the Northern papers. I fear it will have the effect to again agitate the question. I had written so often and desired information and council, that I became truly impatient and vexed. I expected to hear something from Ewing or Stone, but not a word have I received from either. I received a letter a few days ago which gave me more consolation and hope than any yet come to hand, from Henry. Had I received such a letter earlier I would have been content, and would never have acted as I did. I would have succeeded, only for meeting a party aboard, who knew me, before I could arrive at my hiding-place. I was informed on almost immediately, and was taken in custody by the guard. I regret only one thing, being necessitated to inform on the party who had promised to befriend me. It was all done by the mere slip of the tongue, and without reflection; but perhaps it was all providential. He is now free, having made good his escape with a notorious thief with whom he was locked up. I understand, after escaping from the dungeon in which they were confined, they robbed the sutler of fifty dollars in money, as much clothing as they needed, and a plenty of eatables in the way of canned fruits, preserves, meats, etc. Six prisoners made good their escape on the same boat upon which I was so unfortunate. It seems they were too much elated to look farther after my apprehension.

I am taking my present hardship as a joke. I am not put back in the least. I will soon assume my former position, or one equally respectable. The only thing connected with my present attitude is the name, and not the reality. I have no labor to perform, yet I am compelled to answer roll-call, and to sleep in the guard-house at night. This will not last longer than this week. Write soon, give me all the news, and continue to send me papers. I have received several from you, Frank, and some have been sent from New York by unknown parties, which afforded me considerable recreation. Give my love to all at home, and send this, after reading, to Frank, so that she may know that I am well, etc. I am sorry Tom is going to leave so early. I am under the greatest obligations to him for interest and kindness manifested. I am in hopes my release won't be long deferred, when I shall be able to see you all.

Samuel Mudd

12-22-1865: Mrs. Mudd's Christmas Letter to President Johnson

Source: Mudd, Nettie, *The Life of Dr. Samuel A. Mudd*, 1906. Fourth Edition, Page 148.

Three months had passed since Dr. Mudd was placed in the dungeon after his escape attempt in September. He and his companions in the dungeon, Sam Arnold, Edman Spangler, Mike O'Laughlen, and Colonel Grenfell, wore irons while working outside the dungeon during the day, and received food which was worse than the already low-quality fare at Fort Jefferson. Mrs. Mudd wrote this Christmas-time letter to President Johnson in an attempt to improve Dr. Mudd's treatment, and she succeeded. Not long after she wrote, Dr. Mudd and the others were released from the dungeon and their irons removed.

Bryantown, Maryland, December 22, 1865

His Excellency, Andrew Johnson
President of the United States

Dear Sir: I hesitate to address you, but love is stronger than fear, timidity must yield. I must petition for him who is very, very dear to me. Mr. President, after many weeks anxious waiting for news from my innocent, suffering husband, Doctor Samuel Mudd, last night's mail brought the sad tidings, he with others, by orders from the War Department, were heavily ironed, and obliged to perform hard work. The plea for this cruel treatment is, that the Government is in possession of news of a plot, originating in Atlanta or New Orleans, for the rescue of the said prisoners. The food furnished is of such miserable quality, he finds it impossible to eat it. Health and strength are failing. To my poor intellect, it seems an ineffectual plan to put down a plot by avenging upon the prisoners the acts of others. I suppose Secretary Stanton knows better. It strikes me very forcibly, your Excellency is ignorant of this order.

I saw you in September, and although I felt I was not as kindly treated as others, I looked into your face, and if it is true that "the face is an index to the heart," I read in it a good, kind heart that can sympathize with the sufferings of others. I marked the courteous manner you addressed ladies, particularly the aged. These things encouraged me to pray you to interpose your higher authority. The setting of a leg is no crime that calls for forgiveness. I ask you to release him, and I believe you will do it. I beg you in the name of humanity, by all that is dear to me, in the name of his aged and suffering parents, his wife and four babies, to immediately put a stop to this inhuman treatment. By a stroke of your pen, you can cause these irons to fall and food to be supplied. By a stroke of that same hand, you can give him liberty.

Think how much depends upon you. You were elected the Father of this people. Their welfare is your welfare. Then, in the name of God, if you let him die under this treatment, he an American citizen, who has never raised his arm, nor his voice against his country, can these people love you? Forgive me, I speak plainly, but my heart is very sore. You say, "women are your jewels," you hope for much from their prayers. I do not love you, neither will I ask the Almighty to bless you; but give back my husband to me, and to his parents who are miserable, - the wealth of my love and gratitude will be yours. My prayers shall ascend in union with my little children who are in happy ignorance, daily looking for the return of their "Pa." To him who has said, "suffer little children to come onto me," God of mercy I pray you, touch the heart of thy servant, make him give back my husband. Could you look into our household, it would give you a subject for meditation.

In the Doctor's childhood home, there is his father, who is old and infirm. When he hears the name of his boy, his lips tremble, but he thinks it is not manly to yield to tears, besides, he has confidence in you. His mother has scarcely left her sick room since his arrest. "She waits" she says, "to see him"; then like Holy Simeon, "she is willing to die." Pass from this to my little household. I, a wife, drag out life in despondency. I, who was shielded from every care by him who is now suffering living death, am miserable and have to battle with this overwhelming trouble. I am the mother of four babies, the oldest, seven years, the youngest, but one. The third, a delicate boy requiring constant care. I have confidence in you and feel you will grant my request.

Very respectfully yours,
Mrs. Dr. Samuel A. Mudd

01-01-1866: Dr. Mudd's New Year's Day Letter to Mrs. Mudd

Source: Mudd, Nettie, *The Life of Dr. Samuel A. Mudd*, 1906. Fourth Edition, Page 154.

Dr. Mudd wrote this New Years Day letter while he was still in the dungeon. He rather joyfully tells of being able to attend Mass twice, going to confession, and receiving communion from visiting priests. He asks to be kept informed of what is happening on their farm, but warns about family members writing anything the authorities would consider offensive, as that would only result in their keeping him in prison longer.

Fort Jefferson, Florida, January 1, 1866

My Darling Frank:

Today being New Year, I have no better means at my command of spending the time appropriately than dropping you a few hasty lines to afford you all the consolation that lies in my power. On the morning of the 28th, Bishop Verot, of Savannah, and the Reverend Father O'Hara arrived here about 6 o'clock. Soon word came that they desired to see me; my chains being taken off, I dressed in my best, and was soon ushered into their presence with my usual guard of honor. I found them preparing to say mass, and had the happy fortune of being present during the divine service.

After service I had a short conversation with Bishop Verot and Reverend Wm. O'Hara. I received the contents of the letter formerly addressed to Father O'Hara by Sister Joseph - a cross, a scapular, etc. In the evening I had the pleasure of listening to a very learned and practical lecture from the Bishop. After the discourse, I repaired to my quarters, took my usual supper, said my beads, and enjoyed for a time a promenade up and down my gloomy quarters, when a rap at the the door was heard, and my name called. On going to the door, I found our most pious and venerable Bishop had called to bid me goodbye; he intended leaving in the morning. I had given the subject of confession my attentive thought during the day, and remarked to the Bishop that I regretted I was not allowed the privilege of confession that evening; he said then, if I desired, he had the permission already accepted, and I had the satisfaction and happiness to confess to the Bishop. The next morning I went to communion. Mass was said by the Bishop, Father O'Hara serving as before. After Mass I bade the good and pious old man good-by, and received his blessing. I have not language at my command, my darling, to express the joy and delight I received on the occasion of this unexpected visit. Father O'Hara will remain a week, and I am in hopes I will have the happiness of again communing before he departs; I have made application. I heard Mass yesterday. There are many Catholics among the citizen laborers, and we have quite a large congregation, nearly all going to communion. I have now, my darling wife, but one affliction, viz: uneasiness of mind regarding you and our precious little children. Imprisonment, chains and all other accompaniments of prison life, I am used to. I believe I can stand anything, but the thought of your dependent position, the ills and privations consequent, pierce my heart as a dagger, and allow me no enjoyment and repose of mind. I have apprehensions as from the idle, roving, and lawless negroes that roam unrestricted through the country. Be cheerful, my darling, and be ever guarded.

The papers I notice are filled with horrible, most infamous and degraded crimes perpetrated by these outlaws. When you write, inform me what disposition is made of the farm, horses, cows, sheep, etc., and whether any portion of land has been reserved for yourself to cultivate. Will Old

John remain with you, or Albin? Consult, my dearest, with Pa and Jere, and try to remain comfortable and free from a dependent position. Give me all particulars that you deem worthy, and that can be written with propriety, for letters are inspected before handed to us. Disappointment produces more pain than the pleasure of hope and release, so my darling when you write again, say nothing illusive, and advise Henry and Fannie to refrain from alluding to what is not certain or reliable. It is all supposition, and I can suppose as well as they. The Court who sent me here, I know well never contemplated the carrying out of the unheard-of sentence, considering the slight foundation for even the suspicion of crime, so, my darling, I do not stand in need of any of these vagueries. Life and everything in this world is uncertain and changeable, and we will little know what other trials and crosses Providence may have yet in store for us. I have endeavored to the best of my ability to conform to all the duties required by our holy religion; my conscience is easy, and if death should visit me here (which I pray God to deliver me from), I am in hopes it will not find me unprepared.

Live strictly agreeable to the dictates of your conscience and religion and the trials we have endured may yet rebound to our earthly advantages; if not, I am in hopes we will meet in heaven. I forgot to mention previously I had also the privilege of making the jubilee. The month of December was appointed by the Bishop for the province.

Tell Henry and Fannie I'll answer their letters by next mail. I fear a copy of a former letter of Fannie's has been sent to the War Department., at least a copy was made of it. The Provost Marshal so informed me. I know not whether it was sent to the War Department. I fear imprudent talk and writing will yet dispose the mind of the President not to listen to your appeals in my behalf. Be careful, my darling child, and refrain as much as possible from expressing any angry indignation toward the ruling powers, or using opprobrious epithets toward my known prosecutors. Such conduct can have only the tendency to protract my stay here by keeping up agitation and excitement, if nothing else. Parties can have but little regard for my welfare, who were ever indulging in idle and injurious expressions. I feel that I should be perfectly satisfied to remain the balance of my days only in your and my little ones' company. My constant prayer is - God be merciful to us and grant me a speedy release, and a safe returned to my family. Write often, don't await answer, for months could intervene between the reception of letters.

How much I regretted to learn of the sad accident that occurred in your old home. My heart is often softened by the memory of our happiest days. It was within its hallowed walls that we first indulged in the hope of a blissful future, but alas! to what gloom have we arrived.

Good-by, my darling wife and little children.

Yours devotedly,

Sam

03-05-1867: Dr. Mudd's Letter to Mrs. Mudd

Source: Mudd, Nettie, *The Life of Dr. Samuel A. Mudd*, 1906. Fourth Edition, Page 226.

Dr. Mudd wrote this letter after almost two years at Fort Jefferson. It will be another two years until he is released. He mentions the marriage of Jere Dyer and M.C. Jeremiah Dyer is his wife's brother, who has helped her in many ways during the two years since Dr. Mudd was arrested. M.C. is Dr. Mudd's sister, Mary Clare Mudd.

In his letter, Dr. Mudd mentions John Surratt. John Harrison Surratt was Booth's right-hand man, involved in every aspect of Booth's bizarre scheme to kidnap President Lincoln. Like Sam Arnold and Mike O'Laughlen, Surratt had concluded by March 1865 that Booth's plan was impractical, considered the plot closed, and had moved on with his life. Or so he thought.

On the day Booth assassinated Lincoln, April 14, 1865, Surratt was in Elmira, New York on assignment as a courier and spy for the Confederate Secret Service. When Surratt learned of the assassination, and saw his name in the newspapers as one of the alleged conspirators, he fled across the border to Canada where friends hid him for several months. In September 1865, he sailed to England and then made his way to Rome where he obtained a position as a Papal guard under the assumed name of John Watson. Discovered, he fled to Alexandria, Egypt where he was finally arrested and brought back to America, arriving on February 19, 1867, almost two years after the assassination.

Surratt was charged with the murder of President Lincoln and scheduled to stand trial in the criminal court of the District of Columbia. He would not be tried by a military commission as his mother had been. Dr. Mudd hoped that he would be called to testify at Surratt's trial, freeing him for a while at least from the misery of Fort Jefferson, but that was not to be.

Surratt's trial began on June 18, 1867 and ended with a hung jury on August 10, 1867, deadlocked at 8 to 4 for acquittal. Testimony that Surratt had been in Elmira, New York on the day of the assassination saved him. As John Surratt went free, Dr. Mudd, Sam Arnold, Edman Spangler, and Michael O'Laughlen remained prisoners at Fort Jefferson.

Fort Jefferson, Florida, March 5, 1867

My darling Frank:

Yours of February 12th reached me this morning, bringing me the desired news of all well and hearty. You gave expression to despondency, and asked for something cheering and consoling from me. How willing this would be accorded were it in my power, even the sacrifice of this miserable life, could it be of benefit to you and our little ones.

By referring me to the newspaper for information regarding my situation, you seem no better acquainted than myself with the difficulties in the way of my release. The altered relation which you apprehend will take place with the marriage of Jere, is very natural. It will be impossible for him to extend his former love, care and attention, and to this extent, my darling Frank, is the principal source of your gloom and anxiety. When I think of your dependent state, the trials, inconveniences, and sufferings you have to endure, my heart bleeds and my soul seems ready to leap from this tenement of clay, and rush to the aid and comfort of you and all; but, alas! how impotent are all my efforts, and how inescapable of affording you and our little ones assistance at no distant day, - a hope that would enable me to bear with more resignation the grievous trials to which I have been subjected. I am debarred from all friends and advisers, being yet under close guard, not allowed to hold conversation with any one outside my immediate roommates. How then is it possible for me to form any idea of the future, or to extend to you any hope of our speedy union? I have naturally looked to you and Jere for information and hope, but in vain, to receive anything satisfactory.

Jere has written but seldom, and when he did, I could arrive no nearer the truth than before.

We have received papers up to the 23rd instant. They make mention of the arrival of Surratt, and his being surrendered to the civil authorities. I am in hopes his trial will be speedy and impartial, and have the effect to clear away many of the mists that surround the tragic affair and lead to my early release from this place of exile and misery, and our once more happy union. To this end, my darling Frank, are all my fondest anticipations centered. Be patient, be prudent; in a word, be a good child, and let nothing occur that will tend to mar the pleasure and happiness of which we mutually dream, and God, upon whose justice and mercy we rely, will not permit a much longer delay. When you informed me in a previous letter that Jere and M.C. were to be married, I was truly in hopes I would be home in time to wish them in person a joyous union, and more happiness than has fallen to our lot. It now devolves upon you to perform this both pleasing and gloomy duty.

I wrote Mr. Stone on the 1st of December last and directed the letter to Washington, D.C., thinking he would take his seat in the recent Congress; it was returned to me yesterday. I suppose he takes his seat today by the new arrangement. Seek advice and counsel from him and Mr. Ewing and see whether something can't be effected through the Legislative Department, the Judicial and the Executive having failed. General Hill is of the opinion that, as soon as Surratt arrives, the Government would send for us; God grant his prediction may prove true.

Try and find out from Mr. Ridgely when he intends taking further action, and what hopes he has of success. There seems to be no mode of redress except through Congress, and they appear to have shut up the portals of felicity, both human and divine, and thrown away the key. Let me know at what time he thinks he will be able to succeed. You have made many guesses when I would be home, which has only the effect to increase my misery; but try once more and see how near you can approximate the truth, If it is one, two, three or four months, or the same number of years, give me the view of counsel. Cut out of the papers all the proceedings in the trial of Surratt as they appear, and send to me by mail.

Your devoted husband,

Sam

Three weeks after Dr. Mudd wrote this letter, the New York Times of April 16, 1867, noted:

It seems that John Surratt is treated very differently from his mother and those who were tried with her for complicity in the same crime. He has the full liberty of the corridors of the prison, is visited by his sister every day, and is subjected to no rigor not absolutely required for his safety. His mother was brought into Court daily handcuffed, and neither she nor any of those arrested at the same time were allowed were allowed any kind of freedom during their confinement. This difference in their treatment is doubtless due to the different tone of public sentiment which prevails now from that which prevailed then. While the crime is held in the same abhorrence, there is not the same feverish eagerness for vengeance which then prevailed. There is also a reaction in the public mind from the extreme rigor which then sanctioned, if it did not require, the trial of the assassins and their alleged accomplices, by a military commission instead of the civil tribunals of the land. Public opinion would not now tolerate the trial of Surratt by martial law. He will have, what was denied his mother, the full benefit of all the provisions which the common law makes for the rights of persons accused even of the slightest crime.

04-16-1867: Dr. Mudd's Letter to Tom Dyer

Source: Mudd, Nettie, *The Life of Dr. Samuel A. Mudd*, 1906. Fourth Edition, Page 233.

Tom Dyer is one of Mrs. Mudd's two brothers. Raised on the Dyer farm near the Mudds, he crossed the Potomac and enlisted as a Private in the Confederate Army on September 7, 1863 at Orange, Virginia. When General Robert E. Lee surrendered on April 9, 1865, Tom Dyer, like thousands of other Confederate soldiers, considered the war over and made his way back home. He was captured[95] in Bryantown on April 25, 1865, just four days after his sister's husband, Dr. Sam Mudd, was arrested in connection with the Lincoln assassination. Tom was released on June 21, 1865, and went to live with his brother Jere Dyer in Baltimore. In a letter Dr. Mudd wrote to Jere Dyer on October 5, 1865, he said "I am sorry Tom is going to leave so early. I am under the greatest obligations to him for interest and kindness manifested." Tom Dyer then moved to New Orleans, from where he sent Dr. Mudd moral support, clothes, food, and money while he was in prison. Dyer worked as a New Orleans travel agent with the firm of Yale & Bowling.[96]

The following letter was carried to Tom Dyer by a former Confederate soldier who had been serving time at Fort Jefferson for shooting a Negro prisoner. Dr. Mudd's cavalier dismissal of the shooting as something the Union government should not be concerned with, shows that he still had not shed the instincts of a former slave master.

Fort Jefferson, Florida, April 16, 1867

My dear Tom:

A favorable opportunity presenting, I avail myself to let you hear more directly from me. I have written you on several occasions, but have never received a reply in acknowledgment, consequently fear you do not get them.

Mr. Waters has kindly consented to take this to you in person and present my best wishes for you and all our kind relatives. Waters has just been released, having been sent here for shooting a negro prisoner, in discharge of his duty while in the Confederate service, and for which the Federal authorities had no right to take cognizance. His case though is only one of the many thousand unlawful acts which they have committed, and still continue, upon a brave and defenseless people. You see, notwithstanding the disclosures made by Butler in Congress a few days ago, and the charge made by Frank Blair of a similar nature, no investigation is made or permitted. My sympathies increase rather than diminish when I consider the unjust, tyrannical, humiliating exertions and measures demanded of a defenseless people. A day of reckoning surely will come, but I fear too late for the present generation to bear witness of an offended God and justice.

---

[95] Civil War Prisoner of War Records. Digital image, ancestry.com. Selected Records of the War Department Relating to Confederate Prisoners of War, 1861-1865; (National Archives Microfilm Publication M598_110); War Department Collection of Confederate Records, Record Group 109; National Archives, Washington, D.C.

[96] New Orleans, Louisiana Directories, 1890-1891. Ancestry.com.

The last letter received from Frank was dated March 19th. At that time they were all well. Surratt's trial was expected to come off in the present month, and it was believed we would be sent for by the government, to be tried again in conjunction. We are here yet, and have very little hope of this small boon being offered us. The cause of the government is too weak to expect to gain any advantage, therefore we expect to remain here so long as the government is in the hands of its present occupants. I send you a verbal message by the bearer. If you can, prudently, let me hear from you in regard.

Colonel St. Ledger Grenfel is kept in close confinement under guard. A few days ago, being sick, he applied to the doctor of the Post for medical attention, which he was refused, and he was ordered to work. Feeling himself unable to move about, he refused. He was then ordered to carry a ball until further orders, which he likewise refused. He was then tied up for half a day, and still refusing, he was taken to one of the wharves, thrown overboard with a rope attached, and ducked; being able to keep himself above water, a fifty pound weight was attached to his feet. Grenfel is an old man, about sixty. He has never refused to do work which he was able to perform, but they demanded more than he felt able, and he wisely refused. They could not conquer him, and he is doing now that which he never objected doing.

Remember me to all, and believe me most truly yours,

Sam

09-04-1867: Letter from Fort Jefferson Surgeon Major J. Sim Smith

Source: Record Group 94. Records of the Adjutant General's Office, 1780's - 1917, Medical Records: 1814-1919. Reports on Diseases and Individual Cases, 1841-93, Papers Relating to Cholera, Smallpox, & Yellow Fever Epidemics, 1849-1893. U.S. National Archives, Washington, D.C.

The day after he wrote the letter below, Dr. J. Sim Smith, Fort Jefferson's physician, was stricken with yellow fever and died on September 7th. The Commanding Officer, Major Val Stone, placed Dr. Mudd in charge of the fort's hospital until Dr. Daniel Whitehurst arrived from Key West to take charge. Sixty year-old Whitehurst had worked as the fort's doctor some years earlier. Mudd and Whitehurst worked side by side until the epidemic was over. A new Army doctor then arrived to relieve them.

Fort Jefferson
Sept 4th 1867

Genl,

Since my last report up to the present about twenty five more cases have occurred - of these, two have died making three deaths in all. Among those taken since my last report is Lt. Paul Roemer, Commanding Co. K and Acting Sr Asst & C.S. He was taken during the night of the 30th but did not notify or send for me until between three and four o'clock in the morning. He was very ill and is still quite so but improving I think.

The day after my last report to you the wind died out and since that time until yesterday we had little or no breeze and the average temperature has been a little more than eighty nine (89°) degrees. The result of this condition was very manifest yesterday in the fact that six cases recurred with an aggravation of all the symptoms. But during the day a strong breeze from the north east sprang up and has been blowing with occasional squalls ever since and today or rather since last evening no additional cases have occurred. I have established a Quarantine Hospital upon Sand Key consisting of two hospital tents, two wall tents and a temporary frame building thirty five by twelve feet. This last is the remains of the Hospital originally on the Key, built there during the war at a cost of fourth thousand dollars and complete I understand in all its appointments. This when I arrived at the Post had been torn down and the lumber used to build a theatre at the fort. Sand Key is a little island about an acre in extent a mile and a half North East of this Post.

There are now fourteen cases of yellow fever in Hospital about half of whom are convalescent. This morning by my advices the Commanding Officer detached Co. L and ordered it into encampment upon Bird Key which is a mile and a half to the South West of the Fort and if the other Keys were approached in rough weather I would advise him to detach another company.

The casemates in which three of the Companies are quartered are quite damp but airy and cool. A curious fact connected with the appearance of the disease at this place is that the only case last year at the Post occurred in the person of a Private of M Company who died but so far this year not a single case has occurred in that Company but has been confined to of K, I, and L. My hospital at Sand Key is under the charge of Acting Steward James T. Moses, Prvt. Co. L 5th Arty, who has proved so far a valuable and efficient man but if the number of cases should increase I shall send there Hospital Steward W.W. Wathes U.S.A. on duty at this Post - whose conduct during the epidemic is worthy of the highest commendation.

In the three cases in which death has occurred a very distressing hiccough has appeared about twelve hours preceding death. I would again call attention to the very unsatisfactory manner that this Post is supplied with commissary stores and must protest against it in the most earnest manner. Our supplies are received by a steamer which arrives at this point once a month and the supplies she brings are limited in quantity and indifferent in quality. Our supplies should be derived direct from the Northern markets with which we have direct communication every ten days. In this way our stores would reach us in a direct manner of good quality and in such quantities as are needed. Now as the perishable articles are first shipped from the North to New Orleans and thence back to this place, the loss is I should judge at least one third especially in the articles of flour. In point of economy of transportation I am quite sure that the expenses of transporting commissary stores from New York or Baltimore to Key West would not be as great as sending them by a special steamer from New Orleans.

I am Sir
Very Respectfully
Your Obdt Svt
J. Sim Smith
Asst Surg & Brvt Maj USA

J.J. Milhau USA
Med. Dir. 3rd Mil. Dist.

09-13-1867: Dr. Mudd's Letter to Mrs. Mudd

Source: Mudd, Nettie, *The Life of Dr. Samuel A. Mudd*, 1906. Fourth Edition, Page 259.

Fort Jefferson, Florida, September 13, 1867

My darling Frank:

It is now nearly 11 o'clock at night, and though tired and worn from constant attention upon the sick and dying, having buried two today, I cannot refrain from letting you share the gloom which surrounds this seeming God-forsaken isle. Although three-fourths of the garrison have been removed, the epidemic seems to increase with unabated fury. The first three or four days of my attendance in the hospital we were not visited with a single death. Since then the number has largely increased. The most experienced nurses have been seized with the disease. It is impossible to obtain suitable nurses to bestow the attention required, and seven unfortunate beings have been ushered into eternity, without a kind word or ministering angel of religion. Our hospital being insufficient to hold the numbers, a second, then a third, and yesterday the fourth, were provided, and they are all filled. We have scarcely well ones enough to attend the sick and bury the dead. They are not suffered to grow cold before they are hurried off to the grave.

Doctor Whitehurst, who was expelled from the island in the beginning of the war, on account of the sympathies of his wife, is now an incessant laborer from Key West. He is quite an old man, but has endeared himself to all by his Christian, constant, and unremitting attention at all hours, even when duties seemed not to require. I remain up every night until eleven or twelve, and sometimes later. He is up the balance of the night, and there never was greater accord of medical opinion. He did not arrive here for several days after the duties of the physician of the Post had devolved upon me by the illness and lamented death of Dr. Smith, and I assure you I felt much gratified when my conduct had met with his approval, being almost without any experience in the treatment of the disease, and having nothing to govern me other than the symptoms which the dread malady presented. By this accident I am once more restored to liberty of the island at all hours, day or night. Every officer of the Post is down with the disease, and but one remains to perform all the duties. He is a newcomer from Baltimore, and recently married. His name is Lieutenant Gordon. Little or no guard duty is performed, and but little difficulty presented to those who might be disposed to escape. I have resigned myself to the fates, and shall no more act upon my own impulse. Not one of the prisoners has as yet died, and those that take the disease passed through it without any apparent suffering.

Mrs. Stone, the wife of the Commandant, is quite sick with the fever. She is a patient of Doctor Whitehurst. He manifests some anxiety in her regard, and I fear the disease will overcome her and she will be numbered among its victims. I am well acquainted with her. No deaths have occurred since yesterday morning. There are three very low, and their cases present a doubtful issue at this time. I am very well, and have no fears of the disease. My manner gives confidence to all around, and has a tendency to revive the flagging spirit. I am greatest in danger. I fear the boat may leave, so shall post right away.

Good-by.

Sam

12-03-1867: The Butler Commission

Source: Benjamin Butler Papers, Manuscript Division, Library of Congress, Washington, D.C.

In 1867 the U.S. House of Representatives established a special committee to investigate the Lincoln assassination. Chaired by Representative Benjamin F. Butler, the committee was largely controlled by Republicans who had become alienated from President Johnson because of his lenient treatment of the defeated South, including his large-scale pardons of Confederate officials. Butler was one of the most vigorous proponents of Johnson's impeachment during 1867. In November 1867, after the yellow fever epidemic had safely abated, the Butler Committee sent an investigator, William H. Gleason, to Fort Jefferson to interview Dr. Mudd, Spangler, and Arnold. O'Laughlen had died in the epidemic. Dr. Mudd, an avid follower of political events in Washington, was well aware of Butler's efforts to impeach President Johnson, the only person in the world who could free him from Fort Jefferson. Dr. Mudd was not about to do or say anything to alienate the President. He initially refused to give any statement at all to Gleason, but at the urging of the fort's commander, provided Gleason with the following short declaration:

Mr. Wm. H. Gleason

Sir, considering my present situation, I doubt the propriety of making a detailed statement, but in answer to your request and by the advice of Major Andrews, our kind commandant, I submit to the Committee whom you have the honor to represent the following brief declaration, which I believe covers every point of your enquiry, viz:

1st - I never heard at any time during the war or since a desire expressed favorable to the assassination of the President.

2nd - I never had the least knowledge or suspicion that the murder of the President was contemplated, by any individual or band of men previous to the commission of the horrid deed.

3rd - I was not acquainted with Mrs. Surratt, and to the best of my knowledge, never in her company.

4th - I knew Booth and John Surratt, but not intimately.

5th - I did not know either Arnold, O'Laughlen, or Spangler, Payne alias Powell, Herold, or Atzerodt, and never heard their names mentioned in any connection whatever, previous to the assassination.

Saml A. Mudd

Subscribed and sworn to before me this 3rd day of December AD 1867

W H Gleason
Notary Public

Arnold and Spangler also provided statements to Mr. Gleason, but neither the statements of the three men nor other inquiries made by the Committee shed any new light on the Lincoln assassination. The Committee ceased operation without taking any actions.

12-14-1867: Official Army Report of the 1867 Yellow Fever Epidemic

Source: Record Group 94. Records of the Adjutant General's Office, 1780's - 1917, Medical Records: 1814-1919. Reports on Diseases and Individual Cases, 1841-93, Papers Relating to Cholera, Smallpox, & Yellow Fever Epidemics, 1849-1893. Box 3 of 7. U.S. National Archives, Washington, D.C.

Report of a Board of Officers convened at Fort Jefferson Fla in pursuance of the following Order.

Head Quarters Fort Jefferson Fla
December 14th 1867

Special Order No. 233

A board of officers will meet on the 16th of December, or as soon thereafter as may be practicable to collect and report facts in relation to the epidemic of the year 1867, and to propose the proper means of avoiding any injury to the service by the appearance of disease in the Tortugas Islands, in future.

The Board will not be limited in the field of examination or recommendation, and will take the evidence wherever it may be necessary.

Detail for the Board

Bvt. Major A.H. Smith, Capt. and Asst. Surgeon 1st Lieut Paul Roemer 5th Artillery, Actg. Asst. Surgeon Edward Thomas U.S. Army

By Order of Major George P. Andrews
(syd) Paul Roemer 1st Lieut 5th Arty
Post Adjutant

The board met December 16th 1867 in pursuance of the above order, all the members being present, and proceeded to collate evidence from persons present during the epidemic; from the records of the Post and of the Hospital; by personal inspection of the fort and the vicinity; and, as the result of these investigations respectfully reports as follows: the subject of these investigations consists of an Epidemic of Yellow Fever which occurred at Fort Jefferson, Dry Tortugas, Fla, beginning on the 19th of August and ending on the 14th of November, 1867, furnishing 270 cases and occasioning 38 deaths.

Fort Jefferson is in Lat. 24° 38' N. and Long. 82° 53' W. It is constructed upon a coral island, 3 1/2 feet above the level of the sea. The island contains about seven acres, nearly the whole being occupied by the fort.

At the depth of two feet brackish water it is obtained. The only sources of procuring fresh water are the rainfall which averages 39.38 inches annually, and two condensers for evaporating sea water.

The present available surface of roofing would yield an average of 2,500,000 gallons. If the buildings now in process of construction were properly roofed the yield would be about an average of 3,500,000 gallons annually. There are ample cisterns. The condensers are capable of yielding about 6,000 gallons per day.

The facilities for supplying fresh meat to the troops are exceedingly defective. The cattle for beef are usually brought from the vicinity of Tampa, Fla, and are very inferior when purchased. They are then subjected to a passage of about seven days in the hold of a schooner. On arriving they are placed upon a small barrier island in the vicinity of the fort and fed upon dry forage to which they are wholly unaccustomed. By the time they are slaughtered, it is rarely that a full grown bullock will dress three hundred pounds. The supply of this meat wretched it as it is, often is deficient. When at the best, but three rations in 10 days to a man can be afforded, but it frequently happens that no fresh meat can be had for days at a time, on account of deficient transportation, and the difficulty of getting estimates approved in time to take advantage of the sailing of the chartered steamers. This is owing to the isolated position of the post and the infrequent and uncertain communication with the mainland.

The greater portion of the troops are quartered in the casemates which are very leaky and constantly damp. In that portion of the fort where the fever first appeared the walls are slimy and covered with a green mold. Notwithstanding these disadvantages the general health of the Post, in past years, has been remarkably good. From January 15th, 1866, to August 15th, 1867, the means ratio of sick per 1000 mean strength was 66.30. Among the prisoners during the same period the ratio was 70.10. The principal diseases have been intermittent and remittent fever and diarrhea. A considerable number of cases of "dengue" or "break bone fever" have occurred during the summers. Although but little actual sickness occurs, as a rule, yet the climate produces a remarkable deterioration of bodily strength. The Superintendant of the laborers in the Eng Dept states that it is customary in making up labor estimates to allow two men for the same amount of work as is performed by one man at the North; and that in practice these estimates always fall short, three men not accomplishing more work than one man is accustomed to perform in the northern States. A remarkable example of this effect of the climate occurred here a few days ago. A piano which was handled with ease by three men in New York required fourteen to carry it here, and they were obliged to put it down every few rods, and rest.

These being the general facts bearing upon the health of the garrison, the special circumstances which may have influenced the late epidemic, are the following:

Firstly and Chiefly - the prevalence of Yellow Fever in the West Indies, at Key West, and at numerous points along the Gulf Coast;

2nd The arrival in May and June of about 100 unacclimated recruits;

3rd An unusual fall of rain during the months of June, July, and August, amounting to 37.20 inches, within about two inches of the average fall for whole year;

4th A remarkably persistent wind from the S.E. commencing about the 20th of May and continuing almost without intermission until the 1st of September. This direction of the wind is very exceptional, it's course being generally from the N.E.;

5th The moat along two faces windward of the fort was in an unfinished condition, and had filled in to such an extent that the bottom was exposed at low tide. The stench at such times is represented as being very decided;

6th The connection of many of the privies with the sewers had become interrupted, and a great amount of filth had consequently accumulated in the vaults. Immediately preceding the outbreak of the fever an attempt was made to clean out these places, which attempt however was abandoned, as the resulting effluvia were so overpowering that the further prosecution of the work during the warm weather was deemed hazardous.

On the 19th of August the first case of Yellow Fever occurred. The patient was a member of Co K's 5th Arty then quartered in casemates on the south side of the fort overlooking the unfinished portion of the moat previously referred to. On the 20th the second case occurred, also from Co "K", while quartered in the same locality. The next three cases were also from this company. On the 25th the Schr. Matchless arrived from Tampa, having on board a case of Yellow Fever. This was the six case. The patients had all been removed to the Hospital on the east side of the fort, in the immediate vicinity of which Co "L" was quartered. On the 23rd Co "K" was removed into casemates on the east side of the fort adjoining Company "L". On the 25th the disease broke out in the latter Company. It next appeared among the servants in the officers quarters. Co "I" quartered in the barracks adjoining the Hospital was then attacked. Co "M" on the north side of the fort escaped for nearly three weeks, when on the 7th of September 30 cases occurred in the company.

In addition to the above there were 58 cases of relapse, making in all 270 cases.

On the fourth of September Co "L" was removed to Bird Key three quarters of a mile from the fort. After the removal none were attacked, except those whose duties called them to the Post.

On the 1st of September a Hospital was established on Sand Key, two miles from the fort. A small building capable of accommodating about ten patients was already on the island, having been erected some years before as a smallpox hospital. Three hospital tents were added. Twenty six patients were treated at this place, all of whom had taken the fever before they were sent from the fort. Seven died.

On the 5th of September Bvt. Major J. Sim Smith, Asst Surg., the Medical Officer of the post, was taken sick. He died on the 8th. During his illness Dr. Mudd, a prisoner, was placed in charge of the hospital by the Commanding Officer and rendered faithful and efficient service until the arrival of Dr. Whitehurst from Key West, September 7th.

On the 8th of September Co "K" was removed to Loggerhead Key and encamped. On the 21st Co "L" was for greater convenience transferred to the same place from Bird Key. But one case occurred at Loggerhead, while the disease continued to rage with unabated severity at the Fort. This encampment was continued until the close of the epidemic. The supply of provisions & water was derived from the Post.

The disease reached its height about the 20th of September, and gradually declined until about the last of October, the last case occurring the 14th of November.

The total number of cases of officers, soldiers, citizens, and prisoners, amounted to 270. The number of deaths was 38. The mortality among the recruits coming from the North who had been here but a few months previous to the outbreak of the fever, was in every instance very much greater than among those who has spent a winter here.

Of the 54 prisoners at the Post, 44 had been here upwards of a year. Of these one died or 3.33 percent. Of the other ten prisoners who had been here but a few months, one died making 10 percent.

Of the men detailed as cooks and nurses in the Hospital, not one escape disease: - four died.

The facts which have been presented to the Board lead them to concur in the following recommendations:

1st That unacclimated troops should never be sent to this Post except to arrive in the months of November, December, and January;

2nd That care should be taken to have always at least one company of thoroughly acclimated troops at the Post, to act as cooks and nurses, and to perform fatigue duty in the event of an epidemic of Yellow Fever;

3rd That the barracks be finished and the men removed from their present damp and unhealthy quarters in the casemates;

4th That the sea wall be completed as soon as possible and the moat dredged so that the bottom will not be exposed at low tide;

5th That the connecting sluices between the privies and the sewers be opened, and if necessary enlarged, and the outlets of the sewers be carried across the moat so they may discharge outside the sea wall and not as at present into the moat;

6th That the temporary wooden buildings in the interior of the fort be removed;

7th That the Post Hospital should not be erected on the site contemplated in the original plan; viz. within the Fort between the officers quarters and the barracks, but outside of, and to the leeward of the Fort, where there is a very favorable ground for that purpose. As proposed in the original plan the hospital, besides being in the closest proximity to the quarters of the officers and men, would be enclosed on three sides by lofty structures which would completely shut out a free circulation of air;

8th That a supply of ice sufficient to provide for its liberal use in case of sickness be furnished before the approach of summer. There is a well constructed ice house here capable of holding 200 tons;

9th That in the event of the reappearance of Yellow Fever in the vicinity the requisite means be on hand to construct summer quarters for the troops on one of the neighboring Keys;

10th That a small steamer should take the place of the schooners now in the employ of the Q.M.D. in order that prompt communication may be had with the mainland and the procuring of suitable supplies be facilitated;

11th That at least during the summer there be two Medical Officers at the Post, and two hospital stewards;

12th That the fact a grave cannot be dug to a greater depth than 1 1/2 or 2 feet without filling in with water renders a proper interment of the dead, in the ordinary manner, difficult if not impossible. It is therefore recommended that vaults be built above ground having separate cells, each of which should be large enough to contain one coffin. These cells can be hermetically sealed, and the remains of the dead, it is believed, be better preserved for removal afterwards by relatives or friends. We would also add in the recommendation that Loggerhead being the most desirable Key for the location of barracks should have erected upon it one of these vaults to contain not less than twenty separate cells, for the reception of the remains of those dying there, and Long Key 1/4 mile distant from the fort should have another to contain not less than thirty cells in which to deposit the dead from this place. The Commanding Officer states that these vaults can be easily and cheaply constructed.

In conclusion, we would say that of the origin of the disease that not much can be determined with certainty, but it appears, from all the evidence we have been able to collate, reasonable to believe that it originated here, - was caused by deficient and bad drainage, and the consequent accumulation of a great quantity of decomposed animal and vegetable matter, - was aggravated, in all probability, by damp & unhealthy quarters, and the unusually great amount of moisture in the months of June, July, and August, last.

The exemption of the troops at Loggerhead would seem to indicate that the poison was confined within the limits of the fort, and, at the same time, to throw some disproof upon the commonly advanced theory that this disease is wafted by the wind.

A.H. Smith
Capt & Asst. Surgeon, U.S.A.
Paul Roemer, 1st Lt. 5th U.S. Arty.
Edward Thomas, A.A.Surg. USA Recorder

12-25-1867: Dr. Mudd's Letter to Dr. Whitehurst Regarding Epidemic

Source: Weedon and Whitehurst Family Papers, Manuscripts Department, Southern Historical Collection, University of North Carolina, Microfilm call number 1-4485.

Dr. Mudd wrote this letter shortly after the end of the 1867 yellow fever epidemic at Fort Jefferson.

Fort Jefferson, Tortugas, Fla.
December 25th, 1867

Dr. Whitehurst
My Dear Friend,

I received yours of the 13th, but being again detailed in the Carpenter Shop & the speedy going out of the boats, I was unable to reply. It would be absurd in me doctor to attempt to instruct you as to the course of treatment etc. pursued - for the sound of suffering and affrighted humanity was no sooner heard, than the impulses of your own kind and generous nature led you to be one of us - & whose constant watchful attention day and night will be ever gratefully remembered by every resident of the Post during that gloomy period. I will state as near as I can the time I was placed in charge of the Hospital & leave you to report - feeling satisfied whatever remarks you may make in connection with the visitation of the fever here will meet with my earnest approval.

I was detailed in the Hospital about the fifth or sixth of September - not having kept a record, I can't state with certainty. There were in the hospital at the time about twenty cases - I attended Dr. Smith, his wife and Lt. Roemer until relieved by you. Not being connected with the health department at the commencement of the fatal malady I am not able to state the first case or the manner of its inception.

In regard to the nature of the disease I differ with the authors - I look upon it as eminently a Typhoid affection, & rather the Superlative of the latter - Yellow Fever might be considered to true Typhoid what the malignant or congestive chill is to Bilious Remittent or Intermittent.

Owing to the services rendered by me - the soldiers drew up a petition, which I believed was unanimously signed with a view to my release - anything that you can do to lessen the prejudice caused by an unlawful and slanderous court shall be kindly cherished and reciprocated by myself and distressed family.

Wishing you and your kind family a happy Christmas and New Year, I am very truly

Your friend, Samuel A. Mudd

P. S. Doctor Thomas gave me a short but flattering letter which I forwarded to my friends in Maryland to be made use of as they might deem most proper. The Convention of Physicians of Maryland has memorialized the President in my behalf - a Committee of five was appointed to wait upon the President to make known the sense of the Convention. Please excuse this hasty scrawl - I am sorry it's not in my power to give you a full report of all the cases - to do which, I would have to refer to the Hospital books not at my command. Hoping to hear from you soon. I am yours - Samuel A. Mudd

12-31-1867: Dr. Whitehurst's Letter to Dr. Crane

Source: Samuel A. Mudd Pardon File B-596, RG 204, U.S. National Archives, College Park, Md.

Dr. C.H. Crane
Asst. Surgeon General
U.S. Army
Washington

Sir.

I have the honor of acknowledging receipt of copy of a petition, signed by soldiers of the 5th U.S. Artillery at Fort Jefferson, Fl. in behalf of Dr. Mudd, a state prisoner thereat, and referred to me by order of the Surgeon General for remark incident thereto.

On the morning of 7th August last, at 2 o'clock, I was called on by 2nd Master Thorpe & Dr. Cornick, and was informed that there was much apprehension felt at Fort Jefferson, in consequence of fever existing there; and I was asked if I could not go down; to which I replied, if the situation of my sick of Engineer Hospital, as well as private patients, would admit of leaving that I would cheerfully do so.

At daylight I commenced visiting my patients, and received at the same time, a note from Major Stone, importuning me to come over, as Dr. Smith was extremely ill, and they were all in great affliction. An appeal of this character could not pass unheeded, and turning my sick over to the care of another, I left for Fort Jefferson, arriving there at 10 o'clock that night, and immediately visited Dr. Smith, whom I found in the wildest phrensy. As soon as Major Stone entered, he sprang at him, and demanded that he should be allowed to see his wife, then laying ill in the next room.

I had iced water poured over the head, and in a short time, he fell off into a gentle slumber - awakening at 12, with returning cerebral disturbance, and at 2 of the morning of the 8th I closed his eyes - dying without a struggle.

Dr. Mudd was and had been in attendance on Dr. Smith, as well as Mrs. Smith. Dr. Mudd, at 6 o'clock called on me, and remarked "that he had been doing medical service, from the emergency of events, and as I had come down, he would now retire." Favorably impressed with his services, I asked him to continue them, which he did, visiting the sick with me, taking down prescriptions, putting them up, and attending to the various duties which the increasing sick required at his hands.

The Hospital Steward, Wythe, was convalescing, with a sick wife and child, and altho' as efficient as he could be, under such circumstances, he had continued claims upon his attention, in supplying cooks and nurses; for those of one day were patients the next, and thus his duties were exacting in the extreme. Incidentally, I would remark that I found Grenfell a volunteer nurse with Dr. Smith; and after his death in the hospital; and I must say that his attention and kindness was most continuous - to many a sick soldier, their return to health was the result I have no doubt of his continued devotion.

On my arrival, I found a hospital at Sand Key, and that the island was used as a burial place of the dead. The island was small, and had been used during the war for a similar purpose, leaving really but little room for new interments. The hospital tents were located over, and surrounded by graves, and the small wood building, tho' not so much, was still subject to the same objections. As the communication which I made daily with the island was liable to interruption, and as the sick continued to improve, I thought it best to discontinue the use of the island for that purpose and on the 15th Sept. it was abandoned. From the first development of fever (Aug 18th) there were 27 cases treated, and 6 deaths on Sand Key. In removing the convalescents, and ceasing to make a further use of Sand Key, the most important consideration was that the weather was boisterous, and a hurricane might occur at any moment, a contingency which would have been fatal to all the occupants thereon.

The companies at Sand Key were removed to Loggerhead, and the depressing influences of burials was thus removed from among the soldiers stationed there.

Major Stone and Lieuts Orr & Gordon frequently spoke to me in relation to Dr. Mudd, and they expressed themselves, warmly commendations in his favor, as well also in favor of Grenfell, and that they desired reporting to the Government their excellent conduct, and asking its benignant recognition in their behalf.

These gentlemen were all victims of the disease and it seems but just to their memories that opinions so formed and expressed should be made a matter of record.

I believe that these remarks will explain all sought for by the Surgeon General in relation to Dr. Mudd; and in conclusion, I feel that I should be unfaithful to a common humanity did I fail to recognize his useful, unwearying and continued service in a period of sorrow and deep distress.

I have the honor to be
Very Respectfully,

D.W. Whitehurst M.D.

02-29-1868: Major George P. Andrews Letter to Dr. Samuel A. Mudd

Source: Samuel A. Mudd Pardon File B-596, RG 204, U.S. National Archives, College Park, Md.

Fort Jefferson, Florida
February 29th 1868

Dr. Saml A. Mudd

Dear Sir,

As you wish me before leaving this post to state my knowledge of your conduct and services I most cheerfully do so.

I took command June 3rd, 1867. Everything went on as usual until about Sept 5, 1867 the yellow fever appeared in epidemic form and Dr. Smith USA, the only Post Surgeon was among the first taken sick. Then you took charge of the sick, made many valuable alterations in their treatment, and devoted all your time, energies, and professional skill to their benefit. The result was very favorable and was so recognized by all the survivors. Your changing the mode of treatment and "blanketing" patients so as to bring the period of fever under your full control, was regarded by the medical gentlemen with whom I conversed as a bold and valuable alteration, and seems to have produced the very best results. Your entire treatment of patients met with most friendly criticism from all medical gentlemen who were made acquainted with it, and with the very great difficulties under which you undertook the management of the sick.

While at Key West, commanding the Sub-District, a memorial signed by nearly every non-commissioned officer, and many other persons, recommending, that, for your valuable services, your sentence should be remitted, was sent to me. I examined it carefully, and finding that it was perfectly proper, I sent it forward to Col. Sprague, Comdg Dist. of Florida. I have heard no more of that paper, which I regret, as I hoped it might do you some good.

In my opinion your valuable services during the sickness should entitle you to very kind and generous consideration and I still hope that you may receive it. Your whole course, during my stay there, has met with kind feelings from every officer and soldier who has been placed in contact with you, and you merit, and may always depend upon, my most sincere good wishes and earnest exertions in your behalf.

Very Respectfully
Yr Obt Servt

Geo. P. Andrews
Major 5th Artillery
Comdg Post

04-13-1868: Lizzie Smith's Letter to President Johnson

Source: Samuel A. Mudd Pardon File B-596, RG 204, U.S. National Archives, College Park, Md.

Many letters were written to President Johnson asking him to pardon Dr. Mudd for his work during the 1867 yellow fever epidemic at Fort Jefferson. This letter was written by the widow of Dr. Joseph Sim Smith, Fort Jefferson's physician, and one of the first casualties of the epidemic. When Dr. Smith died, Dr. Mudd stepped in and began ministering to the sick and dying. Smith's wife and son also contracted yellow fever. His son died, but his wife survived to write this letter.

To His Excellency Andrew Johnson
President of the United States

Sir

I have the honor to address a few words to you in behalf of Dr. Mudd, prisoner at Ft. Jefferson, Dry Tortugas Florida.

Feelings of deep gratitude to him for his great kindness and attention to my late husband and only son, both of whom were victims to the yellow fever which raged so fearfully at the Fort last September, and also to me during my illness with the same disease prompts me to address a petition to you for his pardon and release.

He did not spare himself during the prevalence of the epidemic and absence of other medical aid, as was sometimes the case, especially during the illness of my husband and myself but was ready and anxious to render any assistance in his power to the sufferers. And to the last of my child's life, he was near him trying to relieve his dreadful suffering.

I shall ever remember his kindness in that trying time, and beg of you, if it is possible, to grant his pardon and allow him to return to his family in Maryland. He surely deserves some return for his services, and he has suffered enough in prison and hospital to atone for any wrong he may have done during the late war. Hoping this liberty may be pardoned, and the request granted,

I am,

Very Respectfully
Your Obedient Servant

Lizzie C. Smith
Widow of late Brvt. Major & Asst. Surgeon
Jos. Sim Smith U.S. Army

April 13th, 1868
159 Putnam Avenue
Brooklyn N.Y.

02-08-1869: Dr. Samuel A. Mudd's Pardon

Source: Samuel A. Mudd Pardon File B-596, RG 204, U.S. National Archives, College Park, Md.

This is the full text of Dr. Mudd's pardon:

Andrew Johnson
President of the United States of America.

To all to Whom these Presents shall come. Greeting:

Whereas, on the twenty-ninth day of June in the year 1865, Dr. Samuel A. Mudd was by the judgment of a Military Commission, convened and holden at the City of Washington, in part convicted, and in part acquitted, of the specification wherein he was inculpated in the charge for the trial of which said Military Commission was so convened and held, and which specification in its principal allegation against him, was and is in the words and figures following, to wit:

And in further prosecution of said conspiracy, the said Samuel A. Mudd did, at Washington City and within the Military Department and military lines aforesaid, on or before the sixth day of March, A. D. 1865 and on divers other days and times between that day and the twentieth day of April A. D. 1865, advise, encourage, receive, entertain, harbor and conceal, aid and assist, the said John Wilkes Booth, David E. Herold, Lewis Payne, John H. Surratt, Michael O'Laughlen, George A. Atzerodt, Mary E. Surratt and Samuel Arnold and their confederates, with knowledge of the murderous and traitorous conspiracy aforesaid, and with intent to aid, abet, and assist them in the execution thereof, and in escaping from justice after the murder of the said Abraham Lincoln, in pursuance of said conspiracy in manner aforesaid:

And whereas, upon a consideration and examination of the record of said trial and conviction and of the evidence given at said trial, I am satisfied that the guilt found by the said judgment against the Samuel A. Mudd was of receiving, entertaining, harboring, and concealing John Wilkes Booth and David E. Herold, with the intent to aid, abet and assist them in escaping from justice after the assassination of the late President of the United States, and not of any other or greater participation or complicity in said abominable crime;

And whereas, it is represented to me by respectable and intelligent members of the medical profession, that the circumstances of the surgical aid to the escaping assassin and the imputed concealment of his flight are deserving of a lenient construction as within the obligations of professional duty, and thus inadequate evidence of a guilty sympathy with the crime or the criminal;

And whereas, in other respects the evidence, imputing such guilty sympathy or purpose of aid in defeat of justice, leaves room for uncertainty as to the true measure and nature of the complicity of the said Samuel A. Mudd in the attempted escape of said assassins;

And whereas, the sentence imposed by said Military Commission upon the said Samuel A. Mudd was that he be imprisoned at hard labor for life, and the confinement under such sentence was directed to be had in the military prison at Dry Tortugas, Florida, and the said prisoner has been hitherto, and now is, suffering the infliction of such sentence;

And whereas, upon occasion of the prevalence of the Yellow Fever at that military station, and the death by that pestilence of the medical officer of the Post, the said Samuel A. Mudd devoted himself to the care and cure of the sick, and interposed his courage and his skill to protect the garrison, otherwise without adequate medical aid, from peril and alarm, and thus, as the officers and men unite in testifying, saved many valuable lives and earned the admiration and the gratitude of all who observed or experienced his generous and faithful service to humanity;

And whereas, the surviving families and friends of the Surgeon and other officers who were the victims of the pestilence earnestly present their dying testimony to the conspicuous merit of Dr. Mudd's conduct, and their own sense of obligation to him and Lieut. Zabriskie and two hundred and ninety nine noncommissioned officers and privates stationed at the Dry Tortugas have united in presenting to my attention the praiseworthy action of the prisoner and in petitioning for his pardon;

And whereas the Medical Society of Hartford County, Maryland, of which he was an associate, have petitioned for his pardon, and thirty nine members of the Senate and House of Representatives of the Congress of the United States have also requested his pardon;

Now, therefore be it known that I, Andrew Johnson, President of the United States of America, in consideration of the premises, divers other good and sufficient reasons me thereunto moving, do hereby grant to the said Dr. Samuel A. Mudd a full and unconditional pardon.

In testimony thereof, I have hereunto signed my name and caused the Seal of the United States to be affixed.

Done at the City of Washington, this Eighth day of February, A. D. (Seal) 1869, and the Independence of the United States the ninety third.

ANDREW JOHNSON, By the President

04-19-1869: Letter from Dr. Mudd to Dr. Whitehurst after Pardon

Source: Weedon and Whitehurst Family Papers, Manuscripts Department, Southern Historical Collection, University of North Carolina, Microfilm call number 1-4485.

Dr. Mudd wrote the following letter to Dr. Whitehurst shortly after arriving back home from Fort Jefferson. St. Catherine was the name/address sometimes used for Dr. Mudd's farm.

St. Catherine, Charles Co. Md.
April 19th 1869

My Dear Friend,

I arrived at my home on the 20th March. Since then I have had scarcely an uninterrupted moment - being constantly besieged by friends & strangers. Several reporters have visited me & notwithstanding my resolution & endeavors to be reticent they have gleaned sufficient to pen a long letter to "the Herald" filled with misstatements & etc. I felt much grieved when I saw one remark relative to the treatment of Fever etc. I am made to claim an overdue success. Let me assure you my dear friend that I have on no occasion sought distinction for the small part performed by myself during the prevalence of Fever at the post - nor have I spoken of the subject with a view to detract from the noble & skillful services of yourself, or attaching credit to myself. The private soldiers through kind feeling made my conduct whilst in the hospital the basis of a petition for my release; and anything they could say that would tend to soften public opinion I had no objection, believing the object desired thereby would be effected. Whatever fame has been attached to my name belongs entirely to you. My duties were simply as nurse & dispensor of medicines, if as such, was worthy of mention, the greater praise is due you since I could not have occupied the position without your appointment.

I mailed the letter given me for your son from Baltimore, not being able to call. I wrote to him a day or two after and notified him of the letter & the health of yourself & kind family - also extended invitation to visit myself or Brother in Law in Baltimore, whenever his vacation or studies permitted.

I met on my arrival in Baltimore, our Governor and many of the prominent men of the city & state. I had no chance to speak relative to your request. I have since talked with many friends on the subject & they tell me the President is selecting all his appointments from the most Ultra Radical ranks & any advocacy of your claims by them they feared would result in your injury. I shall visit Baltimore in the course of a week or two & will try to get some of our Fraternity to visit the Secretary personally in your behalf. Remember me kindly to Mrs. Whitehurst & little ones, Father Allard & asst, Mr. Mallory, Mr. Mareno & others - & accept for yourself my highest regards & friendship.

Very truly etc.
Samuel A. Mudd.

06-24-1869: Edman Spangler's Account of Life at Fort Jefferson

Source: New York World Newspaper, June 24, 1869.

Edman Spangler and Samuel Arnold were pardoned on March 1, 1869, released from confinement at Fort Jefferson on March 21, 1869, and arrived back in Baltimore on the steamship Cuba on April 6th. Two and a half months later, the following article, written by Spangler, appeared in the New York World newspaper.

Washington, June 23.

Edman Spangler, who was tried and sentenced by a military commission in May 1865 on a charge of being engaged in the plot to assassinate President Lincoln, and pardoned by President Johnson, has prepared the following statement, asserting his innocence of all knowledge of the crime, and detailing the cruelties practiced on the prisoners before and after conviction. Spangler was a scene-shifter at Ford's Theatre, and was on the stage when John Wilkes Booth shot Mr. Lincoln and jumped from the box. He also at times took care of Booth's horse. The evidence against him was of the flimsiest character, not being even circumstantial, for it did not appear in that trial, or in the subsequent civil trial of Surratt, that Spangler had any connection whatever with any of the other so-called conspirators. Most everybody believed him innocent then, and the Military Commission doubted his guilt by sentencing him to six years at the Dry Tortugas, and giving the others a life term. The Military Commission was organized to convict, and it convicted. Abundant testimony is now at hand to show the vast amount of perjury of that trial - perjury exacted by fear and dictated by malice. Spangler's allusion to the witness Weichmann being in the abduction plot is important. Weichmann's testimony, it will be remembered, hung Mrs. Surratt. The following is the statement sworn and subscribed to:

Statement of Edman Spangler

I have deemed it due to truth to prepare for publication the following statement - at a time when I hope the temper of the people will give me a patient hearing - of my arrest, trial, and imprisonment, for alleged complicity in the plot to assassinate the late President Lincoln. I have suffered much, but I solemnly assert now, as I always have since I was arraigned for trial at the Washington Arsenal, that I am entirely innocent of any fore or after knowledge of the crime which John Wilkes Booth committed - save what I knew in common with everybody after it took place.

I further solemnly assert that John Wilkes Booth, or any other person, never mentioned to me any plot, or intimation of a plot, for the abduction or assassination of President Lincoln; that I did not know when Booth leaped from the box to the stage at the theatre, that he had shot Mr. Lincoln; and that I did not, in any way, so help me God, assist in his escape; and I further declare that I am entirely innocent of any and all charges made against me in that connection. I never knew either Surratt, Payne, Atzerodt, Arnold, or Herold, or any of the so-called conspirators, nor did I ever see any of them until they appeared in custody. While imprisoned with Atzerodt, Payne, and Herold, and after their trial was over, I was allowed a few minutes exercise in the prison yard. I heard the three unite in asserting Mrs. Surratt's entire innocence, and acknowledge their own guilt, confining the crime, as they did, entirely to themselves, but implicating the witness, Weichmann, in knowledge of the original plot to abduct and with furnishing information from the Commissary of Prisoners Department, where Weichmann was a clerk.

I was arrested on the morning of the 16th of April, 1865, and with Ritterspaugh (also a scene shifter) taken to the police station on E street, between Ninth and Tenth. The sergeant, after questioning me closely, went with two policemen to search for Peanut John (the name of the boy who held Booth's horse the night before) and made to accompany us to the headquarters of the police on Tenth street, where John and I were locked up, and Ritterspaugh was released. After four hours confinement I was released, and brought before judges Olin and Bingham, and told them of Booth bringing his horse to the theatre on the afternoon of the 14th of April (1865). After this investigation I said: "What is to be done with me?" and they replied: "We know where to find you when you are wanted." and ordered my release. I returned to the theatre, where I remained until Saturday, when the soldiers took possession of it; but as the officer of the guard gave an attache and myself a pass to sleep there, we retired at 10 P.M., and at 1 A.M. a guard was placed over me, who remained until 9 A.M. Sunday morning, when I was released. I did not leave the theatre until Sunday evening, and on our return this attache (Carland by name) and myself were arrested by Detective Larner. Instead of taking us to the guard-house he said he would accompany me home to sleep there, but we all went to Police Headquarters on Tenth street, and when Carland asked if we were wanted, an officer sharply said "No." I returned to the theatre that night, and remained the next day till I went to dinner, corner Seventh and G streets. That over I remained a few minutes, when Ritterspaugh (who worked at the theatre with me) came, and meeting me, said: "I have given my evidence, and would like now to get some of the reward."

I walked out with Ritterspaugh for half an hour, and on returning to lie down left word that if anyone called for me to tell them that I was lying down. Two hours after I was called down stairs to see two gentlemen who had called for me. They said that I was wanted down street. On reaching the sidewalk they placed me in a hack and drove rapidly to Carroll Prison, where I was confined a week. Three days afterward, Detective, or Colonel, Baker came to my room, and questioned me about the sale of a horse and buggy (which belonged to Booth), and I told him all about it freely and readily. On the day following I was called into the office of the prison in order to be recognized by Sergeant Dye, who merely nodded his head as I entered and then he left. (Dye subsequently testified that he was sitting on the steps of the theatre just before Booth fired the shot, and to seeing mysterious persons about.)

I was allowed on the fourth day of my imprisonment to walk in the prison yard, but from that evening I was closely confined and guarded until the next Saturday at midnight when I was again taken to the office to see a detective, who said: "Come Spangler, I've some jewelry for you." He handcuffed me with my arms behind my back, and guarding me to a hack, I was placed in it and driven to the navy yard, where my legs were manacled and a pair of Lillie handcuffs placed on my wrists. I was put in a boat and rowed to a monitor, where I was taken on board and thrown into a small, dirty, room, between two water closets, and on a bed of filthy life preservers and blankets, with two soldiers guarding the door. I was kept there for three days. I had been thus confined three days on the vessel when Captain Monroe came to me and said: "Spangler, I've something that must be told, but you must not be frightened. We have orders from the Secretary of War, who must be obeyed, to put a bag on your head." Then two men came up and tied up my head so securely that I could not see daylight. I had plenty of food, but could not eat with my face so muffled up. True, there was a small hole in the bag near my mouth, but I could not reach that, as my hands were wedged down by the iron. At last, two kind-hearted soldiers took compassion on me, and while one watched the other fed me.

On Saturday night a man came to me and, after drawing the bag so tight as to nearly suffocate me, said to the guard, "Don't let him go to sleep, as we will carry him out to hang him directly." I heard them go up on the deck, where there was a great rattling of chains, and other noises; and while I was trying to imagine what was going on, and what they intended to do, I was dragged out by two men, who both pulled me at times in opposite directions. We, however, reached a boat, in which I was placed, and rowed a short distance, I could not say then where we stopped, for my face was still covered. After leaving the boat, I was forced to walk some distance, with the heavy irons still on my legs. I was then suddenly stopped, and made to ascend three or four flights of stairs; and as I stood at the top waiting, some one struck me a severe blow on the top of the head, which stunned and half threw me over, when I was pushed into a small room, where I remained in an unconscious condition for several hours. The next morning someone came with bread and coffee. I remained there several days, suffering torture from the bag or padded hood over my face. It was on Sunday when it was removed and I was shaven. It was then replaced.

Some hours after General Hartranft came and read to me several charges; that I was engaged in a plot to assassinate the President, and the day following I was carried into a military court and still hooded before all of its members. I remained but a short time, when I was returned to my cell for another night and day and then again presented in this court. Mr. Bingham, Assistant Judge-Advocate, read the charges against me, and asked if I had any objection to the court, and I replied "No," and made my plea of "not guilty." They then wished to know if I desired counsel, and, when I answered affirmatively, General Hunter, the president of the court, insisted that I should not be allowed counsel. He was, however, overruled, but it was several days before I was permitted legal aid, the court in the meantime taking evidence with closed doors. On every adjournment of the court, I was returned to my cell, and the closely-fitting hood placed over my head. This continued until June 10, 1865, when I was relieved from the torture of the bag, but my hands and limbs remained heavily manacled.

On one Sunday, while I was confined at this place (the Washington Arsenal), I was visited by a gentleman of middle stature, rather stout, with full beard, and gold-framed spectacles. He noticed my manacles and padded head. I afterwards learned that he was Mr. Stanton, the Secretary of War. It is proper to state that when the hood was placed on me, Captain Munroe said it was by order of the Secretary of War. My first thought was that I was to be hung without trial, and the hood was preparatory to that act.

The first time I ever saw Mrs. Surratt was in the Carroll Prison yard, on Capitol Hill. I did not see her again until we were taken into court the first day at the arsenal. My cell was on the same corridor with hers, and I had to pass it every time I was taken into court. I frequently looked into her cell, a small room about four feet wide by seven feet long. The only things in her cell were an old mattress laid on the bricks and an army blanket. I could see the irons on her feet, as she was generally lying on the mattress, and was the last one brought into court. She occupied a seat in court near the prison door. The seat was twelve inches high, and the chains between the irons on her feet were so short that she had to be assisted to her seat. She was so sick at one time that the court was compelled to adjourn.

On the 17th of July, about midnight, I was conveyed to a steamboat, and arrived the next day at Fortress Monroe, and was thence taken to the gunboat Florida. The irons on my arms were temporarily removed, but Captain Dutton, in charge of the guard, ordered heavy Lilly irons to be placed on me, when General Dodd, chief officer in charge, more humanely countermanded his order and had the irons again removed from my arms. I was placed for security in the lower hold of the vessel, and compelled to descend to it by a ladder. The rounds were far apart, and, as the irons on my feet were chained but a few inches apart, my legs were bruised and lacerated fearfully. The hold where I was confined was close and dirty, but after two or three days I was allowed on deck in the daytime, but was closely guarded. I was allowed to speak to no one of the crew. We arrived at Fort Jefferson, on the Dry Tortugas, and were handed over to Colonel Hamilton, commanding, who placed me until the next day in a casemate. The next day I was brought before Colonel H., who informed me that he had no more stringent orders concerning me than other prisoners confined there.

I managed to get along comfortably for a while, though to some of the prisoners the officers were very cruel. One man by the name of Dunn, while helping in unloading a government transport, got hold of some liquor and imbibed too freely, for which he was taken to the guard-house and tied up to the window-frame by his thumbs for two hours. General Hill then ordered him to be taken down and be made to carry a thirty-two pound ball, but as the hanging had deprived him of the use of his thumbs, he was unable to obey. The officers, however, put two twenty-four pound balls in a knapsack, and compelled him to carry them until the sack gave way from the weight of the iron. He was then tied up by the wrists and gagged in the mouth by the bayonet from 8 P.M. until the next morning. He was then taken down and thrown into the guard-house, but was so exhausted that he had to be removed to the hospital. It was decided to amputate three of his fingers, but this was reconsidered. He lost however, the use of his thumb and two fingers. This punishment was inflicted by Major McConnell, officer of the day, and was carried out by Sergeant Edward Donnelly.

Another poor prisoner named Brown, was once excused by the doctor from work on the plea of illness, but the Provost Marshal insisted and finding him too ill and lacking strength made him carry a thirty-two pound ball. He staggered under the weight and was compelled from weakness to put it down. He was then taken to the wharf and with his legs tied together and his hands tied behind him, a rope was placed around him and he was thrown into the water and then dragged out. This was done three or four times, he begging for mercy most piteously. He was finally jerked out of the water and ordered to return to his ordinary work. The poor wretch crept off apparently thankful for any escape from such torments. Captain Jos. Rittenhouse was officer of the day, and his orders were carried out by Corporal Spear.

During the latter part of last October I was placed in irons and compelled to work with an armed sentinel over me. I did not know the reason for this, for I was unconscious of having given offense, and had conformed to every regulation. I was then closely confined and allowed to communicate with no one for four months. The pretense for this, I afterwards learned, sprang from an attempt of Dr. Mudd to escape.

Colonel St. George Leger Grenfel, aged 65 years, was taken sick and went to the Doctor to get excused from work. The Doctor declined to excuse him. He then applied to the Provost-Marshal, who said that he could not excuse him if the Doctor couldn't. Grenfel then tried to work and couldn't. They then took him to the guard-house, tied him up for half a day, and then took him to the wharf, tied his hands behind him, tied his legs together, and put a rope around his waist. There were three officers, heavily armed, who drove spectators from the wharf; I could see and hear from my window. The Colonel asked them if they were going to throw him into the water, and they answered "Yes." He then jumped in, and because he could not sink, they drew him out and tied about fourth pounds of iron to his legs, and threw him into the water again, and after he had sunk twice they pulled him out again, and then compelled him to go to work. The officers who had him in hand were, Lieutenant Robinson, Lieutenant Pike, and Captain George W. Crabb, assisted by Sergeant Michael Gleason, and assistant storekeeper G.T. Jackson, who tied the iron on his legs. Captain Samuel Peebles tied up Grenfel for saying that "he was capable of doing anything." Colonel Grenfel was forced to scrub and do other menial work when he proved he was so ill as to have refused to eat his rations for a week. All of the officers hated Grenfel on account of a letter which appeared in a New York paper, which they said Grenfel wrote, about tying up the prisoner Dunn - which letter was truthful, as others and myself were witnesses to the details it related.

One very stormy night, Grenfel with four others, escaped in a small boat and was evidently drowned near the fort. His escape was discovered but the storm was so severe that it was deemed too dangerous to pursue them, although a steamer was at the wharf. Grenfel frequently declared his intention of running any risk to escape, rather than, to use his own words, "to be tortured to death at the fort." These are only two or three instances of the many acts of cruelty practiced at the fort. During my imprisonment at Fort Jefferson, I worked very hard at carpentering and wood ornamental work, making a great many fancy boxes, &c., out of the peculiar wood found on the adjacent islands; the greater portion of this work was made for officers. By my industry in that direction, I won some favor in their eyes. I was released in March of the present year by executive clemency.

(Signed) Edman Spangler

06-25-1873: Newspaper Article by Dr. Mudd on Epidemics & Infection

Source: Baltimore Sun, June 25, 1873

Dr. Mudd continued to study and write about yellow fever after he was released from Fort Jefferson. It was not an academic exercise. Yellow fever, cholera, typhoid fever, malaria, and similar diseases continued to plague the population during his lifetime. Almost every issue of the Baltimore Sun and other southern newspapers carried current stories about these diseases. Only a few days before Dr. Mudd's article appeared in the Baltimore Sun, the Sun printed a story about the steamship Liberty, the same ship which had carried Dr. Mudd home from Fort Jefferson in 1869. The Liberty was being held in quarantine in Baltimore harbor because passengers were sick with yellow fever.

Since scientists had not yet discovered the causes of these diseases, and therefore their effective treatment, there was, as Dr. Mudd says "a wonderful diversity of opinion" concerning their treatment. Dr. Mudd's article was only one of many contributed to the newspapers by concerned physicians and scientists on the cause and prevention of these diseases. It would be almost two decades after Dr. Mudd's death in 1883 that Dr. Walter Reed and his fellow researchers would show that yellow fever was transmitted by infected mosquitoes. After that discovery, yellow fever was able to be controlled by mosquito eradication programs. In 1937, Max Theiler discovered a yellow fever vaccine, for which he received the Nobel Prize.

Epidemics and Infection

A Distinctive Line of Difference Between Contagion and Infection Drawn, and the Means of Preventing Epidemics of Infection.

By Dr. Samuel A. Mudd.

Nature is made up of like causes, producing similar effects. The diseases known as contagious producing contagious of their kind, and the poison of infectious producing infectious of their kind. They are as distinct from each other in their pathological character as the different species and variety of animals, and bear no relation, except as to their medium, in evolving cause and extension. The human or animal system evolves the germ directly in contagions, and disease is communicable by contact with the disease. But in the case of infections, no germ is evolved from the disease, therefore no number of sick - not even ten thousand confined to one apartment - is sufficient directly to generate its poison and consequent extension. Owing to this fact the efforts of physicians have been vain to discover a method of inoculating typhoid fever, yellow fever, cholera, etc.

An example tending in proof of what I have alleged, is furnished by the fact that all physicians agree as to the contagiousness of small-pox and measles, when a wonderful diversity of opinion exists in regard to typhoid fever and yellow fever. This diversity is due in the first place to education and secondly, to treating these diseases of infection in different localities at the same time without an endeavor to separate the cause from the effect or considering the point of origin.

All medical writers, in speaking of infections, use the word infectious as applied to disease. Infectious is proper when applied to matter, but no greater mistake can be made when applied to the diseased body, for it implies that the disease is capable of generating its cause, which is as impossible as that a burn from a hot iron should produce the heated metal, or salvation produce the globule of mercury. There is then no such thing as an infectious disease, and isolation from one to ten thousand is its plainest proof. Infected disease seems to be most proper and expressive of the true pathological condition.

Infection spreads from bed to bed that have been for a length of time exposed to the action of human effluvia, and not from local miasma or from individual to individual, as, no doubt, a large majority of the public and profession suppose. The error regarding the origin of the diseases, particularly that of yellow fever, has led, within my own knowledge, to serious, fatal consequences, for had the very worthy surgeon of the post at the Dry Tortugas, in 1867, understood whence the poison arose, and the matter of its augmentation, we would have been spared the spread of the fever and the sacrifice of his own and many other valuable lives by removing at once from the fort the company of soldiers and all its property, in which the disease first made its appearance, and pointed out the presence of the poison. The surgeon caused the company to be removed from the quarters where the disease began, believing that it was caused by emanations from the unfinished moat in front, and ordered the portholes to be closed to prevent the admission of the supposed deadly miasma within the fort. The company, however, was quartered, with all its property, bedding, blankets, etc., in the southeasterly portion of the fort, which, instead of cutting short the fever, caused its more rapid spread through the garrison and prisoners by the prevailing southeast wind.

We learn from this that had the surgeon removed only the men, and left the property behind, the disease would have been checked, for then only those who went in these quarters would be liable to attack, and the disease, instead of manifesting an epidemic form, would appear accidental or sporadic. And had he removed all the beds and property of the company from the fort, and had the quarters swept and washed, and clean beds and bedding supplied, no more cases would have resulted.

A knowledge of the nature of infection is invaluable to every government - general or municipal - to prisons or boarding schools, and particularly to every master of a ship, for whenever the bedding and apartments are kept clean by soap and water, and the regulation enforced of not admitting anything aboard ship in the shape of clothing but what has been recently washed and thoroughly dried, no fear can be entertained of the breaking out of cholera, yellow fever, typhoid or typhus fever etc., on a reasonable voyage. The master could, under these circumstances, convert his ship into a cholera or yellow fever hospital, transport the sick across the ocean, enter port without quarantine, and establish his sick in clean, comfortable quarters in the midst of a populous city without endangering the safety of his crew or the inhabitants of the city.

To give an illustration of infection, when an article of clothing is immersed in a solution of any kind the nature of the solution is imparted, as plainly perceived by our senses in the very colors of silks, cloths, etc., some answering well the effect of contagion - being indelible, and others answering to infection, fading - rendering immunity only for short time. So the human system, when under the influence or exposed to the fumes of mercury, arsenic, lead, etc., the peculiar character of the agent is plainly manifest to the senses. In is then only when the cause is hidden that uncertainty rules. But as the globule or crystal of mercury, arsenic, lead, etc., is not developed by their action upon the system, no fear is entertained by nurses or attendants of contracting the malady. Why, then, cannot we arrive at the nature of an agent, when its effects are similar, though its chemical formula be unknown.

Undoubted proofs from experience and observation have taught me that the germ of all spreading infections common to mankind resides in human effluvia, and man is the victim of his own neglect. When once this germ is generated it reacts or ferments with all such matter whenever it comes in contact, under favorable conditions of moisture and temperature. This is not more improbable than the germ that is contained in the egg of the chicken, turkey, hawk, crow, buzzard, etc., and generated by a longer or shorter duration of a certain continuous heat. The contents of all these eggs are very similar or the same in appearance. Then there is another genus that are hatched entirely through solar and atmospheric influence, namely turtles, snakes, lizard, frogs and insects. So we perceive, after all, that the generation of the germ depends entirely upon the quality of the heat, for we know full well that the eggs of the turkey, chicken, etc., will not hatch in the sand with the alternations of heat and cold, caused through the operation of day and night; and vice versa, the turtle, snake, etc., under the continuous heat of the chicken or turkey. Now for the practical results. Let us destroy the egg and we destroy the germ. Destroy the effluvia and we prevent the generation of the germs or poison which occasions the disease. An epidemic of infection, under these circumstances, can no more arise and extend than a fire burn without fuel. Bear in mind that contagion is the parent of the disease, whereas poison only is the result of a disease of infection, as fire is the parent of a burn, mercury the parent of salivation, and strychnia the parent of convulsions and death.

The yellow fever is eminently a disease of infection, and belongs to the classes of diseases known as typhus and typhoid fevers, and is generated from human effluvia under the peculiar atmosphere of ships in certain latitudes instead of being the product of miasma or emanations from swamps, marshes and vegetable decomposition. The poison that gives rise to the intermittent and remittent fevers, (chills and fever and billious fever) agreeable to all the evidence we have concerning it, does not act as a ferment upon human effluvia. We cannot, therefore, transport its poison. But, on the contrary, we can transport the poison of yellow fever thousands of miles, and under favorable atmosphere and temperature light up a similar epidemic. A wonderful and important difference!

02-25-1878: Bill for the Relief of Dr. Samuel A. Mudd

Source: H.R. 3418, 45th Congress, 2nd Session, U.S. House of Representatives, Washington, D.C.

The five year period from 1873 to 1878 encompassed the third longest economic depression in U.S. history. Bankruptcies and insolvencies were widespread. In rural areas, the downward pressure on prices reduced farm income and created great hardship. Dr. Mudd and his family were not exempt from this hardship.

Congressman Eli Jones Henkle represented the 5th District of Maryland where Dr. Mudd lived. Following the 1867 yellow fever epidemic at Fort Jefferson, the Government paid Dr. Daniel Whitehurst, the civilian doctor whom Dr. Mudd worked under during the epidemic, the sum of $300 for services rendered during the epidemic. $300 at that time is equivalent to $6,000 today. In this Bill, Dr. Mudd is requesting compensation of $3,000, equivalent to $60,000 today, or ten times what Dr. Whitehurst was paid. The Bill died in committee.

H.R. 3418

In the House of Representatives
February 25, 1878

Read twice, referred to the Committee of Claims, and ordered to be printed.

Mr. Henkle, on leave, introduced the following bill:

A Bill

For the relief of Doctor Samuel A. Mudd, of Maryland.

Be it enacted by the Senate and House of Representatives of the United States of America in Congress assembled, that the Secretary of the Treasury be, and is hereby, authorized and directed to pay to Doctor Samuel A. Mudd, of Maryland, or his legally authorized attorney, the sum of three thousand dollars for services rendered to the United States as surgeon and assistant surgeon during the epidemic of yellow fever at Fort Jefferson, Florida, in the year eighteen hundred and sixty-seven.

03-10-1883: Dr. Samuel Mudd's Guide to Health

Source: Baltimore Sun, March 10, 1883

This article was published a month after Dr. Mudd died. The Guide to Health treatise discussed in the article was never published and the original manuscript is now lost. Dr. Mudd's views on the causes and treatment of yellow fever and other diseases were consistent with the medical knowledge of his time, but as we know now, were largely incorrect. It would be almost two decades after Dr. Mudd died that Dr. Walter Reed and his fellow researchers would show that yellow fever was transmitted by infected mosquitoes.

It should be noted that his discussion of the yellow fever epidemic at Fort Jefferson omits any mention of Dr. Daniel Whitehurst, the civilian Key West doctor who voluntarily went to Fort Jefferson at the start of the epidemic and who worked with and supervised Dr. Mudd during the entire course of the epidemic. In a letter Dr. Mudd wrote to Dr. Whitehurst shortly after Dr. Mudd returned home from prison in 1869, he said:

> Let me assure you my dear friend that I have on no occasion sought distinction for the small part performed by myself during the prevalence of Fever at the post - nor have I spoken of the subject with a view to detract from the noble & skillful services of yourself, or attaching credit to myself. The private soldiers through kind feeling made my conduct whilst in the hospital the basis of a petition for my release; and anything they could say that would tend to soften public opinion I had no objection, believing the object desired thereby would be effected. Whatever fame has been attached to my name belongs entirely to you. My duties were simply as nurse & dispensor of medicines, if as such, was worthy of mention, the greater praise is due you since I could not have occupied the position without your appointment.

The complete text of the Baltimore Sun article follows:

> Dr. Samuel A. Mudd, of Bryantown, Charles County, Md., completed a short time before his death a treatise upon epidemic and endemic diseases, intended for the use of families and legislative bodies, State and municipal, entitled "The Family's and the Nation's Guide to Health." The manuscript of the work is still in the hands of the widow of Dr. Mudd, and to her THE SUN is indebted for the privilege of its perusal and the publication of the following extract of its interesting contents. including his experience with the fearful yellow-fever epidemic that ravaged the Dry Tortugas in 1867, during the period of his unjust confinement there, from July 1865 to April 1869. Dr. Mudd's familiarity with the contagious diseases and the diseases of infection common in the United States extended over twenty years, and entitles him to speak with considerable authority upon the subject of which he treats. Writing for the public, he has freed his language from technical terms, intelligible only to physicians, and produced a brief work which merits publication, and is sure, if published, to prove to the general reader an agreeable and instructive work, although in some respects its conclusions may be disputed by the profession.

> It gives what has been much wanted, an analysis which enables anyone to draw a distinct line between "the two forms of disease propagation known as epidemic contagion and epidemic infection" - terms which, like the things they designate, are generally confounded with each other.

> The terms endemic and epidemic, so often used indiscriminately, are also placed in distinct contrast. As the intelligent application of sanitary precautions must depend upon a clear apprehension of the difference between germ-bearing diseases and non-germ-bearing diseases,

and the modes in which they are originated, it may be fairly said that Dr. Mudd's work in elucidating these matters is of national interest, whether tending to controversy or not.

City councils and State Legislatures will find his suggestions, and particularly the body of quarantine regulations which he draws up, valuable for guidance or suggestion in legislation. In a private letter defining the scope and and object of his little book, Dr. Mudd says in this regard: "I have framed a quarantine law, the simple and the inexpensive provisions of which, if carried out, make it impossible for yellow fever, Asiatic cholera, typhus or any other of the epidemic diseases of contagion or infection to be introduced into any of our ports, or for them to occur even in climates where they are known to be indigenous." Farmers engaged in stock-raising and those interested in their transportation by rail or ship will find presented to them "the means by which they can distinguish a disease of contagion from one of infection, and the proper mode in which to prevent, with little cost and labor, the transmission of the malady from one animal to another."

Theory of Disease Germs

Physicians will note that in view of the fact that exhaustive experiments undertaken to prove the existence of disease-producing germs in the blood or viscera of persons suffering from yellow fever have failed to disclose the existence of germs of any kind, and in consonance with the large body of facts within his own experience, Dr. Mudd originates a theory of his own, novel to the profession and suggestive of experiment by microscopists. This theory, which underlies most that the doctor has to say in regard to diseases of infection, is briefly this - that yellow fever and certain other diseases result from the development of disease germs, not in the person, but in the concrete effluvia of the body such as perspiration and other exhalations of the skin, &c., which have for some time defiled the clothing, bedding and hair. Under suitable conditions of temperature and moisture, found in hot climates, the fermentation set up by these germs in the filth of clothing &c., renders it a poisonous substance, and this poison, being taken into the body, deranges its functions. But the germ itself finds no lodgment or development in the body, as in certain other diseases it undoubtedly does. It results that yellow fever cases may be isolated, provided only that the patient be well washed from head to toe and his clothing be scoured and steamed. In an environment of clean clothes yellow fever, typhus, Asiatic cholera and other diseases of that type are not infectious. Cleanliness may, therefore, with regard to them, be said to constitute the whole doctrine of health for persons brought into contact with the sick. "Diseases of infection of the epidemic form are caused by the action of specific germ upon human effluvia and such diseases do not propagate themselves, being effects incapable of self-propagation."

Malarial Fevers

Dr. Mudd thinks malaria not due to germs: "Miasmata, arising from the swamps, &c., are in themselves innocuous. The fevers known as malarial fevers are developed only when the miasma (which I consider to be only moisture) in contact with volatile human effluvia under favorable conditions of heat and moisture, produces an action similar to fermentation, and from this, and this alone, the so-called malarial disease results."

Possibly there is a specific germ in the exhalations of swamps &c., but it finds its proper habitat and development in the filth of soiled clothes and bedding, not in the person. Hence malarial fever is not contagious, and is escaped by persons who know how to exclude the cold, damp air of the morning, sleeping within doors, and using clean linen. Fires morning and evening to warm the air of apartments and prevent chilling and the condensation of the so-called miasmatic poison (in reality the moisture) of the air, are important auxiliaries to health. The view that the free air over any infected area becomes poisoned, whether by typhoid fever, yellow fever, or malarial exhalations must be discarded in toto, since, if correct, it would necessarily follow that the mortuary report of any community after a season favorable to disease should embrace very nearly its whole population.

The supposed extensive vitiation of the atmosphere, if it occurs at all, has been taking place since the beginning of the world, and by this time should have made a breath of air as fatal as the rankest gas of the laboratory. The fact is that an exhalation from any given locality is, with the motion of the winds, speedily rendered innocuous by dilution and destroyed by contact with sunlight, seas and mountains. As long, however, as the opinion prevails that endemic and epidemic diseases of infection arise from a tainted atmosphere, no curative or preventive measures will be adopted, it being obviously impossible to combat a universal poison. There is no rational ground for sanitary precaution, and no proper measures can be fixed upon, until it is understood that epidemic and endemic diseases originate for the most part indoors, by the condensation and decomposition of the volatile emanations of animal and vegetable substances in conjunction with human effluvia which has found lodgment in clothing and bedding.

Sewer gas is hurtful or innocent according as it finds in inhabited apartments filth of person or clothing, rendered by some lapse of time suitable for the development of germs to which its virulence is attributed. Moisture, or dampness combined with sudden cold, is an important requisite to the condensation of the substances floating in the air, which produces disease. When the air is dry, and the temperature is equable between day and night, condensation is slow and scarcely perceptible. Such conditions obtain during parts of the year; those seasons are healthy. Localities also which are so favored by circumstances as to be dry and equable in temperature are exempt from chills and remittent fevers, although places not far distant, less favorably situated, are famous for their unhealthiness.

A Terrible Experience

Dr. Mudd thus graphically depicts his own terrible experience:

In July 1865 I was sent to the military prison at Fort Jefferson, better known as the Dry Tortugas, an island of coral formation in the Gulf of Mexico. Tried by a court-martial, an unlawful tribunal constituted for the purpose of conviction - the same that hanged an innocent woman - I was convicted in the testimony of paid and perjured witnesses of a crime the conception of which I never harbored or entertained. By such a tribunal, I was pronounced guilty of complicity in the assassination of President Lincoln, when all the world knew - and the members of that iniquitous and law-defying military commission knew it as well - that my only offense consisted of setting the leg of a man whom I did not at the time know to be a fugitive from justice, and with whose insane act I had not the slightest sympathy. I had done merely an act of charity, from which no true physician would shrink, no matter what the consequences might be. For this I was banished, under life sentence, from my wife and children, from home, friends and society; immured in the gloomiest and distant prison in the United States. For this I was bound in chains like some savage brute, denied for a long time healthy sustenance, and forced at the point of the bayonet to perform menial and offensive offices, which I will forbear mentioning. The iron entered my soul. Even now, though on restoration to my family and social circle I am brought back to life and to some portion of all that was lost by four years of banishment, yet the recollection of those years of mental and physical suffering, and the nature of what I endured on that barren coral reef,

179

accursed and plague-smitten, rises before me at times like a horror of great darkness, and will never be effaced as long as memory remains.

Fort Jefferson is an irregular hexagon, containing within its walls about three acres - not of ordinary ground, but coral sand. It is distant from the Florida coast about ninety miles, and nearly as far from Key West and Cuba. The temperature is high there all the year round, advancing in the summer to an average a little above 90 degrees Farenheit in the shade, and in the winter rarely falling below 65 degrees. The surrounding water of the gulf exercises an equalizing influence upon the atmosphere. The drinking water in use is made from the sea water by distillation, which separates the salt and other impurities. Cistern water is more pleasant to drink, but the water so obtained is, I believe, healthy enough in that climate. The fort is surrounded by a moat, which in its turn is inclosed by a circular stone wall, called 'the breakwater.' The water in this moat is - or was in 1867 - about six feet deep. A portion of the moat, however, at that time remained to be dug out. When, on the 18th of August, 1867, the yellow fever broke out, there were stationed at the Dry Tortugas four companies of the Fifth United States Artillery, a few civilians employed in the Engineering Department, and about 200 'guard' prisoners. These last consisted of deserters from the Federal army, 'bounty-jumpers' &c. The roll of 'State prisoners' consisted of Messers. Arnold, Spangler, O'Loughlin and myself. There were also some Confederate prisoners, prominent among whom was Col. St. Leger Grenfel, sent there for life by sentence of a military tribunal for alleged complicity in the abortive attempt to release the Camp Douglas prisoners. It is generally supposed that he was drowned in the attempt to escape from the island.

Fighting the Fever

The first symptom of the appearance of the yellow fever was observed, as already stated, on the 18th of August. From that time until the 4th of September, when I took charge of the hospital, it was of a very malignant character and most frequently fatal. It was supposed, and I consider it highly probable, that the germ of the disease was brought in a boat that landed at the island, bringing government supplies. A member of Company K, engaged in unloading this vessel, was the first to take the disease. He died within a few days. Seventeen days after the occurrence of the first case of the epidemic Dr. J.S. Smith, the regular Army surgeon, a gentleman beloved and respected by the garrison, especially by the soldiers, on account of his having them relieved from unnecessary guard and other duty, was attacked with the yellow fever and died soon after, as did also his infant son. Dr. Smith was not under my care until a short time before his death, when, under the hallucination of the disease, he persistently refused to take any medicine or submit to any treatment. By the illness of Dr. Smith, the garrison was left without a government physician. I was the only person on the island possessed of any knowledge of medicine.

For a time I hesitated what I should do in the novel and distressing situation in which we were placed. The sense of deep injury done me by the government and the voice of humanity were tugging at my will in opposing directions. My fellow 'State' prisoners urged me to have nothing to say or do in the matter, one of them remarking: "The yellow fever is a square deal in which the keepers take an equal chance at death with their prisoners, without regard to age, color or previous condition of servitude." In regard to myself, I could see that there was room for the exercise of discretion, as a cloud of suspicion rested upon me, and I apprehended that in case my treatment should not prove successful, the basest motives would be attributed to me. Putting aside, however, everything but what conscience and professional training taught me to regard as duty, I asked Mr. Arnold, my fellow prisoner, then employed as a clerk at headquarters, to inform

Major Stone, who was in command of the post, that I was willing to devote all the skill and attention I was capable of to the terror-stricken garrison.

On his way to headquarters Mr. Arnold met Major Stone, who was then, as he informed Mr. Arnold, on his way to the casemate where I was confined, to ascertain whether I would take charge of the hospital until the services of another physician could be secured. He expressed himself as much gratified that I had already authorized a tender of my services. From the point of view of the scientist, the opportunities to which I was now introduced were valuable. On a small island where many people were congregated in small space, every facility being offered me and there being every desire on my part to watch the progress of the epidemic it will be admitted that for this purpose I could not have been more favorably situated.

The Fever's Deadly March

From very full notes on each case taken at the time, and from careful observation, I reached the same conclusion with regard to the mode of progress of yellow fever that I had reached some years before from observations of the spread of typhoid fever. I was enabled to follow step by step, from case to case, from bed to bed, from quarter to quarter, the development of the fever and track fully its sinuous course around the fort. As far as propagation is concerned, I found the disease innocuous when isolated from its cause. It is purely a disease of infection. From the evidence subjoined, it will be seen how the disease advanced, attacking one, then another, following the sleepers in their beds in a regular and unbroken order of succession, spreading as the flames of a conflagration is spread by sparks from house to house rapidly in the direction of the wind and slowly against it. Not, however, attacking one here and another there indiscriminately as it would have done had the poison been the atmosphere in and around the fort, but marching from bed to bed and from company to company in a line of unbroken continuity.

When the disease first broke out, the post surgeon, entertaining the not yet wholly exploded idea that it was caused by miasma which he supposed rose from stagnant water in the unfinished moat, had the portholes in the quarter where the disease broke out boarded up 'to keep out the malaria.' The effect, of course, was to prevent the free circulation of the air, and so to intensify the infection. Holding opposite views, I had everything thrown open, and acting upon my conception of the nature of the disease and the mode of its dissemination, I am happy to be able to say that during the time I had exclusive charge of the hospital, I did not lose a single case. On taking charge, I met with difficulties. One was to break up the practice instituted by my predecessor of sending the sick in open boats over a rough sea to Sand Key, a little island some two and a half miles distant, and the other was to induce the commander to send as many as possible of the soldiers not yet sick to some of the adjacent islands out of harm's way.

The first case occurred on the 18th of August, the second on the 20th, the third and fourth on the 21st of August, all four men having occupied contiguous beds. Company K, to which they belonged, was then removed to new quarters to the windward of Company L and the prisoners' quarters. On the 24th, Company K furnished a new case, after which the disease spread rapidly (through a board partition) to Company L and the prisoners. The first two cases in Company L occurred in the beds next to the loosely boarded partition separating it from Company K. Those attacked during the night and following morning it was the custom to take immediately to the post hospital, and thence at 4 P.M. to Sand Key, as said above. Yet up to September 11 not one of the nurses who waited on the sick at the post hospital by day and slept in the same room with them by night was attacked by the fever.

181

After running through Company L and the prisoners' quarters, the disease next attacked Company I, quartered some sixty feet distant from Company L and worked its way regularly in series, not missing a single bed. Two days after some infected bedding was taken into the hospital the nurses there began to fall sick. Next the laundresses, occupying a building seventy yards distant were attacked simultaneously with the first issue to them of infected bedclothes brought into the hospital. Again, as soon as the nurses from the Sand Key Hospital who had hitherto escaped, were assigned duty at the post hospital, where the infected bedding had been admitted, they too fell sick. These various facts, with the order of their occurrence, convinced me beyond doubt that the yellow fever is not 'infectious' not contagious, but is propagated primarily by germinal action in human effluvia contained in blankets, bedding, &c., and that in no case did the diseased person propagate the disease.

When a yellow fever patient, or one suffering from any other epidemic disease of infection, is placed in clean clothing, and clean bed and room, he is incapable of communicating the disease. Under these circumstances the germ may be carried along with the diseased person without danger of propagation, for if there is no effluvia, or filth, for the germ to react upon, it will die as does a fire from lack of fuel.

These conclusions were perfectly confirmed by the facts in the case of Company M and indeed by the whole subsequent history of the disease at Fort Jefferson.

Contrasts and Resemblances

After stating the present attitude of medical science with regard to the germ theory as applicable to epidemic diseases, Dr. Mudd gives for practical use a table in which the contrasts and resemblances of these diseases are clearly set forth. The substance of it is partly given here. By "diseases of contagion" are designated small-pox. measles, whooping cough, mumps, &c., by "diseases of infection", scarlet fever, diphtheria, typhus or typhoid fever, yellow fever, &c. Epidemic contagion proceeds from a specific germ, which primarily propagates itself only in the tissues of membranes of living animals; while epidemic infection proceeds from a specific germ which propagates itself only in the heavy and concrete emanations that have passed off from the bodies of living animals. The germ of epidemic contagion is sui generis, that is to say, the germ that produces disease in man does not propagate in other animals, and vice versa, and does not pass from one species of animal to another. The germ of epidemic infection likewise fails to pass from the effluvia of man to that of animals, and from the effluvia of one species of animal to that of another. The diseases of epidemic contagion are propagated by contact either with the disease or its emanations among the animals to which they specifically belong; those of infection on the contrary are not produced by contact with the disease or its emanations, but result indirectly from the peculiar gas or vapor produced by the reaction of germs on the heavy and concrete matters or emanations of animals, and this only among animals of the same species.

As the germ of epidemic contagion does not develop in dead matter, it may remain therein for an indefinite time with its virulence unimpaired; but the germ of infection, propagating only in dead matter, i.e., in effluvia of long standing, and not in living tissues and membranes, or in clean clothing, may be retained in unimpaired vigor indefinitely in clean clothing or in the hair, and be handled or even swallowed with impunity. The former produces disease only when it enters the body; the latter only when it meets with foul clothing which has remained too long unwashed. The germ of contagion gives immunity from a second attack of the disease which it causes; the germ of infection does not. The germ of contagion is inseparable from the disease, making it impossible to isolate it, while the germ of infection is separable, and may, therefore, be easily isolated. Diseases of epidemic contagion can be inoculated; those of infection cannot be so inoculated by matter taken from the diseased person, but only from matter undergoing germinal fermentation. Diseases of epidemic contagion are "contagious;" those of infections are not "infectious," i.e., their emanations have no effect upon either living or effete matter. The former class of diseases is never sporadic or accidental; the latter are. The former are confined to no particular climate, are governed by no atmospheric changes, except, so far as cold weather, by confining the disease to close rooms, renders it more virulent; the latter, on the contrary, are confined to particular climates and governed by atmospheric changes, and when found beyond a certain zone or latitude are traceable to importation.

The germ producing an epidemic disease of contagion is developed in the disease of the animal, be it man or beast; so that, in its case, we quarantine against the disease (that is the person having it) and its emanations retained mechanically in bedding and clothing. In epidemic diseases of infection, however, the primary cause of the disease is developed in the effluvia, so that, in their case, we quarantine against effluvial deposits, contained mostly in bedding and clothing. Endemic diseases possess no germ, and arise from the use of impure water, air or food, taken in connection with excessive heat, cold or anything tending to suppress the irrespirable transpiration or disorder of the stomach and bowels. Much importance is to be attached to adherence to proper definitions of the words contagious, infectious, endemic, and epidemic.

Quarantine Regulations

I. When a ship enters port, and after the landing of passengers, all bedclothing in use during the voyage shall be removed and washed, or steamed with soap and water, rinsed through clean water, ironed and dried without starching. The beds shall be also removed and washed, and the cabin walls, ceilings and bunks washed.

II. On leaving port the beds for both passengers and crew shall be furnished with duplicate bedclothing which has had ample time to be cleaned and dried.

III. No beds, bedclothing or wearing apparel shall be allowed aboard which does not bear evidence of recent purification.

IV. No one affected with a disease of epidemic contagion, or article of clothing that has been in contact with it, shall be permitted aboard.

V. Epidemic diseases of infection may with safety be permitted aboard by observing the following rules:

1st. All clothing must be taken off, the sick removed to a clean bed or chair, and clean clothing be put on. 2d. The hair and skin of the head must be thoroughly washed with soap and water and wiped dry with a clean towel. This having been done, the sick person may then be carried aboard wrapped in a clean blanket and placed in a clean bed.

VI. Sporadic cases of epidemic infection must be subjected to the treatment prescribed in the previous section before being admitted aboard.

VII. By observing the precautions specified in section III all accidental, scrofulous, tubercular and endemic diseases may be admitted aboard.

VIII. The passengers and crews of ships from infected ports shall be compelled before disembarking to don clean clothing and have their cast-off clothing disinfected. The hair and skin of the head should also have been washed thoroughly and wiped dry with a clean towel.

IX. Importers of dry goods shall keep a room above the ground or basement floor with spacious windows, in which to open and air boxes and bales of clothing before offering them for sale.

X. Manufacturers of textile fabrics shall not permit among their operatives a person living where a disease of epidemic infection or contagion exists.

XI. The commander of the ship shall be required to have a certificate, given by the health officer of the port from which it sailed, showing that the provisions of section 5 have been observed.

XII. Masters of vessels engaged in the transportation of cattle and other stock shall conform to the foregoing rules. and will, in addition, have the quarters set apart for stock thoroughly cleansed after each voyage.

XIII. No diseased cattle or other sick stock shall be admitted aboard ship.

XIV. Animals before being shipped shall have their skin and hair, by combing and washing, perfectly freed from all effete matter.

It may be added that Dr. Mudd's views as to the proper treatment of diseases of the class to which yellow fever belongs took definite shape during his professional experience before the war, at Bryantown, where he treated successfully a number of cases of typhoid fever during an epidemic of that disease. His opinions were formed in part some time before by observations ranging over a great variety of diseases of infection which came under his notice while a student residing, after graduating, at the hospital in charge of the University of Maryland, in this city.

04-18-1892: Cincinnati Enquirer Article Concerning Dr. Mudd

Source: Cincinnati Enquirer Newspaper of April 18, 1892.

George Alfred Townsend was a popular American journalist during the mid-1800s. His articles appeared in newspapers throughout the United States. Some of his articles were written using pen names, including "G.A.T.," "Swede," "Laertes," and "Johnny Bouquet," but his favorite pen name was "Gath."

On April 18, 1892, the Cincinnati Enquirer published a Townsend article, written under the pen name GATH, in which Townsend describes an interview he had with a man named Thomas Harbin in 1885, seven years before the article was published. During the Civil War, Harbin, a former postmaster of Bryantown, helped his blockade-running brother-in-law Thomas A. Jones get mail and people across the Potomac into Virginia. He knew the people and geography of Southern Maryland quite well.

Towards the end of the article, Townsend says:

> He (Harbin) told me that in Bryantown, at the tavern, Dr. Mudd introduced him to Booth, and said that Mr. Booth wanted some private conversation with Mr. Harbin. They took a room on the second floor where Booth went through the Thespian motions of pacing and watching the hallways and escapements. He then outlined a scheme of seizing Abraham Lincoln and delivering him up the same evening in Virginia.

While Dr. Mudd's role in this event seems to have been no more than to say: "Mr. Booth, this is Mr. Harbin. He wants to have a private word with you", some writers have insisted that it proves Dr. Mudd was part of Booth's plot to kidnap President Lincoln. This seems to be a rather extreme interpretation of the article, but the entire article is presented below so you can form your own judgement.

> Washington, D.C., April 17. - John Wilkes Booth lived a considerable time at Washington, the life of a licentious young actor, with unusual social opportunities. He was remarkably handsome, very manly in his address, quite insinuating, treating women like one who had their interests at heart and whose confidence would never be betrayed. His father was not remembered, having passed off the stage in 1852 when Booth was only 14 years old. But Edwin Booth had been on the stage since 1850, and had an excellent reputation, and was five years the senior of Wilkes. Edwin Booth had been especially honored in the North, as Wilkes had been made much of in the South, and it thus happened that Edwin Booth, according to his sister's statement, voted for Abraham Lincoln in 1864, a few months before Wilkes Booth shot him.

> Living around the Washington hotels and theaters, occasionally playing for the benefit of some fellow-actor, and possessing a peculiar reputation on the stage as one who only required to be studious and persistent to surpass his brother in fame. Booth seemed to be always in reserve for something eminent, and the life of pleasure he lived probably cloyed at times upon his feelings. His use of liquor kept him alternately inflamed and despondent. He suppressed his sympathies, except to a few persons, lived a good deal to the injury of families who were ardent for the Union, and had a worthless career, underneath which ran the persistent purpose to be the match or superior of anybody, and, in short, lived the life of an eighteenth century high-treason conspirator under the mild and unsuspecting society of Abraham Lincoln's time.

> Toward the close of the war the Government was compelled by its Generals, such as General Dix in New York City, to carry out sentence of execution upon some irregular partisans who had come

into the United States disguised, and seized steamers, run off railroad trains, set fire to hotels, poisoned the water supplies, and seriously designed to run off the prisoners at Elmira, at Johnson's Island, and further South. One of these persons was John Yates Beall, who came from the immediate region of Charleston, where John Brown had been hanged, and there or later had become acquainted with Booth. Upon this occasion it seems that Booth exerted himself to have Beall pardoned by the President in Washington, but General Dix insisted that this was a righteous execution and was needed to stop such irregularities. Beall was hanged on Governor's Island, and the writer there saw him executed. He was a dangerous man, and one well adapted to excite the respect of a Thespian in warfare like Booth. Not improbably Booth deepened his animosity to President Lincoln after this execution of Beall, which took place at the close of February 1865.

In the previous October, 1864, Booth suddenly appeared at Bryantown Catholic Church upon a Sunday morning. Though he had been a wandering horseback rider in the vicinity of Washington, it seems that this was his first visit to the region over which his crime still exercises, not as he expected the fascination of heroism, but the gloom of social and political misapprehension and stigma. Near the time November winds were sighing and the quail were running in the old worn-out fields Booth came to the house of Dr. Queen southeast of Bryantown with a letter of introduction from one Martin in Canada.

This Martin came from Lower Maryland, and was concerned in the capture of the steamer St. Nicholas very early in the war, and, when the leading pirates of that undertaking at Point Lookout had been seized by the Government and put in Ft. McHenry, Martin, who had also kept a liquor store in Baltimore with a saloon attachment, slipped off to Canada, and there engaged in trading Canadian and American money and adventuring enterprises for the Confederacy, and he finally closed his career by going in with a Scotchman named Alexander Keith, to pass a cargo of goods from the St. Lawrence to the Carolinas. The vessel was found in the Lower St. Lawrence a complete wreck with every thing on her lost, and her supercargo and crew as well. Years afterward, when a German steamship was partly blown up at Bremen by this same Mr. Keith, the old friends of Martin in Canada suspected that Keith had blown him up too, as it was remembered that Keith applied for the large insurance upon the cargo.

As "Thomasson" and Keith were the same, so Martin, commencing his military career by an act of piratical treachery, was the sponsor for Booth, the murderer of President Lincoln. These facts I ascertained from Marshal Kane of Baltimore, who for a good while after Martin's death, acted as the adviser of Mrs. Martin; and he told me that, being upon the retreat of the Rebel Government from Richmond, word was brought in that John Wilkes Booth had killed President Lincoln, whereupon Marshal Kane, who was delirious from a fever, managed to obtain his gripsack to open it and tear up a letter from Martin to John Wilkes Booth, introducing Kane to Booth.

Dr. Queen's family heard Booth inquire about the price of lands and horses in that neighborhood, and say that he was a rich person who had money to put out in the country. The next day Booth was taken to the Catholic Church and there the actor was introduced to Dr. Samuel A. Mudd, the principal slave-holder mentioned, who lived five miles north of Bryantown in the direction of Surrattsville. Of course, Mr. Booth had been to Montreal, and there had participated with the fly-by-nights, such as those who raided St. Alban's, and John Y. Beall, aforesaid, and through his unadjusted mind had run the idea of doing some great performance at Washington City, then escaping into the South, securing his wardrobe from Canada, which he had left there, and starring in his father's great part in "Richard III", "Pescara", &c., throughout the English-speaking countries. These men in Canada, and others he had seen in Washington, had told him about the free intercourse with the South from the lower Potomac ferries. After church that day Booth went into Bryantown, a mile or two distant, and in plain sight, and was introduced by Dr. Mudd at the village hotel to Mr. Thomas Harbin, the Marylander, who was the principal signal officer or spy with the lower Maryland counties.

Toward the close of the war rigorous policing of the lower Maryland country was relaxed or dispensed with as the enemy had been pushed south of the James River and seldom molested the Potomac parts. Harbin, whom I talked to at great length just before he died, about 1885, gave me particulars concerning Booth, which would now be past discovering. He told me that in Bryantown, at the tavern, Dr. Mudd introduced him to Booth, and said that Mr. Booth wanted some private conversation with Mr. Harbin. They took a room on the second floor where Booth went through the Thespian motions of pacing and watching the hallways and escapements. He then outlined a scheme of seizing Abraham Lincoln and delivering him up the same evening in Virginia. He said that he had come down to that country to invite cooperation and partners and intimated that there was not only glory, but profits in the undertaking.

Harbin was a cool man who had seen many liars and rogues go to and fro on that illegal border and he set down Booth as a crazy fellow, but at the same time said that he would give his cooperation.

08-07-1893: Conversation Between Dr. Mudd and Samuel Cox, Jr.

Source: *J. Wilkes Booth, An Account of His Sojourn in Southern Maryland after the Assassination of Abraham Lincoln, His Passage Across the Potomac, and His Death in Virginia*, including handwritten personal notes by Samuel Cox, Jr. Maryland Historical Society, Baltimore, Maryland.

Following is the text of the notes written by Samuel Cox, Jr. on August 7, 1893, recording a conversation between himself and Dr. Mudd in 1877, eight years after Dr. Mudd was released from prison at Fort Jefferson. The conversation took place while Cox and Dr. Mudd were campaigning together for election to separate seats in the Maryland Legislature. Cox won, but Dr. Mudd lost. Samuel Cox, Jr. was the adopted son of Samuel Cox, the farmer who arranged for Thomas A. Jones to help Booth and Herold get across the Potomac River.

In 1877, after Samuel A. Mudd's return from Dry Tortugas and when he & myself were canvassing this County as the Democratic candidates for the Legislature, he told me he knew Booth but casually, that Booth had at one time sought an introduction to him through John H. Surratt on Penn. Ave, Washington. This was some time prior to the assassination, but he had refused and that Booth had forced himself on him shortly afterward and that subsequently Booth attended church at Bryantown where he spoke to him but he was particular in not inviting him to his house, but that Booth came that evening uninvited.

He told me he was not favorably impressed with Booth, and that when Booth and Herold came to his house the night after the assassination, they told him they were just from Virginia & that Booth's horse had fallen soon after leaving the river & had broken his leg, that he had rendered him medical assistance while in utter ignorance of the assassination.

That after he had set the broken leg, he, Dr. Mudd, took letters he had but a short time gotten through the contraband mail for distribution, and that in going to Bryantown to mail them he was surprised to find the village surrounded by soldiers, and upon being stopped by a sentry he was horrified when told the President had been shot the night before, and, upon asking who had shot him the fellow had answered Booth.

He then told me his first impulse was to surrender Booth, that he had imposed upon him, twice forced himself upon him, and now the third time, had come with a lie upon his tongue and received medical assistance which would be certain to have him serious trouble. But he determined to go back and upbraid him for his treachery, which he did. And that Booth had appealed to him in the name of his mother whom he professed to love so devotedly and that he acted and spoke so tragically that he told them they must leave his house which they then did and after getting in with Oswald Swan they were piloted to Rich Hill.

Rich Hill was the name of the Cox farm.

12-18-1902: Samuel Arnold's Account of the Yellow Fever Epidemic

Source: Baltimore American, December 18, 1902

In the brief space of a month after the killing of Winters our small island and inclosure was visited by yellow fever. It made fearful ravages among the limited number stationed there, sweeping nearly every officer at the post away. It struck from earth our best officers and permitted the heartless ones to recover, to repeat again, I suppose, more of their cruelties upon humanity under their command. The ways of Providence are mysterious, and no doubt it was done for some good and wise purpose.

Among the first to succumb to the dread disease was Brevet Major J. Sim Smith, surgeon in charge. Dr. Smith, on his arrival at the post, which was but a few months before, corrected in various instances the abuse and reigning terrors which abounded there. He was, indeed, a man of humanity and kindness, a gentleman by birth and culture — the soldiers' and prisoners' friend and protector, and, his memory lives in the mind and the heart of all by whom he was then surrounded as all that was good, pure, upright, and noble. He worked with untiring zeal whilst the fever raged, until the fatal malady struck him down upon the bed of sickness, where he lingered but three days and died. He received every attention from Dr. Mudd, who, at that period, had charge.

Mrs. Smith was lying in an adjacent room, sick with the fever. Dr. Mudd paid her every attention and worked unfalteringly to save her life. His efforts were crowned with success and she recovered from the disease. During the period of the sickness of Dr. Smith and family there was neither an officer nor an officer's wife that came near them to administer to their wants, their cases devolving upon the care of Dr. Mudd, and faithfully did he perform all that lay within his power.

In a short time the fever proved epidemic, and men could be seen falling down in every section of the fort, as the dread malady seized them. When in former times officers were parading about devising plans wherewith to torture the soldiers and prisoners nothing was seen or heard of them, they keeping themselves closely closeted, a pall like unto death seemingly hanging over the officers' quarters. Fear was depicted upon the countenance of everyone on the island, each looking for his turn next.

Two of the companies were removed to the adjacent islands, thereby being saved from the fever's fearful ravages. Two companies were retained to guard the fort and prisoners. Prisoners had to stand the brunt of the fever, their only safety being in an overruling Providence. Out of the 52 prisoners confined there but two died, whereas the garrison lost in officers and men 37.

Had Coffins Ready

Men at first, when taken sick, were carried to the small key termed Sand Key, upon which a small temporary shed had been erected as a hospital, the commanding officer thinking thereby to prevent the garrison from being infected. Sick patients, seated in a small boat, were conveyed over, confronted by coffins which were piled up in the bow of the boat. This of itself was sufficient to cause alarm, and even to kill the fainthearted, of whom there were quite a number collected on that small area of seven and a half acres.

With but a few exceptions those who were conveyed to the key in the small boat fell victims to the disease, and are buried beneath the sandy soil. When Dr. Mudd was given charge he stated to the commanding officer that it would be advisable to discontinue this practice; that the fever was in our midst, and that it could not be dislodged until the poison had expended itself, advising that all cases be brought to and treated at the hospital. This was acceded to, and, from his manner of treatment in the disease, a great change was soon to be noted.

From this period until the arrival from Key West of Dr. Whitehurst everything was progressing favorably, no death occurring. Dr. Whitehurst, perfectly conversant with the mode of treatment, he having had immense practice in the disease, approved Dr. Mudd's manner of treatment, and it was continued throughout the period the fever raged in our midst. The fever began to assume a more virulent type, and in spite of the untiring exertion of both began to make sad inroads into our numbers.

Everyone now thought of self alone. There was not respect shown by the attendants, they being soldiers taken from different companies, to either the dead or the dying. No sooner had the breath left the body than it was coffined and hurried over to its last resting place, there being a boat, with a crew detailed as the burying party, always awaiting. In many instances coffins were brought into the hospital and placed alongside of the bed to receive the body of some one expected to die, and had to be removed again, the patient still tenaciously clinging to life.

Fear Reigned Supreme

Men less sick were startled viewing these proceedings, it having a tendency to cause their own condition to become worse. During the terrible ordeal of the fever the garrison kept itself, duties being neglected by both officers and soldiers. During its progress the island assumed a different aspect. The island, which before was more like a place peopled by fiends than anything else it could be compared with suddenly became calm, quiet and peaceful. Fear stood out upon the face of every human being.

Some attempted to assume the tone of gaiety and indifference, but upon their faces could be read traces of other feelings. For two months the fever raged in our midst, creating havoc among those dwelling there. During this time Dr. Mudd was never idle. He worked both day and night, and was always at post, faithful to his calling, relieving his sufferings of humanity as far as laid within his power. The fever having abated through the want of more subjects, a contract physician from New York arrived at the post and relieved Dr. Whitehurst of his duties. When the new doctor took charge there were but two or three sick, and they were in a state of convalescence.

Soon thereafter Dr. Mudd was taken down with the fever in his quarters, and during the entire period of his illness was never visited by the New York doctor, the surgeon in charge, he remaining closeted in his room. The only medical treatment received by Dr. Mudd during his illness was administered at the hands of Spangler and myself. True, neither of us knew much about the disease or its treatment, all the experience either possessed being derived from observation during its prevalence, and the mode of treatment having been learned from personal experience in the nursing of patients under our charge.

Treated Dr. Mudd

Dr. Mudd was watched over by us both day and night in turns. We adopted the same method of treatment in his case as had been administered by him in ours, through which he happily recovered. He stated upon his recovery that had it not been for our care and watchfulness he would have died, and, and thanked each of us in unmeasured terms for our friendly consideration.

Dr. Mudd had worked during the prevalence of the yellow fever with an unfaltering zeal, until nature was well-nigh exhausted, relieving in every way at his command and knowledge the sufferings of humanity, but when afflicted himself he was left entirely to the mercies of his God and the limited knowledge of his two companions, which fact had the appearance of a desire for his death on the part of those at the head of affairs.

We felt from the first that we had been transported to Dry Tortugas to fall victims to the many dreadful poisons of malaria generated in that climate. Happily we lived through it all, and I am permitted to give to the world at large some inkling of the many wrongs, tortures and sufferings inflicted upon us during the period of nearly four long years of exile. In the month of October, 1867, the fever having exhausted itself and finally stamped out, and with it, to a great extent, the harsh and rigorous measures which had heretofore been adopted in the manner of our imprisonment, some of the privileges which we had taken during its prevalence were curtailed, but for the most part the others were not countermanded by the officers in command.

The officers who garrisoned the fort at this time, with the exception of two, fell victims to the disease. A lieutenant recovered alone through the kind care and watchful nursing and attention of Colonel Grenfell who remained with him day and night, administering to his slightest want. The officers died of the disease were coffined and borne to their last resting place by the prisoners of the post, no respect being shown by the other officers. Even wives were carried in like manner, the husband remaining in his quarters.

02-11-1909: Mrs. Samuel Mudd's Last Interview

Source: Baltimore News, February 11, 1909

The Baltimore News newspaper of February 11, 1909 carried an interview of Mrs. Samuel Mudd, which she said would be her last, and it was. She died December 29, 1911.

One woman who was made to suffer, without fault of her own, because of the assassination of President Lincoln is still living and is now in Baltimore. She is Mrs. Sarah Frances Mudd, widow of Dr. Samuel A. Mudd, who was sentenced by the Military Commission that tried the alleged conspirators to imprisonment for life in Fort Jefferson, Dry Tortugas, but was pardoned by President Johnson near the close of the latter's term of office.

Mrs. Mudd is hale, hearty and vivacious, vigorous in body and mind, and shows no indication in her well-preserved appearance of having passed through the harrowing ordeals occasioned by the arrest, trial and conviction of her husband more than forty years ago.

Mrs. Mudd claims her residence at the old Mudd homestead in Charles County, where she resided at the time her husband was arrested. She spends much or her time, however, in visiting her children and grandchildren in different sections of Maryland and in the District of Columbia. At present she is visiting her daughter, Mrs. D. Eldridge Monroe, once Miss Nettie Mudd, who recently edited and had published "*The Life of Dr. Samuel A. Mudd*".

Relics in City Home

In Mrs. Monroe's home, 529 West Hoffman Street, Baltimore, may be found a number of interesting articles incidentally connected with the events immediately growing out of the assassination of President Lincoln. Among these articles are the antique davenport on which Booth was laid when his broken leg was set by Dr. Mudd; an inlaid center table, made by Dr. Mudd while he was a prisoner at Fort Jefferson; a ladies' work box, made by him at the same place; a number of shells gathered by him while he was a prisoner and arranged in the form of wreaths of flowers, and much other of his handiwork, all highly finished and giving evidence of his patient toil in his hours of loneliness as a prisoner.

Mrs. Mudd has for many years uniformly refused to be interviewed. When requested to tell her recollections of the events connected with the arrest and conviction of her husband she hesitated about doing so, but finally consented to make a statement.

The Whole Subject Unpleasant

I have already given an account of the visit of Booth and Herold to our home early on the morning of the 14th of April, 1865, which account has been published in my daughter's book. I will not repeat anything I therein stated. Indeed, the whole subject is unpleasant to me. I had much rather let the past rest. I had to go through so many trying circumstances and ordeals and have been so frequently and unwillingly brought before the public that I shrink from again giving an interview. I reluctantly do so only because there have been so many erroneous, indeed, absurd, statements made by irresponsible parties, which have gained currency, that I am constrained to speak in order that, if possible, the truth and only the truth should be made known.

I remember very distinctly what took place at our home on the 14th day of April, 1865. Booth and Herold came on horseback about four o'clock on the morning that date. We were aroused from our sleep. The Doctor went to the door to see who had called at that early hour, supposing that someone in the neighborhood needed his professional services.

Horses Tied in Front of House

The horses on which these two men, Booth and Herold, who gave their names as Tyler and Tyson, had ridden were tied to the horserack in front of the house. The men were then brought into the house, and the Doctor came to my room, stating that one of the men had a broken leg. I did not see either of these men until later the day, as I have stated in my daughter's book. There was no one in our home that night except the Doctor, myself, the children and the children's nurse, a white girl named Nancy Tilly. The children and the nurse were not awakened by the arrival of these visitors.

Frank Washington, a slave belonging to my husband, was the first person to come to the house after the arrival of the strangers. He (Frank Washington) lived in a tenant house not far from our residence. He is still living. He came on that morning at his usual hour, about daybreak, to attend to his duties as hostler. He took the horses of the strangers, led them to the stable and fed them. Washington's wife (Betty), our cook, arrived with her husband. She is now dead. No other person came to our house that morning until the arrival of our old gardener, John Best, an Englishman, who came from his cottage on our farm at his usual hour, about seven o'clock. The Doctor alone received Tyler and Tyson, who afterward proved to be Booth and Herold; there was no one else present. As I have heretofore stated, neither the Doctor nor myself knew who these visitors were until long after they had gone. In fact, it was several days afterward before we really knew.

Very Dark Days

Those were dark, very dark, days when my husband was taken from me, tortured through the semblance of a trial and convicted and sentenced to life imprisonment at Dry Tortugas. Darker still were the days oftentimes while he endured the miseries of that desolate place. It will interest nobody, perhaps, to tell how hard was the struggle I had to make against the most adverse conditions. Yet through all I tried to keep a brave heart, support our children and encourage my husband to hope for his early deliverance from an unjust imprisonment.

I fear I could not have borne up under my trials had there not been the kind friends who gave me sympathy and encouragement that in the darkest moments awakened a more hopeful outlook toward the future. I could not in a limited space name all these friends. A few of them, however, who stand out conspicuously for the noble, Christian friendship they extended me, I cannot well omit to mention.

General Ewing a Good Friend

Foremost among them was General Thomas Ewing (I know he is in Heaven), who defended my husband before the Military Commission, and who was a brave Union soldier. Through all our long period of trial and distress General Ewing was not only my husband's counsel, but his and my sincere friend. I paid him all the fee asked, not an inconsiderable one, yet I truly believe that the least he thought of in his heroic and masterly defense of my husband was the matter of fee for his services. In all the dark days of the trial before the Commission, he tried to cheer my husband and myself with the hope of a successful issue, and he was tireless in his efforts to realize that hope. After the conviction and sentence he was indefatigable in his efforts to secure my husband's release, and wrote me many cheering and hopeful letters.

Another friend, scarcely second to General Ewing, was the late Richard T. Merrick, the eminent lawyer of Washington. Because of Mr. Merrick's well-known sympathy with the South, he was not brought into active participation in the trial before the Commission; but he was consulting counsel and daily conferred with General Ewing in reference to the defense of my husband.

Made Good Defense

I have always believed that so great was the bitterness and excitement at the time, and so intense the desire for victims to avenge the President's death, if it had not been for the unusual but masterly course pursued by General Ewing, aided by Mr. Merrick, my husband, innocent as he was, might have suffered the unfortunate fate of Mrs. Surratt. General Ewing, as is shown in my daughter's book, in his argument against the jurisdiction of the Military Commission to try the accused, had warned the members of the Commission that the time would come when their acts would be judged impartially by posterity, and that it might then be determined that their jurisdiction was an assumption, and any sentence they might impose, only their own unauthorized acts.

General Ewing and Mr. Merrick came to the conclusion that unless the whole of the defense of my husband, including the argument to the jurisdiction and the argument on the testimony, as well as the testimony itself, was preserved in some permanent form and presented to the members of the Commission, that tribunal would likely exercise an unbridled license to condemn and inflict the greatest penalty, without regard to the law or the facts.

Had Record Printed

On the suggestion therefore of Messers. Ewing and Merrick I paid $2,000 to have hurriedly printed and bound 700 volumes, containing the arguments of General Ewing and all the evidence offered in the case against my husband. This work was finished early on the day before the Commission was to announce its decision. On the morning of this day General Ewing walked into the courtroom with his arms filled with a number of these volumes and handed one to each member of the Commission and one to the each party, Judge Advocate General Holt and others, who had been officially connected with the trial.

I was not present on this occasion, but have been told that he incident was dramatic in the extreme. Neither the members of the Commission nor Judge Holt had anticipated it, and received the volumes almost with consternation. They realized that the record had been preserved as to this case in a compact form and by this record future generations would probably judge their acts.

Judge Stone Assisted

Another gentleman to whom I was indebted in my trouble, and whom I shall always remember with gratitude, was the late Frederick Stone of Charles county, afterward a judge of the Court of Appeals of Maryland. He was not employed in the defense of my husband, but took great interest in his case, both before and after his conviction, and gave all the aid in his power. I am indebted to a great many other people for kindness and sympathy, but cannot now name them all.

I passed through many trying, sometimes exciting, experiences, and met with many people whose names are now well known to history. I saw Judge Holt, in the interest of my husband, four or five times. I do not wish to speak harshly of the dead, and shall dismiss Judge Holt by saying of him only that he impressed me as a harsh, unfeeling, insincere specimen of humanity. This, I am sorry to say, is the highest tribute I can pay him. I saw Secretary Stanton only twice in behalf for my husband. My reception by him was, on his part, so cold, unfeeling and, indeed, brutal, that I looked at him in both instances with as much of hauteur as I could command, and deliberately left his presence without any formal leave taking.

Called on President Johnson

I called on President Johnson the great many times. He always treated me courteously, but impressed me always as one shrinking from some impending disaster. He conveyed to me always the idea that he wanted to release my husband, but said more than once "the pressure on me is too great." On one occasion I took a petition to him asking their release of my husband; he told me that if Holt would sign it he would grant the petition. This Judge Holt refused.

Many persons have given statements in regard to the setting of Booth's leg by my husband, few, indeed, none that I have seen, being correct. I read recently of an interview with a person who claims to have held Booth's horse on the morning my husband set Booth's leg. I am sure this party never saw Booth at all, and never saw my husband until after his return from the Dry Tortugas. For myself, I with wish nothing more in relation to these matters than to commit them to the impartial historian of the future. I never again will be interviewed on the subject.

This was indeed Mrs. Sarah Frances Mudd's last interview. She died on December 29, 1911, surviving her husband by almost three decades.

Profile: General August V. Kautz - Reminiscences of the Civil War

Source: August V. Kautz Papers, Manuscript Division, Library of Congress, Washington, D.C.

Major-General August V. Kautz was one of the nine members of the Military Commission that conducted the Lincoln assassination trial. In his *Reminiscences of the Civil War,* Kautz included his recollection of the Lincoln assassination trial:

I left on the 4th of May and reached Washington on the morning of the 6th and, having reported to Genl. Grant, was directed to report my name and address in the city to the Adj. Genl. and await orders. I learned indirectly that I was destined as a member of the Military Commission to try the assassins of the President. It did not transpire fully until the 9th when the first meeting of the Commission took place in a room fitted up adjoining the prison near the Arsenal grounds.

We met, but we did not transact any business. The prisoners to the number of eight were brought in behind a railing. They were masked and chained, and clad in black dominos so that we could not identify the prisoners. The Commission decided that they must be brought in, so that we could recognize the different prisoners, and be able to identify them. The mystery and apparent severity with which they were brought into the court room partook so much of what my imagination pictured the Inquisition to have been, that I was quite impressed with its impropriety in this age. The prisoners were never again brought into court in this costume.

On the 10th the Commission got so far as to swear the members, and have the charges read, and the pleadings of the prisoners entered. Gen. Hunter was the presiding officer. I was the third member in rank and sat on the left of the President. Gen. Lew Wallace sat on his right and Gen. Foster of Indiana sat on my left. There were three Judge Advocates: Genl. Holt, Genl. Burnett and Maj. Bingham. There were some changes; Genl. Comstock met on the first day with the Commission and did not appear again. We had Mr. Pittman and the Murphy brothers as shorthand reporters, and I was surprised at the facility, rapidity and correctness with which the work was done. They were able to read the record as rapidly as any other writing and we were able to make rapid progress. The 11th we met but the prisoners had not yet provided counsel, and we did not do much, but on the 12th we got fairly started and worked all day accomplishing so much that it took two hours of the morning of the 13th to read the proceedings of the previous day.

The leading incident of the 13th was the objection of Genl. Harris, one of the members, to the introduction of the Hon. Reverdy Johnson as Counsel for Mrs. Surratt. The objections were that he had sympathized with the action of the Rebel element in Maryland. Mr. Johnson, when the opportunity was given him to say a few words, his indignation was very manifest by his flushed face, but his remarks were quiet and dignified, and full of irony, and showed the ill-advised nature of the objection in such a light that Genl. Harris must have regretted that he made the objection. If he had any sense of the absurdity of a Court or Commission such as ours, raising an objection to a member of the U.S. Senate, appearing before it as a counsel on the ground of disloyalty. Mr. Johnson did not do us the honor to appear before us again after this insult to his dignity. He did the other members great injustice if he supposed they united with Genl. Harris in his ill advised objection.

The court met as a rule at ten in the morning, and sat until after six p.m. usually, taking a recess about noon for lunch which the Secretary of War had served for us in adjoining room to save time and the necessity of our having to go back to the city. Ambulances were supplied by the Q. M. Dept. to take us to and from the court room to our rooms. This was the daily programme. The weather soon became very warm and the confinement was very trying on account of the number of visitors that were permitted by pass to visit the court room, preventing the free circulation of the air.

On the 16th the court met informally, at the theater where Mr. Lincoln was shot, before going to the court room, in order to acquaint ourselves with the scene of the assassination. This was the only change from the daily routine. We worked very faithfully and there was little leisure, often sitting until seven o'clock in the evening, and rarely adjourning before six, except when no work could be done for want of witnesses which happened occasionally.

The prosecution was continued until the 26th of May when the defense began. The evidence was very clear as to the conspiracy and that all the parties arraigned were connected with it in various ways. The original and avowed object was a conspiracy to kidnap the President, and it was so understood by nearly all concerned. The testimony showed J. Wilkes Booth and John Surratt to be the heads of the conspiracy. The order to kill did not go forth until about eight o'clock p.m. on the 14th of April. There was evidence produced that tended to show that the heads of the Confederate government knew of the conspiracy and also that the agents of the same in Canada were cognizant of it. It was shown that a proposition to kill Mr. Lincoln was made to Jefferson Davis and, over his signature, the paper was forwarded for the consideration of other officials without any adverse comment.

The defense lasted through until about the 19th of June when we began to hear the arguments in behalf of the prisoners. An attempt was made at the close to prove insanity on the part of Payne, who finally defeated the attempt of his counsel by maintaining his sanity, that he knew what he was doing when he tried to kill Mr. Seward. The interest of the case centered mostly about Mrs. Surratt and Payne. Dr. Mudd attracted much interest and his guilt as an active conspirator was not clearly made out. His main guilt was the fact that he failed to deliver them, that is, Booth and Harold, to their pursuers.

Mrs. Surratt was shown to have been active in the conspiracy to kidnap, prior to the capture of Richmond. That she was a willing participant in his death was not clearly made out. My own impression was that she was involved in the final result against her will by her previous connection with the conspiracy. Booth was a fanatic in the matter and craved a notoriety that would appear heroic if he survived the act, and prove martyrdom if he perished. He, no doubt, held most of his confederates in the conspiracy under the impression that it was organized for the purpose of kidnapping, who would have been deterred if they had known that they might be required to kill.

During the many weeks that the court was in session I never saw the face of Mrs. Surratt. She sat behind the railing furthest away, and her face was constantly screened by a large palm leaf fan. I could not even recognize her picture for she was entirely unknown to me. I presume this is the case with every member of the court. All the other members of the court were indelibly impressed on my mind. Harold was a simpering foolish young man, so short of stature that he appeared like a boy and never seemed impressed with the gravity of his position. He must of been simply a plastic tool in Booth's hands.

Payne was a sullen character whose expression rarely changed. He seemed to be fully aware that he had taken a desperate chance and lost, and had the nerve to abide the result manfully. He was manly and strong in every respect, but how much moral character there was in his make up was not apparent on the surface.

Atzoroth looked the hired assassin and the testimony went to show that he failed to perform his part of the compact, which was to kill Genl. Grant, either from want of courage or want of sufficient intelligence. He excited no sympathy from anyone.

Dr. Mudd was the most intelligent looking and attracted most attention of all the prisoners. There was more work done in his defense. His subsequent career showed him to be a man of more character and intelligence that anyone of the prisoners.

Spangler does not seem to have been a conspirator knowingly. He was simply a tool of Booth's and held his horse for him, and cut the stick with which Booth held the door to the box, in which Mr. Lincoln was in at the theater. His greatest crime was his ignorance, and that he did not see the ends to which he was being used.

Arnold was shown to have been associated with the conspirators, but what part he performed and to what extent he was implicated was not shown to the Commission. He was a good looking, amiable young man, who seemed to have gotten into bad company. The same degree and character of guilt applied to McLaughlin.

All of the prisoners had counsel but the greatest effort was made in behalf of Mrs. Surratt and Dr. Mudd. The Hon. Thom. Ewing made an elaborate defense of Mudd and Mr. Johnson, by proxy, defended Mrs. Surratt, through Mr. Aiken.

The members were not released until the 30th of June when the Commission adjourned sine die. The deliberations were not protracted, the last ten days were taken up with time allotted to the counsel and Judge Advocates to make their arguments in the case. The Judge Advocates, under the influence of the Secretary of War, evidently, were very persevering and wanted evidently to have the seven prisoners all hung, and they were very much put out when a paper was signed by a majority of the Commission recommending Mrs. Surratt to executive clemency on account of her sex. We, who signed it, did not deem it wise or expedient to hang her. This paper afterwards became a matter of much controversy. When public sympathy, as we who signed the paper foresaw, had reacted to such a height as to make it desirable for Mr. Johnson to shift the responsibility, he endeavored to do so, by claiming that this paper was withheld from the proceedings, and that he never saw it. This did not seem to be very sincere, in view of the fact that within a day or two after the adjournment of the Commission, the recommendation with the names of those who signed it, and there were five of the nine members, was published in the daily papers.

It was apparent that if John Surratt had been one of the prisoners tried, his mother's life would have been saved. In those early days after the assassination the country seemed to require victims to pay for the great crime. It was apparent to me however, that there would be a reaction and that those who were instrumental in causing her execution would regret that they had permitted Mrs. Surratt to be hung.

The reaction came even before the close of Mr. Johnson's administration and he alleged that the recommendation of the court was not attached to the proceedings when he acted on them. Judge Holt and Bingham, however, denied that any mutilation of the proceeding had taken place and that the papers were intact when submitted to the President.

There has been much controversy over the course pursued by the Administration to punish the conspirators, mostly originating with the adverse political element. Some of my Democratic friends were fond of telling me that when the party got into power again, I would hang for my part in the proceedings. There might be abuse of the slight statutory authority for Military Commissions, but the one organized for the trial of the assassins will never, I think, be styled such by posterity. It was the only way for speedy result which the loyal spirit of the country seemed to demand at the time. The result of the trial of John Surratt by the Civil Courts a few years later, go to show that the civil courts could not have been depended upon for a speedy result in this remarkable case.

Profile: The Ships of Dr. Samuel A. Mudd

Dr. Mudd had seen a lot of ships before the events of 1865. He saw ships in Washington, D.C. when he attended Georgetown college as a teenager, and when he visited D.C. from time to time as an adult. He saw ships in the Baltimore harbor when he attended medical school at the University of Maryland's Medical Department. And he saw ships at Benedict, Maryland, the Patuxent River town where he took his farm produce for sale and shipping. But there is no record of his having ever been aboard a ship until 1865.

During the four years between his arrest on April 24, 1865, and his return home on March 20, 1869, Dr. Mudd would find himself on five different ships, the State of Maine, the U.S.S. Florida, the Thomas A. Scott, the Matchless, and the Liberty.

Following are short sketches of those five ships.

The State of Maine

Dr. Mudd, Edman Spangler, Samuel Arnold, and Michael O'Laughlin began their journey to prison at Fort Jefferson when they were taken from the Washington Arsenal and placed aboard the steamer State of Maine[97] in the early hours of Monday, July 17, 1865. The State of Maine transported them to Fortress Monroe, where they were transferred to the U.S.S. Florida for the week-long journey to Fort Jefferson in the Dry Tortugas, Florida.

The State of Maine was built in New York City in 1848, and then operated by the Bay State Steam Boat Company of Falls River, Massachusetts.

Shortly after the Civil War started, the U.S. Army Quartermaster Corps chartered the 806 ton side-wheel steamer at the rate of $600 per day plus fuel to transport troops from Massachusetts and other northern states to east coast destinations such as Fortress Monroe, Virginia. In 1862, the State of Maine was used to transport troops and supplies for General George McClellan's York-James Peninsula campaign designed to capture Richmond.

Early in the war, the Army was good at getting troops into battle, but it had no effective system for evacuating wounded soldiers from the battlefield. This resulted in many needless deaths and much unnecessary suffering.

The U.S. Sanitary Commission, precursor to the American Red Cross, was authorized by President Lincoln to provide a variety of support services to the Army. The Commission acted quickly to address the evacuation problem by organizing a ground ambulance service.

---

[97] State of Maine Ship Vessel Files, Record Group 92, Box No. 60. Office of the Quartermaster General, Water Transportation 1834 - 1900, U.S. National Archives, Washington, D.C.

State of Maine, Record Group 41, Bureau of Navigation Headquarters Records. Official Number Files 1867 - 1958. Box 145. U.S. National Archives, Washington, D.C.

Olmsted, Frederick Law, *Hospital Transports. A Memoir of the Embarkation of the Sick and Wounded from the Peninsula of Virginia in the Summers of 1862.* Tichnor and Fields. Boston, 1863.

When casualties began to mount from the battles of the 1862 Peninsula campaign, the Army lent some of its vessels to the U.S. Sanitary Commission for use as hospital transports. The State of Maine was one of these ships.

The fourteen ships the U.S. Sanitary Commission operated during the Peninsula campaign were known as the Hospital Transport Service. They evacuated wounded soldiers from landings along the York and James River east of Richmond and transported them to hospitals in Washington, Alexandria, Annapolis, Baltimore, Pennsylvania, and New York.

The Hospital Transport Service was disbanded after the summer of 1862 when the U.S. Army's new medical director, Jonathan Letterman, finally organized an effective Army ambulance and transport service.

The State of Maine continued to be used as a hospital transport by the Army Quartermaster Corps for the remainder of the war, including service as a hospital ship and medical supply vessel during Grant's long siege of Richmond.

On April 18, 1864 the Quartermaster Corps renewed its charter for the State of Maine with its new owners, Borden & Lovell of New York City, at the rate of $400 per day plus fuel. The contract contained an option allowing the War Department to purchase the State of Maine, appraised at $140,000, if it chose to do so. It never exercised this option.

In July 1865, with the war over and and its hospital ship duties no longer required, the State of Maine rested peacefully beside a wharf in the Potomac River at Washington, D.C. However, in the early hours of July 17, 1865 the boilers of the former hospital ship were brought to life once more so that she could make one last trip down the Potomac to Fortress Monroe, carrying Dr. Mudd and his three companions.

The State of Maine reverted to its civilian owners on August 11, 1865. The last record on her is a note by a Port of New York Naval Officer that the State of Maine was "Surrendered New York. Febry 18, 1871 sold to subject of Foreign Power."

Her ultimate demise is unknown.

The U.S.S. Florida

The U.S.S. Florida[98] was built by the William H. Webb shipbuilding company in New York in 1851, for the New York and Savannah Steam Navigation Company. She carried passengers and freight between New York and Savannah until the Civil War started in 1861. The passenger fare was $25, including meals.

The U.S. Navy purchased the Florida for $87,500 on April 12, 1861, the same day the Civil War began with the attack on Fort Sumpter, South Carolina. The Florida was renamed the U.S.S. Florida and converted to a gunboat with the installation of eight 32-pounder smooth bore guns and one 20-pound Parrott rifle.

---

[98] Department of the Navy - Naval Historical Center. *Dictionary of American Naval Fighting Ships.* Washington, D.C. The U.S.S. Florida. Page 418. Also, Heyl, Eric. *Early American Steamers*, Buffalo, N.Y., 1953. The U.S.S. Florida. Page 149.

During the war, the Florida carried out blockade duty along the Atlantic coast, capturing or destroying any Confederate ships she encountered. These included the Confederate ships Emily St. Claire, Calypso, and Hattie. The British side-wheel steamer Wild Dayrell was caught trying to break through the blockade off the North Carolina coast and was destroyed.

The Florida was in New York when Captain Budd received a telegram ordering him to steam to Fortress Monroe, which he did, arriving there about noon on Monday, July 17th. Shortly, the steamer State of Maine arrived from Washington, lowered anchor nearby, and transferred Dr. Mudd, Edman Spangler, Samuel Arnold, and Michael O'Laughlen, plus their Army guards and escorts, to the Florida. A week later, the Florida delivered its passengers at Fort Jefferson.

In 1868, the U.S.S. Florida was sold at auction for $19,000. She was later operated as the merchant steamer Delphine and the Haitian warship Republique. Her ultimate demise is unknown.

William Frederick Keeler was the Paymaster aboard the U.S.S. Florida from 1863 to 1865, including the time Dr. Mudd and his companions were taken to Fort Jefferson. Keeler recorded his service on the Florida in his book *Aboard the USS Florida: 1863-65*, which is still available in many libraries.

The Thomas A. Scott

The Thomas A. Scott[99] was a large 1,052 ton ocean steamship built by the William A. Cramp & Sons shipbuilders in Philadelphia in 1863. The U.S. Army Quartermaster Corps purchased it upon completion for use as a transport.

On September 25, 1865 the Thomas A. Scott arrived at Fort Jefferson from New York by way of Key West to deliver brown sugar and other supplies. Dr. Mudd had been at Fort Jefferson only two months, but during that time he had witnessed the successful escape of eight prisoners who stowed away on the Scott during an earlier visit. When the Scott returned on September 25th, he was ready to try his own escape.

Dr. Mudd was anxious to escape because he had learned that control of Fort Jefferson was being transferred from the 161st New York Volunteers to the 82nd United States Colored Infantry. He was fearful of how the incoming troops would treat a former slave owner.

Dr. Mudd attempted to escape by hiding aboard the Scott while supplies were being unloaded. However, he was quickly discovered and returned to the fort in chains.

At the end of the Civil War, the Government auctioned off the Thomas A. Scott and other no-longer needed ships. She was purchased by Leary Brothers of New York and renamed Saragossa. Subsequent owners were the Baltimore and Savannah Steamship Company, the Miners Transportation Company, and the Bell & Company fruit importers.

The Saragossa sank during an Atlantic coast storm in 1887.

---

[99] Steamship Historical Society of America. *American Ocean Steamships 1850 - 1870.* Providence, Rhode Island. 1986. The Thomas A. Scott. Page 92.

The Matchless

The Matchless[100] was a 170-ton sailing schooner, 99.6 feet long, built in 1859 in Key West, Florida, and used as a slaver before the Civil War. She was purchased by the U.S. Army Quartermaster Corps on June 5, 1863 for $13,500.

During the Civil War, the Matchless was used to transport troops from Fort Myers, Florida to Useppa Island on Florida's Gulf coast. After the war, the Army used the Matchless to ferry mail, supplies, and people between Key West and Fort Jefferson.

When Michael O'Laughlen died during the 1867 yellow fever epidemic, his body was taken from Fort Jefferson to Key West aboard the Matchless, on the first leg of its journey back to O'Laughlen's family in Baltimore.

When Dr. Mudd was pardoned, he sailed on the Matchless from Fort Jefferson to Key West, where he obtained passage on the Liberty for the final leg of his journey home.

The Coast and Geodetic Survey acquired the Matchless in 1885. It was rebuilt in 1895 at a cost of approximately $50,000. The Matchless was the last sailing vessel to be owned and operated by the Coast and Geodetic Survey. It remained in service until 1915. Its ultimate demise is unknown.

The Liberty

The steamship Liberty[101] was built in 1864 by the George Lynn shipbuilders of Philadelphia, for the New York merchants Hargous & Company. Like many other ships built during the Civil War, the Liberty was chartered for transport service by the U.S. Army Quartermaster Corps.

After the war, the Baltimore, New Orleans, and Havana Line used the Liberty to carry passengers and freight between Havana, Key West, Baltimore, and New York. For six months during the latter part of 1868 and the first part of 1869, the Liberty was berthed at the Port of Baltimore undergoing a major upgrade in engines, equipment and passenger accommodations. She resumed service on February 15, 1869.

After his release from Fort Jefferson, Dr. Mudd secured passage on the Liberty at Key West as it sailed up from Havana on its way back to Baltimore. The Liberty arrived back in Baltimore on March 18, 1869.

The Liberty was sold in 1970 to the Baltimore and Havana Steamship Company. In 1875, she was sold to Ward & Company of New York.

The next year, while carrying a load of sugar from Havana to New York, the Liberty sank in a September hurricane off Hilton Head, South Carolina.

---

[100] Department of the Navy - Naval Historical Center. *Dictionary of American Naval Fighting Ships.* Washington, D.C. The Matchless. Page 418. Also, The Army's Navy Series, Ensign Press. 1995.

[101] Steamship Historical Society of America. *American Ocean Steamships 1850 - 1870.* Providence, Rhode Island. 1986. The Liberty. Page 95. Also Heyl, Eric. *Early American Steamers*, Buffalo, N.Y., 1953. The Liberty. Page 235.

Profile: Mary Eleanor "Nettie" Mudd

Sources: Mudd, Richard D., The Mudd Family of the United States; Baltimore Sun, July 11, 1934.

Nettie Mudd was the ninth and youngest child of Dr. Samuel Mudd. She was born January 10, 1878, exactly five years before her father's death. Like many educated young women of her day, she became a school teacher, teaching at the Gallant Green elementary school just a short distance from where she lived with her family on the Mudd farm.

1906 was a big year for 28 year-old Nettie Mudd. She published her book, *The Life of Dr. Samuel A. Mudd*, and she got married. Two important people helped her with the book. One was her mother who was able to provide Nettie with an invaluable first-hand account of her father's life, plus all the original letters her father had written home from prison. The other was Daniel Eldridge Monroe, a 61 year-old Baltimore lawyer who wrote the Preface to her book. Eldridge was a widower whose first wife, Louisa Church, died in 1869, leaving Eldridge to raise their five daughters and two sons.

On December 8, 1906, Nettie married Eldridge Monroe and moved to Baltimore. They had four children. The first two, the twins William Eldridge Monroe and Sarah Frances Monroe, were born September 27, 1907, but died shortly thereafter. James Victor Monroe was born November 7, 1908, and Frances Dyer Monroe was born October 12, 1910. When Eldridge passed away in 1914, Nettie was forced to leave Victor and Frances with her brother Samuel A. Mudd II and his family on the Mudd family farm while she tried to get her life back together in Baltimore. She soon found work as a bookkeeper for Michael Schloss, a Baltimore wholesale clothing manufacturer, and brought her children back home to live with her.

During the depression years, hard times came to Nettie as they came for many other Americans. In order to raise money, she gave many of her prized possessions to Mr. Schloss to sell for her. These included the sofa on which Booth lay while Dr. Mudd set his leg, an ornate inlaid table made by Dr. Mudd, and a number of photos, including photos of Dr. and Mrs. Mudd, and eight photos of Fort Jefferson that Samuel Arnold took in 1898 and sent to her when she was writing her book. Schloss died without selling the items, and in 1934 Nettie sued his estate to recover the items. The sofa and table were eventually recovered and are now on display at the Dr. Samuel A. Mudd House Museum in Waldorf, Maryland. The photos were not recovered.

Not long after this, Nettie told family members that she had lost the original letters that Dr. Mudd had written from prison, and which formed a large part of her book. It may be that the letters were among the items given to Michael Schloss for sale, and not recovered after his death.

Nettie enjoyed visiting her brother's large family back at the Mudd farm as long as she lived. The children especially looked forward to Nettie's visits since she was very skilled at making chocolate candy. Nettie died at 65 years of age on December 31, 1943.

Profile: The Author

Dr. Samuel A. Mudd is my great-grandfather.

My mother's room while she was growing up on the Mudd farm was the very same room Booth rested in when he was at the farm a half century earlier. Her father was Samuel A. Mudd II, the youngest of the four children who were asleep in the Mudd farm house when John Wilkes Booth arrived at 4 A.M. on April 15, 1865.

Growing up in Washington, D.C. in the 1940's, my parents often took my brothers, sister, and me to visit what we knew as "Uncle Joe's Farm". Uncle Joe was Joseph Burch Mudd, my mother's older brother, who continued to run the Mudd farm after his sisters married and left.

We played in the barns where drying tobacco leaves hung from the rafters, and where newly harvested corn was stacked to the ceiling. We gathered eggs from the hen house, and picked fresh tomatoes and other vegetables from the fields. Inside the farmhouse, we shared incredibly delicious farm meals, better than can be found in the most expensive restaurants today. When we went home, Uncle Joe and his wife Helen Louise sent us back with armfuls of fresh country food better than anything that could be bought in stores. In short, we always had a wonderful time when visiting Uncle Joe's Farm.

As we grew older I learned that our great-grandfather Dr. Samuel A. Mudd had once owned Uncle Joe's Farm, had fixed the assassin John Wilkes Booth's leg, had been sent to an island prison for helping Booth, and had been pardoned for saving many lives in a yellow fever epidemic. But that was about all I knew of the Dr. Mudd story. His life was not an important topic of conversation in our family.

As an adult, I read various books on the Lincoln assassination and began to learn that there was more to the Dr. Mudd story than what I had learned as a child. Living in the Washington, D.C. area, I was able to read many of the original historical documents located in the Library of Congress, the National Archives, the Maryland Historical Society, the Maryland State Archives, and other similar places. I have twice visited Fort Jefferson where Dr. Mudd was imprisoned.

I was surprised, and somewhat saddened, after researching the subject for several years, to find out that the family tradition of Dr. Mudd being an innocent country doctor was not the whole story. I was also surprised and saddened to come across books that painted Dr. Mudd as a complete villain. Neither of those positions is historically accurate. I have written this book to try to present an historically accurate account of Dr. Mudd, following the facts wherever they led, without personal spin or opinion.

People have debated Dr. Mudd's role in the Lincoln assassination for the past century and a half, and will undoubtedly continue to do so in the future. I hope this book will help inform that debate in a positive manner.

- Robert K. Summers

Photographs

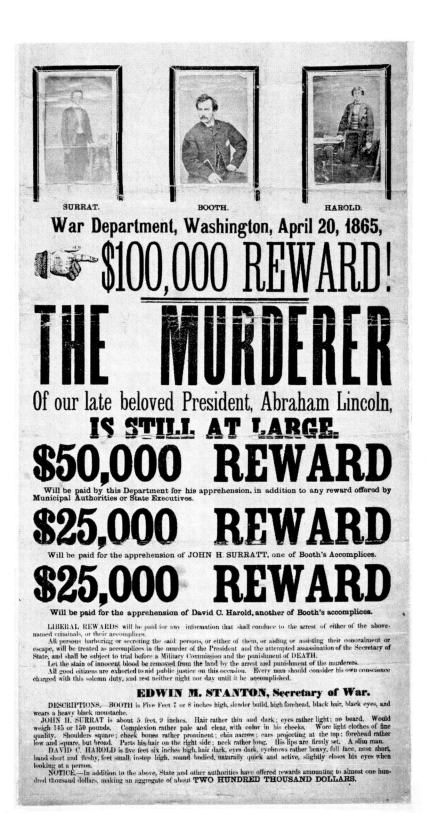

Government reward poster

The Mudd farm house

Dr. Samuel A. Mudd

Mrs. Sarah Frances Mudd

President Abraham Lincoln

John Wilkes Booth

Frederick Stone

General Thomas Ewing, Jr.

David Herold

Lewis Powell

George Atzerodt

Mary Surratt

Edman Spangler

John Surratt

Samuel Arnold

Michael O'Laughlen

Fort Jefferson

Sally Port Entrance

Remains of Soldiers' Barracks. Hospital was on 1st floor.

Sally Port Inside Fort

The State of Maine. National Archives photo.

The U.S.S. Florida at Newport, R.I. U.S. Naval Institute photo

The Thomas A. Scott. National Archives photo.

The Thomas A. Scott. National Archives photo.

The Matchless. U.S. Coast & Geodetic Survey photo,

The Liberty. National Archives photo.

The Liberty. National Archives photo.

Research Notes

Two persons provided valuable assistance in researching the life of Dr. Mudd. I am indebted to both of them for their advice and encouragement.

The first is Michael W. Kauffman, author of *American Brutus: John Wilkes Booth and the Lincoln Conspiracies*. Mike generously shared his encyclopedic knowledge of the Lincoln assassination and Dr. Mudd's role in it.

The second is U.S. National Park Service Chief Ranger Mike T. Ryan. Mike is the Park Service's foremost expert on Fort Jefferson and Dr. Mudd's imprisonment there. He very generously shared his expert knowledge of this part of Dr. Mudd's life.

Specific source documents are cited in the body of this book, in page footnotes, and in the header of each historic document in the Source Documents section of this book.

A major source of information about Dr. Mudd's life is *The Life of Dr. Samuel A. Mudd*, published by his daughter Nettie Mudd in 1906. It may be found at many libraries, purchased at amazon.com, or read and downloaded at books.google.com. Note however, that there were four editions of Nettie Mudd's book, and the Google book is the first edition. This book, *The Fall and Redemption of Dr. Samuel A. Mudd*, uses the fourth edition of Nettie Mudd's book as a source.

There are four major printed accounts of the Lincoln conspiracy trial:

1. *The Assassination of President Lincoln and the Trial of the Conspirators*, Benn Pitman. Moore, Wilstach & Baldwin. New York. 1865.

2. *The Trial of the Assassins and Conspirators at Washington, D.C., May and June 1865 for the Murder of President Abraham Lincoln*, T.B. Peterson & Brothers, Philadelphia. 1865.

3. *The Conspiracy Trial for the Murder of the President and the Attempt to Overthrow the Government by the Assassination of its Principal Officers*, Benjamin Perley Poore. J.E. Tilton & Company. Boston. 1865.

4. *Trial of the Assassins and Conspirators for the Murder of Abraham Lincoln*, Barclay & Company. Philadelphia. 1865.

Benn Pitman's book, *The Assassination of President Lincoln and the Trial of the Conspirators*, is the official Government version of the trial, and is the one most used and cited by researchers. It was authorized by Secretary of War Edwin Stanton, endorsed and approved by the members of the Military Commission, and certified as accurate by Colonel Henry L. Burnett, the Special Judge Advocate of the Military Commission.

The Pitman book is organized by topic, e.g., Defense of Samuel A. Mudd, and contains a handy alphabetical index of witnesses with the page number of their testimony. It is the easiest of the four books to work with, and is the most easily obtained. It can be found at many libraries, borrowed through inter-library loan, purchased at amazon.com, and even read online and downloaded at books.google.com.

While Pitman's book is a highly accurate account of trial testimony, and the easiest to work with, it does not contain the literal word-for-word trial testimony provided in the Peterson and Poore books. The word-for-word testimony often provides additional background information that aids understanding. Unfortunately, the Peterson and Poore books are hard to find. The Barclay book, a condensed account of the trial proceedings, is also hard to find. Many libraries offer an inter-library loan service which your librarian can use to obtain these books for you.

If you cannot obtain one of the above books, you can read the word-for-word account of the trial online at footnote.com. It is a bit tedious to read online, but it is all there. The U.S. National Archives has provided footnote.com with the entire contents of its official word-for-trial trial records contained on National Archives microfilm publication M-599.

Research Locations

U.S. National Archives
700 Pennsylvania Avenue, NW
Washington, D.C. 20408

U.S. National Archives
8601 Adelphi Road
College Park, MD 20740

Library of Congress
101 Independence Ave, SE
Washington, DC 20540

Georgetown University
Lauinger Library, Special Collections Division
37th and N Streets, N.W.
Washington, D.C., 20057

Maryland State Archives
350 Rowe Boulevard
Annapolis, MD 21401

Maryland Historical Society
201 W. Monument Street
Baltimore, MD 21201

Fort Jefferson
Dry Tortugas National Park
P.O. Box 6208
Key West, FL 33041

Dr. Samuel A. Mudd House Museum
3725 Dr. Samuel A. Mudd Rd.
Waldorf, Md 20601.

Southern Maryland Studies Center
College of Southern Maryland
8730 Mitchell Road
La Plata, MD 20646

James O. Hall Research Center
Surratt House Museum
9118 Brandywine Road
Clinton, MD 20735

Bibliography

Researchers studying the life and times of Dr. Samuel A. Mudd will profit from reading any of the books below, not only for their main content, but also for the wealth of references to additional source material contained in their notes, footnotes, and bibliographies. We all stand on the shoulders of those who have gone before us. These books can usually be obtained through your local library, or by searching online at google.com.

There are a number of other books on Dr. Mudd which tend more towards personal opinion and speculation. Those books have not been included in this bibliography, which is intended for the use of serious researchers.

The Life of Dr. Samuel A. Mudd, by Nettie Mudd

The Mudd Family of the United States, by Dr. Richard D. Mudd

American Brutus: John Wilkes Booth and the Lincoln Conspiracies, by Michael W. Kauffman

Memoirs of a Lincoln Conspirator: Samuel B. Arnold - edited by Michael W. Kauffman

Thomas A. Jones: Chief Agent of the Confederate Secret Service, by John M. and Roberta J. Wearmouth

Lincoln's Assassins: A Complete Account of Their Capture, Trial, and Punishment, by Roy Z. Chamlee, Jr.

The Assassination of President Lincoln and the Trial of the Conspirators, by Benn Pitman

Trial of the Assassins and Conspirators at Washington, D.C., by T.B. Peterson and Brothers

The Conspiracy Trial for the Murder of the President and the Attempt to Overthrow the Government by the Assassination of its Principal Officers, Benjamin Perley Poore. J.E. Tilton & Company. Boston. 1865.

Trial of the Assassins and Conspirators for the Murder of Abraham Lincoln, Barclay & Company. Philadelphia. 1865.

Jesuit Slaveholding in Maryland, 1717 – 1838, by Thomas Murphy, S.J.

Slave Narratives from the Federal Writers' Project, 1936 - 1938, Maryland. Library of Congress. Applewood Books, Bedford, Massachusetts.

Colored Volunteers of Maryland, Civil War, 7th Regiment United States Colored Troops 1863 - 1866, by Agnes Kane Callum, Mullac Publishers, Baltimore, Maryland.

One Million Men: The Civil War Draft in the North, by Eugene C. Murdock

Patriotism Limited - 1862 - 1865 - The Civil War and the Bounty System, by Eugene C. Murdock

Doctors in Blue, by George Worthington Adams

The Mighty Revolution – Negro Emancipation in Maryland 1862 – 1864, by Charles L. Wagandt

Reconstruction, 1863-1877, by Eric Foner

A True History of the Assassination of Abraham Lincoln, by Louis J. Weichmann

The Bicentennial History of Georgetown University, 1789-1889, by Robert Emmett Curran, S.J.

Colonel Grenfell's Wars: The Life of a Soldier of Fortune, by Stephen Z. Starr

The Assassination of Abraham Lincoln, by Osborn H. Oldroyd

Fort Jefferson and the Dry Tortugas National Park, by L. Wayne Landrum

Pages from the Past – A Pictorial History of Fort Jefferson, by Albert C. Manucy

Fort Jefferson Research Memorandum No. 6, by Albert C. Manucy, 1938

Lincoln Collector: The Story of Oliver R. Barrett's Great Private Collection, by Carl Sandburg

Bleeding Blue and Gray, by Ira Rutkow

American Ocean Steamships 1850 - 1870, by the Steamship Historical Society of America, Princeton, Rhode Island

Early American Steamships, by Erik Heyl

The Union vs. Dr. Mudd, by Hal Higdon

The Army's Navy Series - Dictionary of Transports and Combatant Vessels, Steam and Sail, Employed by the Union Army, 1861-1868, compiled by Charles Dana Gibson and E. Kay Gibson

Hospital Transports, by Frederick Law Olmsted

Civil War Medicine, by Alfred Jay Bollett

The Army Medical Department, 1818-1865, by Mary C. Gillett

The Travels, Arrest, and Trial of John H. Surratt, by Alfred Isaacson

Index

Arnold, Samuel
  Arrested, 28
  History, 30
  Quit Booth's kidnap plot, 31
  Convicted, 42
  Describes trip on USS Florida, 44
  Assigned to clerical work, 50
  Cared for Dr. Mudd during epidemic, 5769
  Pardoned, 73
  Account of yellow fever epidemic, 189
Atzerodt, George, 24, 32, 37, 38, 42, 113, 117, 128, 154, 165, 168
Booth, John Wilkes
  Kidnap plot, 17
  at Dr. Mudd's farm, 18 ff.
  at Samuel Cox farm, 20
  at Thomas Jones farm, 22
  at Garrett farm, 28
Budd, Captain William, 44, 121, 124, 125, 202
Cox, Samuel Jr., 22, 188
Cox, Samuel, Sr. 20, 22, 39
Dana, Lieutenant David, 22, 23, 104, 105, 132
Dutton, Captain George, 43, 44, 119, 120, 121, 123, 125, 170
Dyer, Jeremiah, 10, 12, 19, 51, 52, 56, 73, 137, 146
Ewing, General Thomas, 26, 36, 39, 45, 51, 55, 72, 104, 109, 110, 113, 140, 147, 193
Fort Jefferson, 44 ff.
Grenfell, George St. Leger, 54 ff., 63, 140, 142, 161, 162, 191
Harbin, Thomas, 18, 185
Hartranft, John F. 34, 35, 170
Herold, David
  Escaping with Booth, 19 ff.
  Captured, 29
  Executed, 42
Johnson, President Andrew
  Pardoned Dr. Mudd, 72, 165
Kautz, August V., 34, 36, 196
Liberty, steamer, 73, 200, 203
Lincoln, President Abraham
  Assassinated, 19
Lovett, Alexander, 22, 23, 24, 25, 100, 103, 114, 128, 129, 132
Matchless, schooner, 73, 157, 200, 203
Mudd, Dr. George
  Dr. Samuel Mudd's Preceptor, 9
  Told of two strangers, 21
  Reported two strangers to Lieutenant David Dana, 22

Mudd, Dr. Samuel A.
  Education, 7 ff.
  Met John Wilkes Booth, 17 ff.
  Arrested, 24
  Old Capitol and Arsenal Prisons, 31
  Trial, 36
  Fort Jefferson, 44 ff.
  Pardon, 72, 165
  Later life, 77 ff.
Mudd, Jeremiah, 16, 40
Mudd, Sarah Frances, 10, 109, 110, 132, 192
O'Laughlen, Michael
  Arrested, 22
  History, 30
  Quit Booth's kidnap plot, 31
  Died of yellow fever, 65
Powell, Lewis
  Arrested, 22
  Executed, 42
Smith, Dr. Joseph Sim, 64, 151, 157, 160, 161, 163, 164, 180, 189
Spangler, Edman
  Arrested, 22
  History, 29
  Pardoned, 73
  Lived at Dr. Mudd's farm, 75
State of Maine, hospital ship, 44, 123, 200
Stone, Frederick, 36, 51, 72
Surratt, John
  Introduced to Booth by Dr. Mudd, 40
  In Elmira, New York, at time of assassination, 24
  Reward poster for, 24
Surratt, Mary
  Arrested, 24
  Executed, 42
Thomas A. Scott, transport steamer, 52, 137, 200, 202
U.S. Sanitary Commission, 200
U.S.S. Florida, 44, 118, 126, 200, 201, 202
Weichmann, Louis
  In Old Capitol Prison, 32
  Testimony of, 40
Wells, Henry H., 25 ff., 99
Whitehurst, Dr. Daniel, 65, 66, 68, 69, 70, 79, 151, 153, 157, 160, 161, 167, 176, 177, 190
Yellow Fever Epidemic, 64 ff.